Knowledge Without Boundaries

Mary Lindenstein Walshok
Foreword by Daniel Yankelovich

Knowledge Without Boundaries

What America's Research Universities Can Do for the Economy, the Workplace, and the Community

Jossey-Bass Publishers • San Francisco

Substantial discounts on bulk quantities of Jossey-Bass books are available to corporations, professional associations, and other organizations. For details and discount information, contact the special sales department at Jossey-Bass Inc., Publishers. (415) 433-1740; Fax (800) 605-2665.

For sales outside the United States, please contact your local Paramount Publishing International Office.

TCF   Manufactured in the United States of America on Lyons Falls Pathfinder Tradebook. This paper is acid-free and 100 percent totally chlorine-free.

Library of Congress Cataloging-in-Publication Data

Walshok, Mary Lindenstein.
    Knowledge without boundaries : what America's research universities can do for the economy, the workplace, and the community / Mary Lindenstein Walshok. — 1st ed.
       p.   cm. — (The Jossey-Bass higher and adult education series)
    Includes bibliographical references and index.
    ISBN 0-7879-0086-9 (acid-free paper)
    1. Education, Higher—Social aspects—United States.
    2. Research—Social aspects—United States. I. Title. II. Series.
    LA227.4.W35   1995   94-48038
    378.73—dc20   CIP

Figure 3.3 is reprinted by permission of the *Wall Street Journal*, © 1986 Dow Jones & Company, Inc. All rights reserved worldwide.

FIRST EDITION
HB Printing   10 9 8 7 6 5 4 3 2 1

The Jossey-Bass Higher and
Adult Education Series

Contents

**Part Two: Organizing and
Disseminating Knowledge
to Serve Public Needs**

Foreword

Up to a few years ago, the leaders of our great research universities were able to look out at the tidal wave of public criticism sweeping over other institutions with a certain smugness. Since the 1970s, institutions such as the criminal justice system, the health care system, primary and secondary education, the legal profession, journalism, big business, and big government have all been headed toward a crisis of legitimacy. The public has cast doubt both on their good faith (accusing them of serving themselves rather than their constituencies) and on their effectiveness (accusing them of doing a poor job in accomplishing their mission).

For years, our institutions of higher education had remained exempt from these criticisms. They were, therefore, unprepared for the harshness of the criticisms when they did flood in from all sides. In recent years, our universities have been accused of pursuing esoteric research (an echo of the 1960s), of standing aloof from the concerns of the public, of raising their fees so unconscionably and irresponsibly as to place higher education out of the reach of people with average incomes, of gobbling up scarce resources in a self-indulgent, self-serving fashion while failing to contribute to the society's most urgent problems, of multiplying an obsessive form of specialization that makes it impossible to deal with real-world issues, of living in a subculture cut off from the mainstream—isolated, contemptuous of average citizens, and subversive of the values of society as a whole.

The response of the universities has been largely defensive: some academics and administrators feel misunderstood, others brush aside and ignore public criticism because it is ill informed. The most frequent response is a feeling of powerlessness. University leaders acknowledge some degree of institutional lag. They acknowledge the need to transform their universities in the light of a new global economy, a knowledge-based society, ever scarcer resources, and a troubled moral climate. But all too often they respond to this challenge in a passive fashion, almost as if renewal were someone else's responsibility.

One can sympathize with those who approach the task half-heartedly: the public's criticisms *are* distorted, and universities are already so complex that their leaders find themselves constantly juggling and balancing diverse interests and values. They find it difficult to know what new direction their institutions should take, and even more difficult to drag them along the new path.

Enter Mary Lindenstein Walshok—a very different kind of leader. Her book *Knowledge Without Boundaries* will, I am confident, serve as a model for the leaders of other institutions as well as those of higher education. It is a wonderfully constructive response to the concerns of the larger society. Importantly, it contains all of the elements needed to counter the crisis of legitimacy that threatens higher education, especially its crown jewel—the hundred or so great research universities that constitute one of the glories of our civilization.

Walshok does not pander to the critics of higher education. She defends the focus of the research universities on basic research, as opposed to a more utilitarian preoccupation with "relevance." And she persuasively argues her case on the critics' own grounds, namely, that this focus will in the long run best serve the public interest.

At the same time, she acknowledges the need for our research universities to recognize that the Cold War era of unlimited resources and equally unlimited respect for their particular forms of expertise is over. Her book not only advances a new vision of renewal for universities in the emerging knowledge society of tomorrow, but it also develops a strategic plan for achieving it and, astonishingly, is full of down-to-earth, practical examples of how this vision and strategy can be accomplished.

The book's title, *Knowledge Without Boundaries*, says it all. Walshok argues that the walls now erected between academic fields of study within the university—while productive for research and the expansion of new knowledge—have made it difficult for that knowledge to be understood and utilized by a society grappling with global economic competitiveness, an underskilled workforce, and fragmenting democratic institutions. She further asserts that universities' increasingly specialized and esoteric approach to knowledge must be better organized and communicated in new ways when the goal is to address social and economic issues. There is a misfit between how universities currently organize and use knowledge and how society taps into knowledge and expertise in its daily economic and social struggles.

Walshok's central point is that knowledge cannot and should not be simply warehoused in universities but rather applied and consumed across all dimensions of society. The book provides exciting examples of how some of the nation's most respected research universities—Wisconsin, California, Chicago, Penn State, and Johns Hopkins—are connecting the work they do to the needs of society. These examples demonstrate the capabilities that research universities have to generate, interpret, and link knowledge to the complex economic, organizational, and community challenges that confront advanced industrial societies. Walshok's analysis of the changing meaning of knowledge lifts her book above the level of a leadership study and gives it a scholarly dimension. I share her discomfort with the popular tag *information society* as the label for the age that is emerging. Universities pursue knowledge and truth, not mere information. But, increasingly in this postmodern era, traditional forms of knowledge are subject to radical questioning.

She has internalized the postmodern critique of knowledge and drawn from it all the right lessons about what to preserve and what to change. For today's universities to assume that they alone have a monopoly on true knowledge, and that other forms of knowing occupy lower rungs in the hierarchy, is an epistemological conceit that diminishes the authority and credibility of the university. It is a tribute to the breadth of Walshok's vision that her conception of the university embraces an immense variety of forms of knowing other than the academically correct ones.

Her combination of responsible leadership, great practicality, and depth of analysis will attract readers in many other fields, as well as higher education. Mary Walshok has written a remarkable book.

February 1995   Daniel Yankelovich

Preface

The late 1960s, when I was a graduate student in sociology at Indiana University, were a heady time of civil rights and antiwar activism even in the conservative Midwest. I rented an apartment from a professor of Serbo-Croatian studies, who from my point of view was involved in a world of teaching and scholarship totally irrelevant to the needs of a society being torn asunder by civil unrest. If I'd had my way then, the university would have phased out esoteric fields such as his and increased support for applied social studies relevant to the more immediate needs of the day: poverty, civil rights, the war in Vietnam, and larger questions of the emerging third world.

Fortunately, I didn't have my way. With the end of the Cold War and the unraveling of the fragile union of Soviet states, those professors of Serbo-Croatian studies—students of the language, culture, and history of Eastern European peoples—and the knowledge they have been developing about this region of the world have moved to center stage. As I read the daily headlines and watch CNN and "Nightline," I am grateful for the intellectual resource those professors represent as we grapple with the vexing problems of ethnic warfare in places such as Bosnia and Herzegovina.

Similarly, in the world of my graduate days, professors and students interested in aggregate data analysis of major social trends worked tirelessly on Monroe calculators, keypunch machines, and card sorters, all brought together in the auditorium-sized computer centers needed to run their cross-tabulations and statistical tests of validity. Today I sit looking out my bay window at the Pacific Ocean and work on my small Powerbook™ personal computer, which is linked to worldwide data banks, colleagues, and programming capabilities unimaginable just twenty-five years ago. In my personal life, my husband and I, entering our fifties, are shielded from many of the physical and emotional costs of aging that affected parents and loved ones when we were young—heart attacks among men in their forties, stress and physical discomfort at menopause for women—thanks to medical innovations such as angiograms and estrogen replacement therapy.

What these few examples represent for me is the extraordinary social benefit of the ongoing research and scholarship that we as a nation support primarily through our great research universities. In contrast to the European model, we have allocated growing amounts of public funds and have vested in universities rather than freestanding institutes the primary responsibility for the development of new knowledge and the provision of advanced education and knowledge. As a consequence, America's major research universities have made unique contributions to society well beyond the education of young people through degree programs. Research universities have developed into major centers of expertise for business, government, and industry; many are centers of new ideas and intellectual movements in the arts, humanities, and social sciences; their research in the sciences has been a primary resource in the development of the post–World War II economy and in the development of the new technological products and enterprises shaping the global economy of the next century. Even though the professors of Eastern European studies, electrical engineering, and cardiology whose work gave rise to the benefits I have received as a citizen did not begin their research with an "application" or a use in mind, the nature of the discovery and development process is such that in a rapidly changing market economy at least, ideas and innovations eventually connect to needs and markets.

Today, however, the university is facing another crisis of relevance, not unlike that of the 1960s. This time, its focus is society's need for more effective, and in particular more rapid, economic and human resource development initiatives to meet global challenges in a world order no longer determined by the threat from military superpowers. Once again, certain voices publicly question the social value of "esoteric" research and teaching and their relevance to the social and economic challenges of the here and now. The difference today is that with the expanding production of new knowledge worldwide and the acceleration of technological, economic, and social change in recent decades, the role of knowledge in all human endeavors—the economy, the workplace, the community—has become more pervasive. Thus research universities, as the society's major sources of expertise and new knowledge, must find ways to make their resources more up-to-date and accessible to growing publics who need knowledge, without compromising their autonomy in the process of discovering and developing that knowledge.

Purpose

I have written *Knowledge Without Boundaries* because I believe it is not only necessary but possible to do just that. The purpose of the book is to address two critical issues affecting the relationship between research universities and the knowledge needs of a post-industrial society. The first is the increased importance to our continued economic and social well-being of the new knowledge being generated and organized by the nation's research centers. The second is a suggestion for how research universities can build better linkages between the expanding knowledge within both the university and in society and can increase the applications and accessibility of that knowledge. Although the institutional focus of the book is primarily the more than one hundred research universities that develop most new knowledge, the concern expressed here for the distinct and important role of new knowledge in economic development, workforce readiness, and civic culture has clear implications for the missions and interrelationships of the more than thirty-five hundred other institutions of higher education throughout the United States. There is a need in advanced industrial societies to continually link new knowledge to all institutions of higher learning as well as to society generally. This book offers examples of how selected research universities create contexts and settings that allow for communication about and evaluation of the discoveries and innovations coming out of some of our finest institutions. The new knowledge they are developing most certainly includes the scientific breakthroughs and technological developments that will drive the new industries and job requirements of tomorrow. Just as important, that knowledge pertains to the new social forms and diverse cultural values affecting communities today and in the future.

Overview of the Contents

A case for the continued and unique importance of research universities in modern society can be made, as I have suggested, through exploration of two fundamental issues. The first is the issue of properly defining and integrating the *apparently* competing knowledge needs of off-campus publics with the traditional teaching and research mission of American higher education. The second is the issue of identifying appropriate institutional mechanisms to serve the expanding need for knowledge among the public without diminishing resources for traditional teaching and research activities. The four chapters in Part One address the first issue, and the four chapters in Part Two, the second.

Chapter One offers a working definition of how the book treats the concept of knowledge in a postmodern society and the dilemmas and opportunities that research universities face. Chapter Two follows that theoretical introduction with a discussion of three spheres of human activity for which knowledge is an increasingly critical resource—economic growth and expansion, social development through enhancing human capacities across the life span, and support for a vital civic culture in a democratic society.

Chapter Three provides an overview of demographic, social, and economic forces giving rise to constituencies with special knowledge needs to which the work of universities is especially relevant. Chapter Four, which concludes Part One, integrates the ideas and data introduced in the previous chapters into a working summative matrix. The matrix represents a heuristic device for identifying specific knowledge needs by constituency on the one hand and potential programs to serve those needs—in the economy, workplace, and community—on the other. The matrix provides a structure for the chapters in Part Two by pinpointing the types of knowledge needs most appropriately served by higher education—and by research universities in particular.

Part Two offers descriptions of exemplary programmatic responses at major American research universities, with a chapter dedicated to each of the spheres affected by the changes in knowledge described in Part One. These include supporting economic development (Chapter Five), enhancing human capacities (Chapter Six), and nurturing a vital civic culture (Chapter Seven). Programs from institutions such as the University of California, the University of Chicago, New York University, the Universities of Minnesota and Wisconsin, and Pennsylvania State University are described in the context of their benefits to new publics. Each suggests potentially useful and workable institutional strategies for other settings. An underlying theme in the presentation of the institutional examples in Chapters Five, Six, and Seven is that properly designed and implemented responses to off-campus publics can actually enrich the "knowledge work" of the university and enhance traditional research and teaching functions rather than detract from them.

There are many by-products of a commitment to improving the connection between the research university and its off-campus constituencies through carefully designed and orchestrated institutional initiatives. In addition to serving the critical social and economic needs that are detailed in Chapters One through Four, a variety of benefits may directly support the more traditional institutional functions of undergraduate and graduate teaching, basic research, and scholarship. These can include

Enriching the content of basic disciplines

Enriching the substance of the undergraduate and graduate curriculum

Offering matching funds for research and teaching initiatives

Providing access to practice and research settings

Providing access to networks of research or institutionally relevant circles of power and influence

Arranging contributions of equipment and/or facilities for research and teaching

Making education more relevant to the world of work

Bringing together faculty to work in interdisciplinary teams to solve problems

Increasing placement opportunities for student interns and for liberal arts and professional school graduates

Endowing chairs and student fellowships

Supporting on-campus programs in which faculty can engage in programmatic innovations and interactions at low risk

Chapter Eight, the concluding chapter, reintroduces the core empirical and value issues raised in Part One and summarizes the key characteristics of the exemplary research university programs described in Part Two. The purpose of Chapter Eight is to leave the reader with a sense of opportunities and ideas for possible next steps in any institutional effort to serve publics more effectively. This last chapter also identifies organizational and policy issues that need to be addressed. The intent is to provide suggestions rather than a formula, because each campus must determine for itself in what knowledge areas, for whom, and in what ways it can and should connect with the larger society. The book concludes with a matrix that offers a reconceptualization of the role of the research university around the multiple activities supporting knowledge rather than around the "functions" of research, teaching, and public service currently used to describe its mission.

In writing *Knowledge Without Boundaries*, I benefited enormously from more than a dozen years spent moving back and forth between the academic preoccupations of the faculty and the knowledge needs of the community in my role as the leader of a large and innovative extension and public service unit at the University of California, San Diego. I have also benefited from the sociological imagination initially imbued in me as a Ph.D. student at Indiana University in the 1960s. It has enabled me to analyze problems and contribute to solutions with a sensitivity to structural and political forces not typically factored into the sort of work I do. I have also benefited from a long and rewarding association with the W. K. Kellogg Foundation, which introduced me to a world of values and leadership in which the application of knowledge to people's problems has as much integrity as the development of knowledge for its own sake.

Acknowledgments

My initial interest in writing a book about research universities and public needs began while I was a Kellogg fellow in the mid 1980s, during which time I was making the transition from being a person who thought of herself first as a sociologist and second as a university administrator. Through those fellowship years, I realized that my life's work was to be a contributor to the building of institutions rather than to the growth of a single discipline or profession. The institutions in which I have chosen to invest myself personally and professionally are those which link ideas and knowledge with the problems and opportunities faced by ordinary people and practitioners living in a world of constant change and uncertainty. The fellowship allowed me to learn about public service and research universities across the United States, and I am deeply grateful to the foundation for the time and resources it afforded to enable me to grow into my new identity.

In recent years, I have benefited in more ways than I can describe from the opportunity to take part in the shaping and growth of one of this country's youngest and most successful research universities, the University of California, San Diego (UCSD). Its commitment to excellence and innovation, first artic- ulated by its founder Roger Revelle in the 1960s and guided over the last decade by Richard C. Atkinson, have provided a context for untold numbers of faculty members, students, and staff to pur- sue wholly original ideas and highly innovative programs, which are contributing to the development of a unique and responsive university ready for the challenges of the twenty-first century.

In more personal terms, long conversations and deep friendships with colleagues such as T. George Harris, William McGill, Neil Morgan, Charles Nathanson, Phillip Nowlen, William Otterson, Paul Saltman, Harold Ticho, and R. B. "Buzz" Woolley have affected the ways I both think about and behave with regard to the role of the research university in society. My husband, Marco, has more than anyone been a source of important conversations about these issues and an incredible support as I have attempted to juggle full-time administration, teaching and lecturing, parenting, and community service with sporadic periods of research and writing.

Finally, I would like to acknowledge Robin Brien Wittman, my assistant at UCSD, who, over the three years I've spent pulling this book together, has provided incredible technical and moral support. It is no overstatement when I say, "Without her this book would never have been finished." Thank you, all of you.

La Jolla, California   Mary Lindenstein Walshok
February 1995

The Author

Mary Lindenstein Walshok is an industrial sociologist and associate vice chancellor for Extended Studies and Public Service at the University of California, San Diego (UCSD), who has spent the last decade building UCSD Extension into a major force for regional, economic, and social development. Her responsibilities include university continuing education and outreach programs, serving more than forty thousand participants annually; the summer session, serving seven thousand students; and the first low-power television station in the University of California system, UCSD-TV, as well as extension centers in North County and downtown San Diego.

Walshok received her B.A. degree (1964) from Pomona College and her M.A. (1966) and Ph.D. (1969) degrees in sociology from Indiana University. She has been associated with UCSD since 1972 and has remained active as an industrial sociologist while teaching, lecturing, and writing numerous book chapters and articles on education and the world of work, as well as her previous book, *Blue Collar Women*. The present book, *Knowledge Without Boundaries*, synthesizes research that Walshok conducted while a Kellogg Foundation fellow. In it, she relies on her knowledge of innovative worldwide programs that are directed toward stimulating regional economic development, workforce readiness, and entrepreneurship. The recipient of many awards and honors, Walshok is a member of numerous community boards and professional associations.

Knowledge Without Boundaries

Part One

The Role of Knowledge in American Society

Chapter One

Challenges to Universities
in a Society Dependent on Knowledge

This is a book about American research universities and the distinct role they play in the life of this nation. In the United States, we have a unique tradition of investing in our large public and private research universities and have developed them into the central institutions through which new knowledge is discovered, developed, organized, and transmitted. As a consequence, a subset of these institutions now conducts more than 50 percent of our basic research while also educating hundreds of thousands of generalists, professionals, and scholars at all degree levels. These institutions operate a network of multibillion-dollar federal research laboratories and collectively represent the finest and most comprehensive research libraries in the world. They support museums and performing arts programs, enriching the cultural and intellectual life of communities across the nation.

American higher education includes more than thirty-five hundred institutions of higher learning—community colleges, liberal arts colleges, religious colleges, state universities, and innovative special purpose centers of teaching and learning. But it is only at approximately one hundred major research universities where knowledge creation and development, as well as teaching, takes place on a major scale; where the organization of knowledge and preservation of knowledge are as critical to their mission as is transmission of knowledge to students through degree programs; where the production as well as the consumption of ideas is central to their identity. What distinguishes these campuses is the extent to which they have come to be organized and structured to ensure the creation and development of new knowledge for the society as well as the transmission of all forms of knowledge through the education and training of citizens, professionals, scholars, and future leaders.

Knowledge Versus Information

American research universities, by virtue of their central commitment to the development of new knowledge and the organization and preservation of all knowledge, make a unique contribution to society far beyond teaching and credentialing individual students. Knowledge has always been the foundation of human progress. The power unleashed by theory harnessed to experimentation, as celebrated by Bacon in the seventeenth century, has become so ubiquitous as we approach the twenty-first century that the knowledge work these institutions do has become the basis for most forms of social and economic progress. *Knowledge* is a highly connotative and contextual term. Throughout history, it has been the subject of serious analysis and scholarly discourse. Conventional philological and etiological discussions of the term indicate that its meaning can range from the most abstract to the most technical, from the most inclusive to the most concrete.

At times, knowledge is understood to be a very general sort of cognitive awareness and acquaintance with a subject. At other times, the term is used to refer to a very formalized, disciplined, and systematic comprehension of a subject including the procedural steps (methods) relied upon to provide order and coherence to that subject. In this case, the aim is often to break down a particular domain of knowledge into its constituent parts, examining the attributes of those parts and the relationships among them in order to know what the subject entails and how it operates or behaves. Science and technical thinking are often associated with this view of knowledge. There is also the quite popular view of knowledge that links it in fundamental ways to direct human experience of the world and a familiarity with specific and discrete bodies of information gained through that direct experience. This is often referred to as common sense or natural knowledge.

As these contrasting views of what is meant by knowledge indicate, arriving at the meaning of the term *knowledge* ultimately involves engaging major philosophical questions about the nature of cognition, perception, logic, and broader metaphysical issues. For these reasons, most of the social and historical discussions of knowledge rely on a contextual understanding of the term, how it is commonly understood within a particular historical and social milieu. In this regard, the dominant and distinctive character of knowledge in modern society is its highly specialized and technical nature.

Modern society has evolved approaches to knowledge that are highly organized, rule-bound, and reconstructed at their core. This reconstructed quality entails the imposition of external "rules" or "standards" on experience, for the purposes of codifying, confirming, and affirming what constitutes the "known" element associated with a discrete experience. In short, what is perceived, what is understood must be mediated by these rules of evidence that guide the ordering of highly specialized, elaborate, and interdependent complexes of discrete information built up to constitute the "current state of knowledge" on a given topic. Knowledge thus is far more than facts, data, or information. It is the systematic collection, validation, and integration of discrete data according to set procedures and rules. Science, the scientific method, and scientific knowledge best typify the modern understanding of the meaning of knowledge.

Knowledge as we shall use it in this book thus is much more than information. It connotes what is known about a subject based on rules and standards of analysis as well as methods for information gathering. In more commonsense terms, knowledge is information put to work. It is the marriage of theory and experimentation. It is the integration of ideas and experience. Knowledge is what enables people to make judgments, create new products, solve problems, and interpret events. Such a full definition of knowledge clarifies why the use of such a concept as the "information society" is unfortunate even though it may be accurate in many ways. Information is merely discrete facts about circumstances and events, meaningless without a body of principles to organize it, to give it coherence and meaning. Without these principles, any significance or implication for action is unclear. Americans are inundated with information wherever they go. What they need are ways to sort, evaluate, make judgments, and take action. That is what knowledge enables people to do. We are instead bombarded with data and information: Dow Jones averages, opinion polls, population statistics, psychological inventories, and standardized tests. We may be an information society, but what we need to become is a knowledge society: a society composed of people and institutions capable of evaluating and using information for positive social and economic purposes (Schwartz and Neikirk, 1983; Drucker, 1993; Bender, 1993).

The Role of Knowledge in Society

The concrete manifestations of the knowledge society are everywhere, particularly in the economy. In a knowledge-based economy, advanced technology allows the efforts of 3 percent of the labor force to generate agricultural productivity sufficient to feed 300 million people. In a knowledge-based economy, synthetic fuels and fibers are more significant than raw materials such as coal and cotton. In a knowledge economy, labor-intensive assembly lines have been replaced by automated manufacturing and advanced telecommunications, which allow us to overcome the limits of time and space. In a knowledge-based society, formerly separated social groups, cultures, languages, and religions encounter one another through communications media and in public places as well as through worldwide migration. In a knowledge-based society, the continuous development of knowledge for social and economic purposes represents a powerful engine for change and progress that touches the lives of all citizens. Peter Drucker, in *Post-Capitalist Society* (1993), comments that even though everyone recognizes the declining return on traditional resources such as land and raw materials, "how knowledge behaves as an economic resource" is not yet fully understood. "We do not yet have a theory, but we need one. We need an economic theory that puts knowledge into the center of the wealth-producing process. Such a theory alone can explain the present economy. It alone can explain economic growth. It alone can explain innovation" (p. 183).

In addition, as Marshall and Tucker argue in *Thinking for a Living* (1992), technological development in the context of an international economy also means that in a knowledge society, social relations and organizations are continuously changing in order to adapt to innovations and new challenges. Economic success is no longer determined by possession (for example, of raw materials or physical prowess) but by the capacity to generate new knowledge (for example, ideas and processes for synthetic materials) and by the ability of the workforce to apply that knowledge successfully in the production system. Fiber optics, composite materials, and silicon wafers have become the synthetic substitutes for the former material building blocks of our economy, such as coal, iron, steel, oil, and rubber. Still-to-be-created materials, products, and processes lie in our future. People and organizations must continually learn and relearn in order to function in a context of ever-changing requirements and resources. Thus in postindustrial economies, as Drucker says, all work is learning. "In the knowledge society, people have to learn how to learn. Indeed, in the knowledge society, subjects may matter less than the students' capacity to continue learning and their motivation to do so" (1993, p. 201).

Three key developments resulting from the knowledge explosion throughout this century are particularly interesting and challenging, especially to higher education. In a sense, they reflect the democratization of knowledge work, once the exclusive purview of highly trained academics working primarily within universities and specialized laboratories. What we find at the close of the twentieth century is (1) a significant acceleration in the development of new knowledge worldwide; (2) the growth of new and important centers of knowledge development outside traditional research universities and special purpose laboratories in industry; and (3) a growing percentage of highly educated research-oriented experts working in a wide array of social institutions, not just in research universities.

Implications for Research Universities

These developments are directly pertinent to the challenges confronting the American research university in a knowledge society. More and more industries, organizations, and groups are seeking access to the university's knowledge resources. The access they seek is not just to the traditional degree programs and classroom activities. They want access to research libraries, supercomputer centers, wet labs, patients for clinical trials, researchers for verification studies, faculty for advanced and interdisciplinary education. Advanced scientists and professionals in business and industry have an increasing need to effectively manage and use the information and technologies changing so rapidly around them. Community leaders and government officials are seeking resources to analyze and address continually changing social and economic conditions. All workers are facing continual demands to expand their knowledge base.

All these trends have deep and pervasive implications for how universities organize and begin to share their unique knowledge resources. Because most change today is linked to scientific discoveries, technological innovations, and new or unfamiliar social and economic developments, change invariably connects to the work and capabilities of research universities. Derek Bok, former president of Harvard University, observed in a speech at Duke University that "we have come to recognize that all advanced nations depend increasingly on three critical elements: new discoveries, highly trained personnel, and expert knowledge. In America, universities are primarily responsible for supplying two of these ingredients and are a major source for the third. That is why observers ranging from Harvard sociologist Daniel Bell to editorial writers from the *Washington Post* have described the modern university as the central institution in post-modern society" (1990, p. 3).

The general public, however, does not appear as convinced as academics, intellectuals, and journalists that research universities play such a vital and central role. They do not see these institutions as the hubs of activity through which and out of which flows much of the knowledge essential to a complex modern society. This is in large part the fault of universities themselves. They have not only failed to communicate what they do, why they do it, and how it serves the public good in a free market economy of ideas and innovations, but they also have not taken seriously the accelerating cycles of change affecting the society and have been reluctant to recognize the significance of the exponential growth of expertise and knowledge functions outside the university. Thus they have inadvertently created a kind of mandarin culture within the university, just as knowledge and expertise apparently are becoming more democratized within American society as a whole.

That such a sheltered university culture should develop is not surprising, given the enormous public investment and social prestige enjoyed by research since World War II. This was primarily due to the central role of technology in both ending World War II and establishing national security policy throughout the Cold War period, 1946 to 1989. What resulted was a tremendous investment in university-based research and the expansion of all aspects of higher education degree programs, libraries, laboratories, and computer centers. This nation's concern with ensuring a continuous stream of new technology capable of securing its position as the world's leading military superpower gave rise to a basic research culture fueled largely by public monies. The nation's investment grew from 5.2 billion to 26.2 billion dollars between 1953 and 1969

(Marshall and Tucker, 1992). Without that public investment, there would not have been the tremendous growth of Cal Tech and MIT, of the University of Illinois in the Midwest's agricultural heartland, or of Stanford and the nine-campus University of California system. Journalists and technology watchers all recognize that without that investment, there would have been no Silicon Valley in California, no Route 128 in Massachusetts, no Research Triangle in North Carolina, much less silicon chips, satellites, fiber optics, supercomputers, CD-ROMs, and the Department of Defense–launched global Internet. Equally important, our changing view of the world (particularly the third world), the spread of our expanded study of language, history, and politics, of cognitive science and world literatures, have all indirectly benefited from increased investments in basic research fueled by the Cold War confidence in expert knowledge.

Now, with the Cold War over, there is no longer an urgent, survival-based political rationale or social demand for government-sponsored breakthroughs in research and innovation. The implications of this lessened demand are as profound for America's research universities as for traditional industries and defense contractors. The organization, funding, and reward systems of the nation's top research universities (fewer than fifty of which do the majority of the federally funded research) have been profoundly shaped by nearly fifty years of national concern with technological "gaps" in national security. Campuses have developed specialized administrative units, curricula, faculty performance standards, and strategies for interacting with students and local communities (not just government and industry) that have been driven in significant ways by the Cold War agenda. Support for research in science and engineering fields as well as scholarship in the humanities and social sciences benefited from the general confidence in "expert" knowledge fueled by national security concerns. The clear and present danger of communism in a bipolar world gave rise to widespread support for research and innovation and for the authority of experts.

However, the shift in recent years to a concern with economic security and sustainable development in a global context has left the public as well as legislators less confident in determining what sort of expertise is now needed and what sources of innovation will bring needed breakthroughs. Our economic competitors come from many places—Japan, Europe, the seven tigers of Asia, NAFTA. Such a multipolar struggle does not mobilize energy like a bipolar cold war. The threats to our economic competitiveness, internal as well as external—outdated manufacturing processes, increasing ethnic diversity, eroding education in the population—have been too long unattended while we met the technological growth needs of the military industrial complex. With the end of the Cold War, research universities are often perceived as knowing a great deal less about the new challenges related to knowledge applications and economic competitiveness and changing social values than they know about scientific breakthroughs and esoteric knowledge.

The problem with this new, more skeptical view of research universities is that one of the most significant by-products of the Cold War–stimulated research agenda (pursued largely through our major research universities) has been the transformation of our society and our economy into a system of industries based fundamentally on knowledge and innovation, processes and services. Our continuing economic competitiveness, even more than our military competitiveness, is bound absolutely to the continued discovery, dissemination, and application of new knowledge—the core activities of major research universities. New and renewable sources of energy; life-saving and cost-effective medical interventions and pharmaceuticals; environmentally sensitive products and processes; telecommunications breakthroughs with direct benefit to health, safety, and education; the capacity to function in global marketplaces, in multiethnic communities, in a highly educated and skilled workforce; and an informed and caring citizenry—all these are profoundly affected by the new knowledge coming out of our research universities. Today's territorial frontiers are intellectual, not geographical;

today's materials are not coal and iron from the ground but composites synthesized in laboratories; genetic engineering and artificial intelligence are supplanting crop rotation, pesticides, and assembly lines. The raw materials of the twenty-first century will be the discoveries, inventions, and innovations coming out of the development and adaptation of new knowledge. The distinct contribution of research universities to such activity suggests an increased rather than a diminished role for them in the twenty-first century.

What Research Universities Must Do

Two things need to happen before research universities can fulfill this expanded role. First, there must be broader understanding of the past and future benefits of research to the public good, in particular to the future economic well-being of advanced industrial economies. Public understanding of the benefits of new knowledge outside military and health applications is minimal at best. Research universities, long the beneficiaries of an expanding economy and a culture of expertise, have failed to appreciate how complicated it is for the public to understand the connection between research and the public good. For example, the tendency of many research universities to embrace only reluctantly many vital public issues, such as race relations, manufacturing competitiveness, and the quality of public schools, has resulted in the public's seeking expert help for these needs elsewhere. Universities clearly need to better describe and articulate the benefits of new knowledge, but they must also be prepared to broaden their research horizons to encompass areas of knowledge of pressing social value as well as intellectual significance.

Second, research universities need better institutional mechanisms for connecting the new knowledge they develop to the increasingly large and diverse publics who can use and contribute to that knowledge. High-priced industrial liaison programs, self-promoting publications, and lobbying activities will not do the job. What works are program initiatives that facilitate regular and recurrent two-way conversations between the various academic groupings on the campus and the appropriate constituencies in the society. What is needed is expanded participation in policy analysis and discourse on public affairs, as well as an expanded commitment to continuing education and advanced education opportunities for practitioners.

By addressing these two issues—the increasing importance of the new knowledge being generated by the nation's research universities to economic and social well-being and the rising need for better connections between knowledge in the university and knowledge in the larger society—it is possible to see the ways research universities can better serve the knowledge needs of a changing society. How these connections are developed—both within higher education institutions and throughout society—is influenced by the ways academics think about knowledge and factor experiences and expertise outside the academy into the society's total knowledge development and dissemination process. Universities will not organize themselves to serve expanding public needs without a clearer articulation of what these needs are. Universities will not integrate the experiences and expertise of individuals and institutions outside the academy without a deeper appreciation of the invaluable resources they represent. Therefore, this book must explore more deeply the connotative meaning of knowledge. Such an introductory discussion will focus, if only briefly, on the significance of experience-based knowledge, the social benefits of knowledge, and the need for more ways to create networks among the users and producers of knowledge in postindustrial societies.

The Multiple Sources of Knowledge

The point was made earlier that knowledge is more than just information or hunks of raw data. It involves a set of rules and standards essential to our drawing verifiable conclusions and interpretations that produce decision making as well as social and economic innovations. Thus knowledge in modern society has a very strong component of intellectual rigor. However, knowledge—particularly useful knowledge that can be applied in the economy and society— is also something more than highly intellectualized, analytical, and symbolic material. It includes working knowledge, a component of experience, of hands-on practice knowledge, as some describe it. However, many people, especially within research universities, treat experience as separate from knowledge rather than as a form of knowledge. As a consequence, we increasingly dissociate thinking from doing, reflection from action, and theory from practice. In a knowledge-based economy, there need to be contexts in which this separation can be overcome and the variable sources of knowledge— both intellectualized and experience based—can be integrated.

In her much celebrated analysis of the complex workplace transformations resulting from "smart machines" based on new information technology, Shoshana Zuboff (1988) challenges the popular distinction between "brain" and "brawn" power by arguing that judgments relevant to action must draw on two equally valuable forms of knowledge: "intellective" (or intellectual) and "experience based (or hands-on)." *Intellectual knowledge* involves a series of cognitive processes including information gathering, thinking about and "making sense" of things using abstract cues, inferential reasoning, and systemic thinking (p. 95). Intellectual knowledge contrasts with *experience-based* knowledge—knowledge with a content of rationality and utility based on years of experience. This type of knowledge is derived from action and displayed in action. It means knowing how to do, to make, to act on. Examples include everything from knowing how to ski to playing the piano, from preparing a perfect béarnaise to raising flawless orchids, from manufacturing finely crafted electronics equipment to designing stylish automobiles. None of these is a purely mechanistic process. Each relies on some combination of intellectual and experience-based knowledge.

Zuboff's thoughts are not radically new, although they are

framed in terms highly relevant to this particular argument. Fritz
Machlup, the Princeton economist who coined the term *knowledge
society* (1962), emphasized the important distinction between and
the relationship of "mundane knowledge" acquired from everyday
practice on the one hand and more "structured forms of knowledge"—scientific, humanistic, social science, and artistic—on the
other. We have become a knowledge society both because an
increasing percentage of our *industries* are concerned with the generation and transmission of the varied forms of knowledge outputs—such as phones, computers, televisions, calculators, ideas, and
marketing concepts—and because increasing numbers of *occupations* involve activities designed to aid in the generation, transmission, or reception of knowledge—engineers, designers, writers,
accountants, lawyers, and many others (p. 228).

Like Machlup, Zuboff argues compellingly for a concept of
knowledge that is broader than typically understood among scholars. She cites significant studies of industrial workers, managers, and
professionals to support her argument. Sociologists of work and
occupations, as well as researchers interested in management issues
and executive behavior, have long noted the significant experience-
based, action-centered character of problem solving and decision
making. Intellectual skills, the use of data and abstract formulations
clearly come into play; but the repair of a broken machine, an
investment in a new product, or the decision to seek a new market
all draw upon a combination of intellectual, intuitive, and experience-based knowledge (Blauner, 1964; Mintzberg, 1973; Kanter,
1983). Zuboff quotes Chester Barnard's classic work on the "art" of
management, as one way of making this point.

In 1938, Chester Barnard, the executive turned scholar, wrote a
lengthy treatise, *The Functions of the Executive*, that eloquently discussed the implicit, experience-based action-centered quality of
executive skills. In a summary description of the executive process,
he wrote: "The process is the sensing of the organization as a whole

and the total situation relevant to it. It transcends the capacity of merely intellectual methods, and the techniques of discriminating the factors of the situation. The terms pertinent to it are 'feeling,' 'judgment,' 'sense,' 'proportion,' 'balance,' 'appropriateness.' It is a matter of art rather than science, and is aesthetic rather than logical. For this reason it is recognized rather than described and is known by its effects rather than by analysis" [p. 235].

Zuboff goes on to describe the components of this experience-based knowledge as sentience, action dependence, context dependence, and personalism. Quite simply, each represents a dimension of experience that provides data—information essential to making judgments. *Sentience* relates to physical cues in the environment—the touch of the hands on a drill press, the fingers on a word processor, or the seeing and hearing of people in relationships in an office setting. *Action dependence* is simply the actual performance of a task—building a model, formatting discussion, or developing consensus among a group of people with disparate interests. *Context dependence* has to do with the environment in which sentience and action are happening. As it varies, so will the experience and ultimate meaning of a given action. Finally, *personalism* has to do with the personality, intelligence, temperament, energy, and related individual characteristics that implicitly affect the linkage between the "knower and the known," giving knowledge "a sense of interiority, much like physical experience." All of these factors affect how people learn and "know." They represent the frame of reference within which new forms of knowledge, especially intellectual knowledge, are evaluated and used.

There is thus almost a physical component to "knowing because so much of knowing is experienced." There is a sentient character to knowing based on the "laboring body" in skilled industries and histories of interaction in office environments or managerial settings. Over years of experience, workers develop a "felt knowledge" of materials and procedures that is not fully captured by the new smart machines operating the factory floor or modern-day offices. The body and the mind "in action" are sources of skill and knowledge that have to be factored in when more abstract knowledge and information are introduced into social action. Whether in voting behavior, factory production work, or executive-level decision making, information alone is not enough. Knowledge broadly conceived as described here is what is needed, and knowledge comes from many places. That is why research universities, if they are to continue their central role in society, must come up with program models that support the integration of more intellectual forms of knowledge with the experience-based knowledge that practitioners and professionals accumulate.

Holzner and Marx's seminal book *Knowledge Application* (1979), among other works, is relevant to this discussion because of the important observations on the nature of knowledge in a "postmodern" society, particularly with regard to how different groups acquire new knowledge. Holzner contrasts the formal and informal modes of communication utilized by basic scientists with those used by applied scientists and engineers. He points out, for example, that "the mode of distribution of knowledge through formal versus informal channels is interdependent with the context of knowledge use." Basic scientists tend to rely on formal communication. In contrast, "applied scientists and engineers tend to rely relatively more heavily on informal channels and conversations with colleagues," rather than formal journal articles. Holzner reports that "in a comparison between seven professional engineering projects and two scientific research projects in physics, it was found that 51 percent of the ideas in the scientific research came from the formal scientific literature. However, only 8 percent of ideas in the engineering project came from this source. On the other hand, in the engineering projects, respondents reported that 33 percent of the ideas came from vendors of potential equipment or subsystems or from the customers of the products being developed. These sources of information did not play any role in the research projects" (p. 226).

Thus the knowledge people need is acquired differently, given different purposes or uses. Academics assume they make knowledge accessible through formal lectures and publications. For some uses, but clearly not *all*, such means are appropriate. Practitioners appear to rely more on face-to-face exchanges than solitary reading. Holzner emphasizes further that research reveals differences in the "structure of bodies of knowledge as well as in their use," and that these different structures are relevant to how people access information. "Practicing professionals almost inevitably make considerable use of role-embedded knowledge and pragmatic knowledge convergencies around a pattern of activity. The channels of communication and knowledge distribution reflect these patterns. It is interesting how profound the integration is between knowledge search behavior and the structure of bodies of knowledge. It appears to us that this complexity must be kept in mind when one thinks of knowledge diffusion, cautioning against the acceptance of any simplistic model" (p. 226).

Once again, traditional academic models of knowledge diffusion do not factor in these structural differences. Academics often assume that because they acquire knowledge through reading, everyone does. Finally, Holzner suggests important implications for the informal knowledge-acquiring strategies of professional practitioners in comparison to the formal strategies (journals, research reports) of basic scientists: "Because of the greater dependence on informal channels, patterns of communication among professional practitioners are more influenced by interpersonal factors and forms of association. Moreover, these informal communication and interaction systems among applied scientists and professional practitioners are highly influenced by their value systems. This theme recurs particularly in reducing uncertainties among professional practitioners" (pp. 226–227).

The significance of Holzner's points to this discussion of knowledge are clear. Making knowledge available and useful requires attention to the structure of the knowledge and to the knowledge search and acquisition modes utilized by different knowledge users. Basic scientists and engineers may seek out, communicate about, and integrate into their storehouse of knowledge the same information in very different ways. Simply put, those committed to getting knowledge to people who use it need to design user friendly mechanisms when interacting with constituencies outside the academy.

How Knowledge Gets Organized

What all this means for research universities is that any institutional initiatives to connect campus resources with society's needs must include *ways of accessing, sorting, synthesizing, and exchanging information from a variety of contexts in a variety of formats across a variety of frames of reference—intellectual and experience based.* For example, rather than providing only day-long lecture programs where faculty researchers brief practitioners or policy makers on their research, the university might also convene day-long meetings at which researchers from industry or government staffers brief faculty on their activities and concerns. America's current needs for knowledge could benefit from these sorts of two-way exchanges as well as more roundtables and publications that draw upon diverse sources of expertise and multiple forms of knowledge. We rely primarily on formalized one-way forms of communication and dissemination between putative "experts" and putative "students." We do not see the knowledge problem as one of harvesting, organizing, and synthesizing various inputs. This is a problem in everyday workplaces as well as labs and hospitals, in civic life as well as industry.

The key point is that there is a need for what in this volume will be referred to as *mediating institutions* (a concept frequently used by sociologists), communities of discourse spanning the boundaries of action-centered and abstract knowledge. Research universities are uniquely equipped to provide these institutional settings because they have valuable knowledge resources not only in their faculty and classrooms, but in their libraries, advanced computing centers, laboratories, and publishing and media capabilities. Just as important, they have a reputation for neutrality and integrity in the pursuit of knowledge, and as such potentially represent a unique kind of "honest broker" between various special interests. If universities are to fulfill this role, however, they must reframe many of the traditional approaches to teaching and learning currently in place. Universities require significant input and feedback from the full range of knowledge users and providers, not just the experts inside the university, especially if the users represent advanced industries and fields of practice or mature, well-educated professionals.

Mature individuals and organizations have histories. They develop a bank of experiences and knowledge upon which they draw as they encounter "new" information and knowledge. Thus new knowledge is evaluated and integrated within that historical and experiential context in ways that are beneficial to action. Distinctive frames of reference affect how new information and intellectual knowledge is integrated, understood, and used. They must be factored into any initiatives designed to better connect the research university to society.

If universities are to accomplish this connection, they must also understand that the benefits of knowledge, and in turn university public service, are social, not just individual. This in turn means that the university as a whole, not just the individual faculty members within that institution, needs to be measured on the extent to which it serves the knowledge needs of society, as well as on how well it performs teaching and basic research. Right now, all our conventional measures of success in this regard are individualistic: Does a graduate get a good job? Does an individual professor deliver services to the indigent or serve on a city commission? Better social and institutional indicators are needed to replace essentially personal ones. Evaluating the benefits of knowledge, education, and "learnedness" in primarily individualistic terms may accord with the individualism of American culture, but this kind of individualism has clouded our ability to discern and evaluate where the common good lies.

Part of the problem in focusing on the social benefits, not just the individual ones, is that we are a nation of pioneers and rebels from distant lands who came to this place of seemingly limitless natural resources and room for expansion to start anew, to build our private worlds relatively free from the constraints of the class and ethnic barriers in our various homelands. Americans have been fiercely individualistic as a result and have characteristically valued action over reflection, product over process, physical over mental prowess. Americans have characteristically measured themselves by what they can do rather than what they know, by what they have accomplished rather than by what they are or where they came from.

As James Fallows's book *More Like Us* (1989) so poignantly argues, the roots of our achievements as a nation lie in our capacity to continually "reinvent ourselves," to not "know our place," to be a society characterized by heterogeneity, optimism, enormous human effort, and mobility. The traditional view of knowledge and education in such a cultural context, not surprisingly, has been highly utilitarian and individualistic. The general population tends to value know-how, the ability to do things more than the ability to absorb and integrate diverse ideas and information. In fact, in this country peopled by successive generations of immigrants escaping the limits of social class and ethnic boundaries in other nations and religious intolerance in other cultures, struggling to integrate and achieve economic stability, the time-consuming pursuit of formal education has often been seen as a luxury in the face of immediate needs such as earning money just to survive. For generations, children have been encouraged to get ahead, to make a place for themselves, to get a job as soon as possible. Programs of study and college majors are often evaluated in terms of their financial and status payoffs. The general public tends to view the study of highly intellectual fields such as physics, philosophy, or European history as something one can "afford" to do if one does not have to get a "real" job. The intellectual community for the most part also evaluates outputs and success in terms of the achievements of individuals. Universities reward individual faculty superstars who win big research grants, Nobel prizes, elite academy memberships, and MacArthur grants with promotions, perquisites, and press releases. They rarely celebrate the research *outputs* that benefit humankind: the research and education programs that contribute to economic development or the public service programs for a community.

Throughout its expansionist history, animated by a belief in individual freedoms and limitless potential, America was served well by these individualistic and utilitarian values. The nation's incredible natural resources, potential for westward development, and rapid industrialization created opportunities for even the least literate. Today, however, our nation faces new contingencies that call upon new skills and very possibly new animating principles in order to sustain traditions of achievement and mobility. Education and learning are essential to employment, new business development, and wealth creation. They represent not just individual but social benefits. Knowledge and its uses in all parts of life, in all sectors of the industrialized world, is an essential resource on a global playing field made level by equal access to information, technology, and the creative use of ideas. In an era of increasingly scarce natural resources and burgeoning information industries, the quality of the ideas and innovations, the knowledge and skills our human resources possess, represents our most significant national resource. This is the new wealth of nations. America's place in the world community will be strengthened or diminished based on how well she can push the frontiers of knowledge and how effectively the population becomes educated, not only for the workplace but also for citizenship and leadership.

The kind of knowledge needed—the ideas, information, and symbolic systems—is increasingly complex. Basic knowledge and skills such as reading, writing, and numeracy are essential. Literacy counts even in the most simple tasks—unskilled labor, voting, or interfacing with the IRS or the health care system. However, increasing numbers of the population also need advanced knowledge and skills. They need facility with complex technology in the workplace, the ability to understand complicated ballot initiatives on such issues as toxic waste, the ability to coach their children in subject matter not taught or not even extant when they were children—DNA, AIDS, and third-world history and literature. As public issues and world affairs become more complex due to the knowledge explosion and the effects of technology, analytical skills become essential for the exercise of basic citizenship. America's most recent knowledge challenges are, therefore, both similar to and different from those in previous epochs. They require a commitment by the individual to develop analytical as well as basic skills and to be a lifelong learner. However, they also require that educational institutions, including research universities, find better ways to serve the evolving knowledge needs of the public across the life span.

The concept of knowledge offered here has some important implications. First it means that while data and information are valuable and essential resources, their usefulness is limited if unconnected to cognitive skills related to more abstract intellectual knowledge. It also affirms the importance of factoring in more hands-on experience-based knowledge in the development of more intellectually structured knowledge. Individuals and organizations may be expert at gathering and examining one form of knowledge over another, at pursuing a narrow set of intellectual problems in the way academics do, or through hands-on actions in the way practitioners do. However, it is the connections between these specialized preoccupations that are essential in a knowledge society. How a citizen votes, an engineer designs, or a social worker relates to clients can be enriched by making the connections between abstract ideas and lived experience.

Second, this conceptualization of knowledge implies that

knowledge inheres in a variety of places and must be drawn from a variety of contexts. Research laboratories, books, television, and school classrooms are all sources of important information and knowledge. Action settings such as factories and office environments as well as discrete experiences over time, at the individual and organizational level, are also essential knowledge sources. Knowledge is not a fixed resource monopolized by any one set of individuals or organizations but is a fluid and continually transforming resource. Basic research followed by knowledge application and testing results in new data and reconfigurations of information, which in turn give rise to new questions needing answers. Knowledge of such variety and complexity requires systems for tracking, monitoring, assembling, and packaging by specialized individuals for use among diverse constituencies.

The knowledge itself, however, originates from myriad sources, not a single source, even though its organization and dissemination may come from a single place. Increasingly, the working person, the citizen, the leader are each confronted with challenges and demands that require them to call upon information, skills, and knowledge unlike anything they have ever been required to access before. The challenge to a knowledge society is in finding ways to assure continual access to knowledge that derives from both abstract and action frameworks, that crosses subject areas and life experiences, that provides as well the tools for evaluating, integrating, and making judgments in a variety of spheres of human activity. Currently, however, knowledge exchanges tend to be highly fragmented and self-referential. In the expanded vision of how knowledge from various sources gets organized and shared, it would be possible for environmental engineers and attorneys, physicists and high school teachers, medical doctors and social workers to have regular opportunities to interact and learn from one another. It would be possible to overcome the growing insularity of many disciplines and professional fields and enjoy the sort of cross-practitioner and interdisciplinary learning that is so badly needed.

Barriers to New Forms of Knowledge Organization and Dissemination

This challenge is made doubly difficult by the way knowledge has become organized within research universities since World War II. Paralleling the expanded social need for knowledge has been the increased specialization and intellectual rigor of the knowledge development done by research universities. Ever since the late nineteenth century, and particularly during the mid twentieth century, the character of intellectual work has been evolving. Thomas Bender's essays on the history of academic intellectuals in the United States emphasize the extent to which "serious intellectual problems and procedures were largely reformulated, most notably in respect to scientific work and in the analysis of society (social science). Valid knowledge, formerly concretized in individual relationships to nature and society, now seemed to be defined in forms and processes one step removed from direct human experience" (1993, p. 13).

As a result, the values and preoccupations of academic intellectuals today, while highly productive of new knowledge, result in forms of knowledge that are increasingly remote from the public worlds of enterprise and technological development, commerce, social services, and civic culture (Rorty, 1991; Bender, 1993). Overcoming this remoteness without compromising the intellectual gains and academic freedoms secured over the last fifty years is the challenge of the moment. The increasingly esoteric and specialized character of knowledge discovery and dissemination in our research universities, and to some extent in all institutions of formal education, means that the potential social and economic benefits of much new knowledge often falls short because of its inaccessibility.

The rising public skepticism about the value of research universities comes in large part from a concern about the willingness and ability of universities to connect much of this new knowledge to wider communities and to other forms of knowledge essential to social and economic problem solving. For example, family planning among low-income minority youth has not taken hold despite the wealth of technical and sociological knowledge developed by the academy; manufacturing modernization is unlikely to happen without input from industrial users despite important basic research in such things as computer-aided design and manufacturing and composite materials. Many business leaders and government officials have been critical of the slowness with which basic research results and abstract knowledge are absorbed into action spheres where they can serve the economic and social objectives of the nation more effectively. What the nation requires are institutions that have both the capacity to generate new information, technologies, and intellectual knowledge and the mechanisms to ensure the introduction and integration of that knowledge into communities, organizations, and fields of practice that benefit the society and the economy.

Also needed are mechanisms that ensure continuous feedback from these communities to ensure in turn constant improvements in research and scholarly knowledge. Thus the challenges of the knowledge society are not just teaching and learning. They are the problems of research and discovery; knowledge organization, interpretation, and utilization; and the need for continual discourse between diverse knowledge bases. This is why the metaphor of knowledge is so powerful. In contrast to *information society* or the now popular term among professional educators, *learning society*, *knowledge society* suggests the need for a simultaneous commitment to a variety of intellectual and action-based agendas in the service of America's complex knowledge needs. Knowledge requires an explicit social commitment to research, discovery, and intellectual work as well as commitment to teaching and certification of young adults, to lifelong learning, and to hands-on experience. Knowledge work has long been a key feature of the research university and one that may need refocusing as we move into the post–Cold War era.

Many critics of the increasingly specialized character of the research and scholarship that produces so much new knowledge are advocating a complete transformation of the modern research university. They would require that knowledge gained through research be more relevant to specific economic or social objectives (Lynton, 1984; Lynton and Elman, 1987). The issue of knowledge for its own sake versus for the public good is a critical one in a knowledge society. The position of this volume is that the pursuit of knowledge for its own sake has had enormous social benefits, particularly in the richness of information and new technologies currently available societywide. Therefore, we as a nation need to continue to support basic research. Such research clearly has also given rise to trivial projects, useless products, and what some describe as "junk" knowledge. However, research in a knowledge society is what navigating uncharted seas was to the age of exploration, what developing raw materials such as coal and steel were to the industrial revolution, and what drilling for oil meant to the transportation revolution. Explorers, miners, and geological engineers of the past encountered more dead ends, false leads, and hazards than gold mines and gushers. However, the net effect of their efforts was an incredible return on investment if measured in terms of overall progress in the economy, in human health and welfare, and in personal freedom.

Basic research similarly carries a high percentage of inconclusive findings and false leads. However, the percentage of efforts that do yield breakthroughs typically has enormous applied consequences. Consider the myriad applications of laser technology or the agricultural and pharmaceutical implications of DNA. If we overly encumber the knowledge development process with advance claims for relevancy and no longer allow researchers and scholars to freely pursue their own creative ideas, we could endanger the expanding knowledge base and ultimately our ability to address real human problems and to further our competitive position in world markets. On the other hand, something must be done to overcome the increasing remoteness of abstract and intellectual knowledge from society as a whole. One way to respond to the increasing expectations of funders that research be more relevant is to provide outreach to more potential beneficiaries of basic research. Research universities must be able to do outreach as well as basic research, thereby demonstrating their commitment to connect the work they do to the practical needs of society. However, society in turn needs to recognize the difference between outreach and an overly "applied" research agenda. A more applied research agenda may not necessarily produce the results that the society and the economy require.

Capabilities Research Universities Need to Better Serve the Knowledge Society

There clearly need to be initiatives to assure the integration of all the new and disparate intellectual knowledge, as well as mechanisms for assuring its connection to valid and appropriate forms of experience-based knowledge. What is required are individuals and institutional mechanisms (mediating institutions) capable of functioning at the interface of the various specialized worlds of information, at the intersection of theory and practice. What is needed are individuals and institutional mechanisms that can help to harvest, organize, synthesize, and span the intellectual and experiential boundaries that are unavoidable in a complex advanced technological society. Because of the diversity, complexity, and sheer amount there is to be known, it is unlikely that single individuals will emerge to fill these roles. Clearly there are Renaissance men and women who can range from topic to topic, social group to social group, who are equally at home in the company of nuclear engineers, medieval historians, and business entrepreneurs. However, the inevitable separatenesses, yet unavoidable interdependencies, of these various worlds are more likely to be linked through *programmatic initiatives*. Such initiatives should focus on the integration of separate knowledge sources for broader use and facilitate the development of new communities of discourse that are likely to be issues oriented or problem focused. Examples are regional planning, economic development, public school reform, and health care policy. Such initiatives must be based on shared expertise and genuine exchange, not just one-way communications to various publics in classes, degree programs, or technology transfer programs.

Efforts at cross-fertilization and integration already are taking place at our major centers of research and scholarship. In an editorial in the *Chronicle of Higher Education*, Robert Kates, a Brown University professor, describes the growth of faculty-initiated interdisciplinary centers, programs, and institutes on many college and university campuses as an antidote to the narrow focus inevitable in increasingly specialized research-oriented academic departments. He notes that fully one-third of the Brown University faculty are affiliated with one or more of these centers and attributes their growth to the need for cross-disciplinary perspectives on the major questions of the times.

> The institutes and centers exist because almost none of the great questions of science, scholarship, or society fit in single disciplines and many such questions are now pursued collaboratively. Whether they are questions of origin; of particles, life, society, or the cosmos; questions of meaning; of existence, being human, kinship, or symbol; or questions of matter and energy; of atom, cell, family or nation—we quickly run up against the boundaries of our disciplinary structures. And if we ask why people kill others, why hunger persists in a world of plenty, or why great gaps separate rich and poor, black and white, male and female—we quickly find how limited are our disciplinary perspectives [Kates, 1989, p. B2].

Kates further reports that the activities of these centers and programs reach well beyond their affiliated faculty. Fully 70 percent of the 1,300 speakers, conferences, performances, and exhibitions listed in the Brown University calendar in the 1988–89 academic year were sponsored solely or in part by these centers he reports. Centers and programs such as these are institutional initiatives to

span the boundaries between the intellectual and basic research preoccupations of faculty within college and university communities.
They also represent institutional settings that can open up opportunities—not just for experts to communicate "out" but for citizens
and practitioners to communicate "in." Universities need more
cross-disciplinary talk within their own faculties but also need more
conversations between their faculties and the larger society.

Another example of a research university grappling with these
issues is MIT. It established a Commission on Industrial Productivity, which published its findings in the much-discussed book *Made
in America: Regaining the Productive Edge* (1989). The commission's
analysis revealed a growing need for the sorts of know-how and
interdisciplinary knowledge under discussion. In a chapter titled
"How Universities Should Change," the commission recommended
the following: "Create a new cadre of students and faculty characterized by (1) interest in, and knowledge of real problems and their
societal, economic and political context; (2) an ability to function
effectively as members of a team creating new products, processes
and systems; (3) an ability to operate effectively beyond the con-
fines of a single discipline; and (4) an integration of a deep understanding of science and technology with practical knowledge, a
hands-on orientation, and experimental skills and insight" (Dertouzos, Lester, Solow, and the MIT Commission on Industrial Productivity, 1989, p. 157). The list of recommendations concludes
with a plea for the MIT community of faculty and scholars to
increase their "awareness of the critical problems surrounding
national productivity and university education" (p. 165). The
authors of the report (distinguished MIT senior faculty) acknowledged that their "everyday work lives at MIT" insulated them from
the many pressing social and economic issues they were required to
learn about to meet the externally focused goals of the commission.

Another example of the knowledge networking effort is the
university-industry partnership. These partnerships, which are being
developed across the United States, include joint research projects,

regular programs of technical continuing education, manufacturing and industrial extension services, and a wide array of technology transfer activities. They are organized in major schools and colleges of engineering and science in the nearly one hundred major public and private research universities across the United States. However, for the most part, these efforts tend to be organized to support a narrow range of technical (mostly engineering) knowledge needs and too often relate primarily to large companies with significant financial resources. As such, they clearly represent necessary but not sufficient knowledge connections, given the spectrum of technical needs and types of industry in our economy.

Clearly many knowledge boundaries within both the university and the society need spanning. Research universities are uniquely qualified to play a lead role in creating the knowledge connections needed to ensure regular, omnidirectional, and cross-disciplinary exchanges among all the relevant participants in the knowledge society. This is both because of the vast and diverse knowledge resources available to them *and* because of the long institutional tradition of pursuing the qualities of neutrality and "objectivity" in the search for knowledge. It is likely that the products of such connections will be new and different ways of understanding and doing things. It is probable that encounters between various information sources and knowledge forms will be synergistic so as to transform ways of seeing, asking questions, and taking action.

The paucity of knowledge exchanges with such transformational potential lies at the heart of America's knowledge problem. Through specialty magazines, television documentaries, professional associations, university-industrial liaison programs, and extension services, information of all types and varieties is being infused into the nation. The problem is that people are not sure (1) how to sort the diffuse information they encounter, (2) how to connect it to what they already know both intellectually and experientially, or (3) how to provide feedback into the more abstracted "knowledge-producing" systems. Professors of education in many research university programs listen to teachers and practitioners too seldom. Schools of business in research universities tend to interact with a narrow range of well-established corporate entities; philosophy scholarship concerns itself less and less with the humanistic and ethical dilemmas facing a modern society; political scientists talk less and less to civil servants and politicians; sociologists have lost interest in families and working people. There are stellar exceptions in all cases. The primary point is that there is a need for institutional mechanisms to help people temporarily cross the boundaries of their narrow intellectual and experiential worlds of knowledge in order to learn from and with one another, giving at certain points more emphasis to issues of abstract intellective knowledge and at other points more attention to experience and action-based knowledge. In all cases, networks need to be established that can facilitate mutually enhancing encounters.

Discovering how to create and facilitate knowledge networks that give rise to these sorts of encounters and outcomes in a systematic and meaningful way is an exciting and formidable challenge. What is needed are institutional initiatives of a sustained and systematic character to focus on what needs to be known and by whom, where the diverse sources of knowledge lie, and how they can be pulled together in ways that will be useful to all participants. Finally, what must come from the knowledge exchange is a synthesis that can enhance judgment and actions in ways that can translate into clear social benefits.

Universities, foundations, and other not-for-profit educational associations that are as concerned about knowledge discovery as about knowledge utilization are the most promising institutions through which these sorts of efforts can take place. The leadership required is one which resonates as much with the problems and dilemmas of intellectual knowledge as with the problems and dilemmas of action-based knowledge. The discipline and skills involved are intellectual flexibility and facility at building relationships across traditional knowledge boundaries. The central challenges are not so much the problems of teaching and learning as they are problems of formulating issues, mobilizing resources, bringing diverse knowledge stakeholders together, and creating the institutional support systems. Applied research centers, community-focused policy institutes, library networking in the community, industrial liaison programs, technology transfer offices, special purpose institutes, and comprehensive continuing education and extension programs all represent mechanisms through which these kinds of exchanges can take place. The critical qualities required are a formal commitment by a university-based resource, an off-campus entity with knowledge needs and resources to share, staff with appropriate competencies and a clear mission, and continuing funding from a reliable source. (A number of programs at research universities that possess these characteristics are profiled in Part Two.)

The central work of research universities has been and will continue to be the discovery, development, preservation, and diffusion of knowledge. What is different today are the quantity and complexity of knowledge throughout the society and, with that, the expanding constituencies for the knowledge capabilities of the academy. Research universities do not need to change the core of what they do so much as their understanding of and commitment to their growing list of stakeholders. Once they embrace the notion that knowledge inheres in a variety of places in modern society, must be drawn from a variety of contexts, and is not a fixed resource monopolized by any one set of individuals or organizations, they will mobilize to develop stronger connections and more socially relevant networks. Their distinct role as centers of new and evolving knowledge development uniquely equips them to organize and facilitate interaction among diverse knowledge resources in ways that more effectively support economic development, enhance human resources across the life span, and sustain a vital civic culture.

Chapter Two

Exploring the Social Uses of Knowledge

A primary reason for the growing need for knowledge throughout society is the extraordinary achievements of the research and scholarly communities over the last fifty years. All fields of knowledge—the arts, humanities, and social sciences, as well as the biological and physical sciences and professional fields—have been transformed by new research findings and recurring paradigm shifts. Such developments in new knowledge continuously transform both how we understand and how we shape our physical, economic, and social worlds.

Computers have not only transformed data processing, quantitative problem solving, production processes, and inventory control. They have also altered popular and serious music, film and television production techniques, and the leisure time pursuits of children. Biomedical advances in such significant areas as new life support and creation technologies—kidney dialysis machines, artificial heart valves, pacemakers, in vitro fertilization—represent new areas of ethical discourse and analysis as well as new medical technologies. Demographic shifts challenge traditional assumptions and scholarly analyses of minority and majority group differences. Growing Hispanic and Asian populations, for example, seek modification of social and occupational systems framed by assumptions formed in an era of primarily African American and Euro-American domination. Today we live and work in a social environment and a workplace that is essentially knowledge based. An ability to absorb, sort, interpret, and utilize—to "make sense"—of all this new information has become essential for living in an advanced industrial society like the United States. It is no longer simply an issue for job security and advancement.

The types of knowledge needs represented by these transformations can be discussed in terms of three distinct spheres of human activity: the *economy*, the *workplace*, and *civic life*. Understanding the role of knowledge in each sphere provides an organizing framework for understanding the challenges research universities face in maximizing the social benefits of the work they do. It is also possible to describe the effects of knowledge in each of these spheres of human activity in terms that can be readily translated into programmatic initiatives suitable to research universities.

Supporting economic development within the context of a research university is largely tied to the contributions of basic research to the development of new and improved products and production processes, which in turn has implications for how universities structure their technology transfer activities and supports for new enterprise development.

Another distinct role for research universities is enhancing human capacities across the life span by developing workplace competencies and practitioner skills, not just through credentialing and degree programs for young adults, but for already well educated adults and practitioners with advanced education. The challenges here are of three types: (1) educational updates in established fields of practice where new knowledge is growing exponentially (such as engineering, law, and medicine); (2) developmental and interdisciplinary areas of practice for competencies requiring cross-disciplinary knowledge and skills (such as engineering management or teaching English as a second language); and (3) skills in emerging specialized fields of practice that arise as a direct result of rapid technological advancements (such as elementary school computer specialists, toxic and hazardous materials managers, or biotechnology laboratory technicians). At this time, research universities do exceptionally well primarily in the first area. However, in all three categories, a significant component of "new" knowledge and experience affects the workplaces of advanced practitioners. Their recurrent need for ever more advanced skills and knowledge leads them to look to research universities to serve their knowledge needs.

A third knowledge-based activity of increasing importance in advanced industrial society is sustaining a vital civic culture through making essential new and advanced knowledge available to citizens. By creating opportunities for intellectual development through liberal studies programs and contexts for community discourse and analysis of ethical and policy issues affecting social and political conduct, research universities can serve significant community needs. Effective democracy depends on an informed public.

The CEO of the biotechnology company, the mayor of an economically depressed city, the superintendent of public schools, the citizen about to vote on a hazardous waste management strategy, the parent helping his child function humanely and effectively in a multiethnic school all seek ways of understanding issues and arriving at conclusions that will enable them to exercise judgment, make decisions, and take actions until confronted with the next new set of challenges. Growing numbers of people like this seek something different from universities than simply access to formal education and existing degree programs. Life requires them to constantly integrate new knowledge into their everyday activities. They need knowledge that provides a base from which they can make informed and considered judgments upon which they can act. Certification that they have mastered a body of knowledge, which now qualifies them as educated, is only one of an increasingly diverse set of reasons people seek out research universities. In fact, increasingly, research university constituents already possess one or more academic degrees and various forms of advanced certification. Institutions such as the University of California, Harvard University, Johns Hopkins University, and the University of Washington report that 80 percent of their adult and continuing education students already have the baccalaureate degree. The people in this sort of constituency need developmental and refresher education rather than basic skills and introductory courses; opportunities to update their skills and knowledge rather than to secure primary certification; technical and scientific briefings on new discoveries rather than education in the basic principles of physics or biology; or an opportunity to participate in communities of discourse focused on important intellectual, humanistic, and policy issues in some regularized way so they can influence the institutions in which they participate.

Current thinking and writing about the educational and knowledge needs of mature citizens frequently overlook the needs of this growing constituency. The tendency to focus on the need for degrees among adults thus offers an overly narrow picture of the adult learner and a highly utilitarian and mechanistic view of what adults need to know. As a result, research universities too readily point to other more diverse higher education providers as the appropriate settings for mature citizens. Adult learners are often portrayed as impatient with, even antagonistic toward, the central preoccupations of research universities and other centers of knowledge development. Because the needs of adult learners has been so narrowly described by leading commentators on lifelong learning as focused on applied issues or certification requirements, many research university campuses have failed to serve knowledge needs in critical advanced practice areas such as manufacturing, the teaching of math and science in the public schools, or effective health care delivery to indigent and immigrant populations. Surely there are those who only want a patentable discovery, an easy degree or certificate, or a skill-focused workshop. Increasingly, however, the mature constituencies for knowledge are participants for whom knowledge and access to significant intellectual and informational resources represent diffuse social, economic, and institutional benefits in specific sectors of the society, not just concrete personal benefits.

The somewhat more utilitarian view of what it means to build connections between the university and the larger society may in part be a consequence of the recent preoccupation with university and business/industry alliances, about which a great deal has been written over the last decade (see especially Matkin, 1990; Botkin, Dimancescu, Stata, and McClellan, 1982; Eurich, 1985; Lynton, 1984; Lynton and Elman, 1987; Gold, 1981; Dertouzos, Lester, Solow, and the MIT Commission on Industrial Productivity, 1989). These various books and reports have done an excellent job of defining and elucidating the knowledge needs facing our society vis-à-vis the problems of economic vitality. However, the proposals they offer to address new knowledge needs derive from business and industry models that are pertinent primarily to technical needs connected to the workplace, current professional practice, and overall economic development.

More recent academic work on society's knowledge needs has done less to elucidate the more subtle yet vital humanistic and sociological issues connected to our national vitality. It has done less to clarify the knowledge needs of publics concerned with the uses of liberal learning for such purposes as citizenship, cultural understanding, or making ethical judgment. Similarly, little has been written about the nascent and emerging fields of specialization in the world of work for which knowledge of new types and in new configurations is a vital ingredient. Only by acknowledging the broader social uses of knowledge will we see the need to develop programs bridging the work of all parts of the academy to the society and cease defining it primarily as a problem of connecting university resources with business and industry. (Notable exceptions include Dale Parnell's *Dateline 2000: The New Higher Education Agenda*, 1990, which focuses on underserved communities and the problems of civic education; the work of Derek Bok, in particular his 1993 book; and Thomas Bender's *Intellect and Public Life* (1993). Program models for connecting the work of humanists or social scientists to the community, or for mobilizing the resources of research libraries or computer centers for community benefits, will of necessity be different from those set up by research universities wishing to connect to business, industry, and the professions.

The following brief discussion utilizes these three categories of human activity—economy, workplace, and civic culture—as the organizing framework in an attempt to make some distinctions about the connections between new knowledge and its social uses. Each activity may require unique approaches to connecting relevant knowledge resources with the academy and within the society. The character of the knowledge, the nature of the questions being addressed, the best analytical and pedagogical tools to employ, and the characteristics of the people who choose to research, teach, or practice in a given field of knowledge may differ significantly from one field to another. How research universities organize to respond to needs will be affected by these differences. Thus a somewhat academic discussion about ways of thinking about the role of new knowledge in each of these sectors is an important first step in designing any research university program of outreach or service.

Supporting Economic Development

A fuller understanding of the role of knowledge in economic development requires attention to a variety of knowledge development, dissemination, and integration issues. The first of these issues is the ongoing debate over the value to our economy of applied versus basic research. Additional concerns include how we organize our technology transfer and commercialization efforts as well as how we meet the challenges of a workforce in need of continual reeducation.

Value of Applied Versus Basic Research and Education

One cannot pick up a newspaper or magazine, tune in to a news show, or attend a chamber of commerce luncheon without hearing about the need to support U.S. economic competitiveness and the vital role research and education play in that competitiveness challenge. New scientific and technical knowledge are seen as critical to this competitiveness because they represent the sources of the products and industries of the future. Such new knowledge represents the engine for economic development in an advanced society and thus relates to our position in a global marketplace. Popular business magazines, not just economists and social scientists, have embraced the idea of knowledge and ideas as the engines for future economic development, observing for example that "competitive advantage no longer belongs to the biggest or those blessed with abundant natural resources or the most capital. In the global economy knowledge is king. And those nations that excel at creating new knowledge and transforming it into new technologies and products will prosper in years to come (Levinson, 1992).

As Harvard's former president Derek Bok asserts, corporate and government leadership today sees America's colleges and universities as central forces for economic and manpower development, particularly in scientific, technical and professional fields (1990). However, the abstract and specialized character of knowledge development since World War II has led to a growing division of labor in preparing young people for the world of work. Colleges and universities more often provide exposure to the basic knowledge foundations: the theories, methodologies, and literatures characterizing fields of specialization. Business, industry, and the professional workplace are increasingly relied upon to provide the hands-on skill and training needed for successful practice. Many leaders in business and industry are critical of the declining vocational utility of formal degrees and exhort colleges and universities to be more applied and relevant in their curriculum. Educators respond that without the broad foundation provided by liberal arts programs, graduates will not know how to continue their own learning, to ask the right questions, to sort through fragmented information. They will not know how to critically evaluate competing solutions, to formulate interpretations, or adapt to continually changing and uncertain circumstances.

The division of labor between universities and employers that has emerged in the last few decades is one with which we as a nation are becoming uncomfortable. In contrast, nations such as England and Japan regard the function of a university education primarily to be the screening, selection, and general preparation of talented youth. The "real" training and job skills development is the responsibility of the employer. In fact, Japanese employers do not want recruits with specialized and applied skills. Broadly educated new employees allow the company maximum flexibility to assign, reassign, and even retrain people. This practice contributes not only to company flexibility but to the ability of companies to assure more job security in the face of uncertain and changing economic conditions for their employees. It does, however, require companies to make a major and continuous investment in people development well after college completion. The entire Japanese system is built upon a different set of assumptions than our own. The recognition that the ability to learn and adapt is as important as a specific set of skills needs to be more widely embraced by U.S. industry.

Another growing concern goes beyond how far formal education should go in providing the society with not only an educated but a trained, ready-to-work labor force. It relates to the current discussions about the relative economic payoffs of "basic" versus "applied" research and the extent to which we as a nation are adequately exploiting the commercial and economic benefits of research through technology transfer. The critics point out that the United States is issuing fewer patents annually, is losing substantial industries to foreign competitors, and is dealing with an overall decline in manufacturing revenues as a percentage of GNP. One strategy that could stem this spiral decline, they assert, is for our centers of basic research, especially universities, to support new product and enterprise development by accelerating their patent processes, becoming more involved in joint research ventures with industry, and expanding programs in more applied fields such as telecommunications, robotics, and manufacturing engineering. The

1989 MIT report *Made in America* is an especially apt example of this point of view.

Those less critical of research universities point out that while early post–World War II Europe and Asia were in economic shambles, the United States had a virtual monopoly in the industrial marketplace of the 1940s, 1950s, and 1960s. Today the revitalized European and Asian nations are significant competitors, in part because of their more modern practices. Nonetheless, the United States continues to dominate worldwide in invention. Thus these advocates resist the move to applied research for the same reasons their critics want it. They assert that the history of science suggests useful applications, and commercial products emerge not from an intentional set of applied questions but cumulatively from the findings of basic research (Lederberg, 1987; Bok, 1986; Giamatti, 1988). They further argue that unless there is a substantial infusion of new resources to fund equipment and faculty and student fellowships in support of both current and new research and teaching fields in universities, our competitive position will decrease even further.

Martin Kenney, an agricultural economist and author of *Biotechnology: The University-Industrial Complex* (1988a), argues that an overly applied focus and increases in university laboratory–industry ties may actually shrink the knowledge base by making knowledge proprietary and therefore not available to all in the society. Such relations can draw professors away from the teaching and mentoring of students in favor of the more personally lucrative time spent on developing their research for commercial purposes. In fact one of the basic values underlying traditional support for research universities in the United States has been their ability to make new knowledge broadly available to the society through advanced education and outreach. Kenney remarks that "many laboratories formerly producing knowledge for all in society—consumers, workers, farmers, and business people—have become corporate-captive. The result is that the freely available knowledge base is shrunk and there is decreased access to information for those unable to purchase it" (Kenney, 1988b, editorial page).

Nobel Laureate and former president of Rockefeller University Joshua Lederberg made a related but different point at the 100th anniversary meeting of the National Association of State University and Land Grant Colleges in his plenary remarks on basic research. The long history of support for basic research has resulted in innumerable "applications" or social benefits. For that reason, Lederberg asserts, we should continue to trust the process.

> Another challenge to introspection is whether we are doing all we can to accelerate "technology transfer" from academia to industry— a point of special sensitivity in the midst of today's anxieties about economic competitiveness. No one who knows my own personal history will accuse me of indifference to that issue. I will recall an anecdote about my professor, Edward L. Tatum, who completed his Ph.D. in bacteriology at Wisconsin just 50 years ago, and was facing a decision where to work. He was urged to take a position at Iowa, to look into the then "hot" field of the microbiology of butter, one of manifest practical importance. Instead, he went to Stanford, to work with G. W. Beadle on the eye pigments in fruit flies. That became translated within four years into their Nobel prize-winning work on the biochemical genetics of eurospora, indubitably one of the principal foundations of today's biotechnology. It would have been tragic were any industry to have had a veto in deciding what would truly be of greatest industrial consequence. My own experience has been consistent with that theme, that the universities accept the difficult charge of leadership in pointing out where tomorrow's industries will find their greatest opportunities, many of them in the hands of corporations that will need new birth certificates—and so will not yet be at hand as the visible contemporary partners at the time the research is conceived [p. 9, 1987].

The central issue, building on the preceding remarks, is not primarily the need for industry to help define research priorities or conceive basic research strategies, as many today argue. It is rather the need for more timely and effective two-way interactions between the university and industry in order to accelerate technology transfer and technology commercialization between autonomous researchers and industry.

Expanding Supports for Knowledge Discovery and Utilization

Even though there is much debate about priorities and strategies, there is general agreement in all sectors—education, business, industry, and professional fields—that the generation and early sharing of new knowledge is vital to the growth and vitality of the economy. A far-reaching report, *The Role of Science and Technology in Economic Competitiveness*, prepared by the National Governors Association and the Conference Board with support and participation of the National Science Foundation (when Bill Clinton was still governor of Arkansas) provides an excellent overview of the critical role of U.S. investments in research and education in the maintenance and improvement of our competitive position in the world economy. Drawing upon the views of government, business, and university leadership from throughout the United States, the executive summary to the report emphasized that

> The most demanding challenge facing America's leadership today is to restore this country's competitive position in the global marketplace. The pattern of the last fifteen years—slowing productivity growth combined with growing competition from foreign producers—has led to record trade deficits, a decline in real earnings of American workers, and a stagnant standard of living. While there are many reasons for the erosion of the U.S. competitive position, there is a growing national consensus regarding the underpinnings of competitiveness. One area of consensus is that U.S. investments

in research and education will be critical in the long term, as the United States seeks to maintain and improve its competitive position in the world economy [National Governors Association, 1989].

The governors study focused on three primary topics and offered recommendations pertinent to each. These recommendations echo findings from a variety of similar investigations including commissions and studies sponsored by groups such as the Business Roundtable, the Carnegie Commission on Education and the Economy, and the Business/Higher Education Forum. The 1989 governors' report summarized the research and education challenges we face as falling into three main areas: (1) "Marshalling Human Resources"; (2) "Investing in Research and Development"; and (3) "Creating an Innovative Environment; Getting Ideas into the Marketplace." All of the core ideas in this report are finding their way into national policy now that Governor Clinton has become President Clinton. Recent economic and employment figures suggest that the 1990s have the potential of reversing many of the downward trends observed in the 1970s and 1980s.

In describing the challenge of marshalling our human resources, education is underscored as the key to the nation's competitiveness, especially the quality of science, engineering, and mathematics education available at the K-12 level. At the university level, attention is focused on the need for state-of-the-art facilities and equipment, adequate preparation of undergraduate students in the sciences and mathematics, and the ability of colleges and universities to continue to attract and retain qualified faculty. The need for high-level technical training, continuing education, and job retraining was also emphasized—in large part because workers at every level can no longer expect to graduate from school with a skill that will last a lifetime. America needs a flexible workforce as it enters the twenty-first century.

With regard to investing in research and development, the study participants agreed that in order to meet the challenge of economic competitiveness, the United States as a nation must not only make a commitment to its research system, but redefine the relationship between government, universities, and businesses in the conduct of research and the use of research findings. To this end, the 1990s have seen a significant shift in federal funding to create incentives for research universities to become involved in industry-led collaborations and more applied research efforts, as well as basic research.

The report's final concern, and most significant for our purposes, is with the need to create an environment that fosters innovation and gets ideas to the marketplace. Specific suggestions for improving commercialization include such things as developing more accurate indicators of technology transfer so that U.S. strategists have a better grasp of the dimensions of this problem; increasing interaction between technologists at primary manufacturing firms and those in supplier firms; developing a cadre of technology transfer agents or mechanisms that would permit entrepreneurs to acquire and commercialize technology discoveries unused by either major laboratories or university research centers; and providing specialized advice and technical support for small firms seeking to commercialize leading-edge technologies. With the end of the Cold War, nationwide efforts at defense conversion and technology reinvestment (programs begun in the Bush administration and accelerated in the Clinton administration) and concerns about enhanced technology development and transfer have moved to center stage. Most universities are still trying to clarify what role they have to play.

All these concerns directly relate to how knowledge is *the* engine for economic development. Developing our human resources, investing in research and development, and assuring that innovative ideas get into the marketplace (technology transfer) each represent strategies for enhancing the economic vitality of the nation. Universities, industry, and business leaders must participate in new and creative ways if these goals are to be accomplished.

They require new ways of connecting knowledge to primary economic players. Each dimension merits fuller discussion.

Technology Transfer—Getting Research Findings into the Commercial Sector

Technology transfer is a complex issue. There are a variety of established and emerging models of technology transfer, and much has been written about this topic. The traditional view is that research laboratories, and especially universities, contribute to the technology transfer process primarily through (1) the people they educate and send to industry; (2) the consulting that faculty and researchers provide to industry, business, and government; and (3) the patents and licenses emerging from research labs. Over the last decade, a more comprehensive approach to technology transfer and the various transfer mechanisms has surfaced. In the late 1980s, a number of more comprehensive statements emerged, one of which was prepared by Professor Richard Dorf of the University of California, Davis, Graduate School of Management, on behalf of the Lawrence Livermore National Laboratory. Its key points are extracted below.

Technology Transfer: Definition and Examples

Technology transfer means the transfer of the results of basic and applied research from the university to industry for the development and commercialization of new products and processes.

Technology transfer occurs by a variety of mechanisms, some of which are informal and involve traditional university responsibilities, such as training graduate students for jobs in industry. Others are more formal and innovative, and involve the university in relationships with government and industry. The following examples illustrate major forms of technology transfer.

1. *Graduate Students*. All research universities train graduate stu-

dents who take their new knowledge and skills to industry when they complete their graduate education.

2. *Faculty Exchange*. Faculty members consult for industrial clients on an individual basis.

3. *Licensing and Patenting*. The traditional means by which Universities protect their financial interests in the commercialization of new products and processes.

4. *Cooperative Extension*. Agricultural Extension at land grant universities provides the model for new Engineering Extension and Technology Extension services. An example is the University of Maryland Technology Extension Service (TES) established in 1983 as part of the Engineering Research Center. It is especially designed to assist small and medium-sized companies and provides technical assistance as well as a conduit for technology transfer. An example at the University of California is CONNECT at UCSD Extension which brings together interested faculty, local companies and venture capitalists to promote their mutual interests.

5. *University/Industrial Liaisons*. These may take several forms, ranging from contracts between individual companies and universities to state-supported partnerships. Some examples are:

   a. Industry-sponsored contract research. An example is Digital Equipment Corporation's (DEC) support of computer research at universities through equipment allowances, technical expertise, and exchanges between faculty and DEC researchers at seminars and other forums.

   b. Industrial affiliates programs. Individual firms pay a membership fee to gain access to basic research at university labs. A University of California example is the Center for Magnetic Recording Research at UCSD. DEC, Hewlett-Packard, IBM, Eastman Kodak and Honeywell Corporation are among the firms that sponsor research at the Center. Membership fees are scaled so that small companies can benefit from ties to the center as well as large ones. Those paying the full fee are entitled to a broader range of technology transfer programs. Another University of California example is MICRO, in which industrial affiliates provide support for faculty research projects with commercial potential.

c. Special university-industry research agreements. An example is The Washington University Medical School-Monsanto Company Biomedical Research Program. The program is targeted to a specific research problem with commercial potential for Monsanto. Monsanto in turn now provides about $60 million over eight and one-half years to the research venture. The relationship involves a grants program, exchange of scientists and facilities, and seminars and other group exchanges among Monsanto and university scientists.

d. Conferences, workshops, seminars, institutes, etc. Single-purpose events sponsored and organized by university and industry scientists. These events may take place within the context of other partnerships such as those described above or they may stand alone. The California Coordinating Committee for Nonlinear Science (CCCNLS) is a systemwide network of University of California researchers that holds frequent workshops and conferences to which industry scientists are invited.

6. *Non-profit Corporations*. The non-profit corporation allows universities and industrial firms to cooperate through a third-party relationship, maximizing benefits and minimizing risks for both. The California Institute for Energy Efficiency (CIEE), a not-for-profit corporation that would funnel research dollars from California utilities to researchers at the campuses and the labs is an example. CIEE is in its final planning stages. Delta Corporation might be an additional example for biotechnology.

7. *Incubators and Industrial Parks*. These organizations are designed to stimulate regional economic growth as a planned outcome of

technology transfer, and are especially appealing to small companies that cannot otherwise afford start-up costs. Examples are Rensselaer Polytechnic Institute's Incubator Program, Stanford University's Research Park, and North Carolina's Research Triangle (University of North Carolina at Chapel Hill, Duke University at Durham, and North Carolina State at Raleigh) [Dorf, 1987, pp. 7–10].

Expanded views of technology transfer mechanisms such as this one are essential, given demands for accelerated invention and global competition to be the first to get commercial products into the marketplace.

More conventional definitions of technology transfer also tend to conceptualize it as a linear process of discovery, invention, commercial development, and introduction into a marketplace. Part of the current competitiveness problem for the United States may be this tendency to disconnect basic research completely from potential applications, product development, and market needs. A sequential model may have been appropriate in the past, but the increasing interaction between basic research and development in advanced technologies such as telecommunications, computer applications, and biotechnology, for example, requires more early stage interaction between the researchers, adapters, and distributors of new inventions and products. Increasing numbers of industry-based expert scientists and engineers are working on questions parallel to those of the basic researchers, especially in fields such as biotechnology, telecommunications, and the material sciences. Recurrent interaction between researchers could be highly beneficial for both sides. This does not mean the basic research agenda needs to be altered so much as that the intermediate steps between basic research and application need to be identified and acted upon much earlier within industry or in joint university-industry applied research initiatives.

Infusion of new ideas and inventions into industry through

successive waves of graduates is also less effective than we once presumed due to longer periods of education in master's, doctoral, and postdoctoral programs, simultaneous with shorter innovation cycles. In addition, even though young employees and specialists may have more up-to-date technical knowledge and skills than others in the organization, their lack of seniority and political savvy can make it difficult for them to get new ideas and practices into the system. Their lack of experience-based knowledge of the type described by Zuboff (1988) also represents a limitation. Business and industry, just like the university, can become vested in certain products and production techniques. Practices and management systems can become entrenched. Many argue that the American economy is as much in danger of losing its competitive edge because of bureaucratic management systems that discourage or are blind to innovation as because of a lack of technical innovation (see especially Reich, 1992; Drucker, 1982; Marshall, 1987).

Dorf's report points out that with regard to the third traditional strategy—patents and licenses—industry has typically "found it difficult to overcome the legal and bureaucratic barriers and constraints of government laboratories and universities. Most technology has left these laboratories through one or more researchers or faculty leaving and taking the knowledge with them, most often to start a new enterprise. Technology transfer is the exception rather than the rule," Dorf asserts. With a few notable exceptions, the patenting and licensing activities of America's major research centers has been minimal relative to the scale of their basic research budgets. Creating mechanisms to increase the numbers of patents and licenses based on this basic research is a high priority at all levels of government in the 1990s.

A Different Way of Thinking About Technology Transfer

The more contemporary view of technology transfer offered by commentators such as Dorf is to conceptualize it as a dynamic rather than a linear process. It requires a fast-moving interactive circle of researchers, engineers, and manufacturing, marketing, finance, and sales professionals—much like a basketball team in which players pass the ball back and forth as they advance toward the goal. As Dorf states, this contrasts with the more traditional view of technology transfer as a relay race, where each player hands off the baton to the next person once he has run his share of the course. What Dorf's conceptualization offers is a new paradigm for knowledge linkages productive of transforming basic research findings into commercially viable processes and products.

The challenge of the decades ahead is to assure the steady flow of research results and technology to and from industry to assure continued economic growth. This highly interactive process depends on new management techniques that will enable basic researchers as well as established and emerging industries to encourage and embrace innovations. Because more and more of our industrial products and services develop out of lengthy R&D cycles and involve interdependencies between licensed technology in one industry sector with that in another, the enterprise development process is different today than even a decade ago. It is increasingly clear that technology transfer in such an industrial culture is an *organizational* not just a *technical* process. It requires transfer of knowledge across disciplines, professions, industry sectors, regions, and societies. Thus it requires new institutional mechanisms for assuring ongoing exchanges and collaborative efforts supportive of new business development among the various essential knowledge professionals.

Of particular significance recently has been the growth of university-community partnerships to develop geographical clusters of high-technology industries in communities such as Silicon Valley, Boston, North Carolina, and Austin, Texas. Typically, these communities have major research institutions, readily available transportation and communications resources, as well as access to capital, high-quality labor, and marketing and distribution networks. A rich literature is emerging on regional economic development, which is fueled by research and high-technology industries. This literature elucidates the importance of regular social interaction and organizational supports for the varied stakeholders in the technology development process—scientists, engineers and technicians, local officials, investors and entrepreneurs, managers, and business service providers (Bingham and Mier, 1993; Markusen, Hall, and Glasmeier, 1986; Rogers and Larsen, 1984; Scott, 1993; Smilor, Kozmetsky, and Gibson, 1988). In addition, over the last decade, there has been a significant expansion of regional and state-based industrial extension and technology assistance programs dedicated to supporting the transformation, expansion, or both of existing industries and the growth and development of new industries based on new technology developments. These regional and state-based programs exist largely to increase and accelerate the technology development process and are ably described in Gary Matkin's book *Technology Transfer and the University* (1990).

Much is still needed in the way of research, analysis, and clinical studies on which models work and why. There is clearly a need for new models and strategies on how to more effectively connect knowledge discovery to the development of new products and production processes. Some very interesting university-based programs that address these sorts of new needs are profiled in Part Two. They represent examples of how basic research entities can interact with and exchange expertise with potential users of their knowledge in ways which enhance knowledge use simultaneously with preserving unencumbered basic research.

Enhancing Human Capacities Across the Life Span

Just as the purposes of research are being challenged and approaches to technology transfer reconceptualized, so too is our view of what we must do to assure a well-educated and continually re-skilled, reeducated workforce that can keep up with social and technical change. The current workforce competitiveness challenge is not just one of upgrading people's skills. It includes the need for inter- disciplinary and cross-disciplinary skills and for the ability to respond to rapidly emerging new types of competencies and skills.

Workplace Readiness

The need for improved workplace skills and competencies is indis- putably one of the highest priorities this nation faces. Numerous reports have raised the national consciousness about the growing crisis in both basic and advanced skills and literacies in every cor- ner of the labor force. The efforts of Magaziner and Patinkin (1989), Reich (1992), and Marshall and Tucker (1992) have been especially informative. In a detailed piece on the changing eco- nomic landscape written for the *Atlantic Monthly* (1985), James Fallows eloquently describes how the contemporary American "frontiers" are not "vacant tracts of land but the social and eco- nomic fluidity created by industries on the rise." Fallows's piece is a highly relevant and thoughtful analysis of the historically opposing points of view regarding the social and economic consequences of the United States moving toward a high-tech economy and espe- cially increased "productivity" through technology and automation. Fallows points out that "a more productive economy can be won- derful in the abstract and threatening in the concrete," which in part accounts for the strange schizophrenia we feel about it, partic- ularly if people believe "there is a certain amount of work to be done, and if machines do it, people can't" (p. 48).

The United States has a long history of constant economic change and labor force transformations. It began with the decline of the agricultural sector and the rise of industrialization. It con- tinues today with the elimination of two-thirds of all the jobs that existed in our industrialized nation of one hundred years ago, because of declines in manufacturing and production sectors as traditional as textiles and steel and as cutting edge as microchips.

Seminal works such as Barry Bluestone and Bennett Harrison's *The Deindustrialization of America* (1982) argue that the technological revolution is resulting not only in fewer jobs but in fewer "good" jobs. Good jobs provide stability, security, high pay, and benefits as well as interest and challenge. Harry Braverman's classic analysis in *Labor and Monopoly Capital* (1974) argues that even professional jobs are becoming de-skilled in the face of technological advances and bureaucratic forms of organization. More recent work by Magaziner and Patinkin (1989) and Cohen and Zysman (1987), and Marshall and Tucker (1992) continue this focus on the significant risks to the strength of the U.S. economy and the overall quality of life of our citizens represented by the decline of the high-wage manufacturing sector and the expansion of the lower-wage service sector. Many of these social commentators, in addition to calling for support of core manufacturing industries, urge public policies that cushion the negative consequences of workplace transitions as well as initiatives that assure a labor force which is adaptable, mobile, and readily retrained.

More conservative analysts such as Robert Lawrence in his book *Can America Compete?* (1984) point to historical changes in the labor market that suggest that economic changes tend to create more opportunities than they destroy (pp. 53–57). The work of Nobel Laureate economist Wassily Leontief in *The Future Impact of Automation on Workers* (Leontief and Duchin, 1986) suggests that by the year 2000 increases are likely to occur in "good" high-skill/high-wage jobs as well as "bad" low-skill/low-pay ones. Even though the service sector ("bad" in Bluestone's terms) is projected to represent 14.7 percent of the labor force, in Leontief's projective scenarios, skilled crafts jobs are projected to represent 15 percent and professional jobs 19.8 percent, increases of 1.7 percent and 4.2 percent respectively (p. 148). Leontief does project declines of more than 3 percent in managerial categories and 7 percent among clerical workers.

Employment forecasts are problematic because it is so difficult to imagine, much less project, new employment opportunities that may emerge as a result of a new technology. In the era prior to the personal computer, who would have imagined the proliferation of manufacturing, sales, advertising, maintenance, programming, and occupational services it would spawn? Before the massive reentry of women into the American labor force, who would have imagined the proliferation of personal services, householder services, convenience and fast-food services which have exploded in recent decades? In addition, the actual distribution of jobs within a very general category such as services can shift over time. The services employment category includes everything from unskilled fast-food service workers to highly paid accountants and financial planners. Figure 2.1 summarizes occupational growth projections through the current decade.

Many analysts worry more about worker scarcity problems than displacement. In spite of high overall unemployment, the *Wall Street Journal* reports that labor shortages are forecast by various pri-

Figure 2.1. Occupational Groups Expected
to Show Largest Growth, 1986–2000.

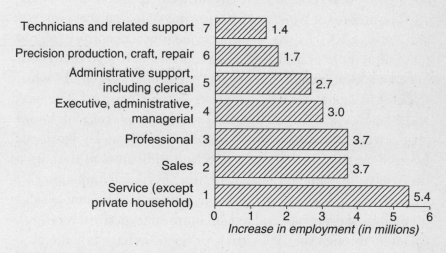

Source: U.S. Department of Labor, Bureau of Labor Statistics, 1987.

vate and governmental analysts. The shortages are primarily because of the decreasing size of the labor force coupled with an increasing "mismatch between the skills workers have and skills employers need" (Sivasy and Hymowitz, 1990, pp. R6–R12). We face a lack of basic reading and math skills in lower-level jobs such as banking, clerking, and word processing. We also are not preparing sufficient numbers with more sophisticated technical skills such as expository writing and advanced computational skills for fields such as sales, computer programming, or accounting. Thus, at many levels of employment, there is a mismatch. There is an emerging national consensus about the educational challenges we need to meet throughout the labor force (including the service sector) if we are to remain economically competitive. *Workforce 2000* (Johnston and Packer, 1987) describes the decades ahead this way: "The new jobs in service industries will demand much higher skill levels than the jobs of today. Very few new jobs will be created for those who can't read, follow directions, and use mathematics." Ironically, "the demographic trends in the workforce, coupled with higher skill requirements of the economy, will lead to both higher and lower unemployment; more joblessness among the least skilled and less among the most educationally advantaged" (p. xiii).

The authors of *Workforce 2000* further state that "between now and the year 2000 for the first time in history, a majority of all new jobs will require post-secondary education." They go on to point out that education and training are "the primary systems by which the human capital of a nation is preserved and increased. The speed and efficiency with which these education systems transmit knowledge governs the rate at which human capital can be developed. Even more than such closely-watched indicators as the rate of investment in plant and equipment, human capital formation plays a direct role in how fast the economy can grow. The simple fact is future jobs of every type will require more education" (p. xxvii). As we move through the 1990s, these projections have not altered.

Former U.S. Secretary of Labor Ray Marshall echoes these sentiments in his book on labor's role in economic policy, *Unheard Voices* (1987), when he notes that

It is widely recognized that the quality of our workforce is a major determinant of productivity, flexibility, and international competitiveness. Indeed, improved knowledge and education are largely responsible for past advances in output and productivity and are likely to be even more important in the future. We should recognize, however, that our current education system is grossly inadequate for world-class competition. Not only must learning systems be improved, but we also need to strengthen the quality of teachers and their role in education and training systems. We must recognize that learning is a lifetime process and not restricted to the first two-and-one-half decades of life. The improvements suggested here will require more resources; but much can be done to improve the productivity of the present system, which costs $453 billion a year, $210 billion of which is provided by private companies. In the long run, it will be very costly *not* to make these changes [p. 1].

Marshall quotes Anthony Patrick Carnevale as concluding that, on the basis of a review of various economic analyses, "people, not machines, are the well-spring of productivity. Since 1929, growth in on-the-job retraining, and increased labor quality through education, training, and health care consistently have accounted for more than three-quarters of productivity improvements and most of the job growth of national income. By comparison, over the same period, machine capital has contributed a consistent and disappointing 20 percent or less" (1987, p. 304). Marshall emphasizes that education is something different from "schooling." Schooling can only get people ready to learn. It determines what kind of learning opportunities an individual will have once he leaves school. Learning and education extend well beyond the years spent in school. In fact, Marshall and Tucker argue, as has management guru Peter Drucker, that the workplace can no longer be seen as simply a producing system; it must be seen as a "learning system" (Drucker, 1993; Marshall and Tucker, 1992). They assert that the most important activity taking place in the American economy is learning. In fact, increasingly, a premium will be attached to adaptability and capacity to learn (the reason we still have cockroaches and no saber-toothed tigers, according to Marshall and Tucker).

In her much more abstractly developed and empirically tested assessment of workplace transformations as a result of the introduction of computers, Shoshana Zuboff argues that all work is "knowledgeable" as opposed to some work that is "intellectual" and other work that is "dumb." Even traditional skilled and semiskilled work, though performed primarily on the basis of "experience-based knowledge" (rather than abstract knowledge), calls upon years of experience and "know-how," which must be developed and shared for the work to get done. The introduction of smart machines (computers) in all work contexts—offices, manufacturing plants, supermarkets—substitutes some of the workers' formerly acquired experience-based knowledge with abstract knowledge, which creates a profound need for "re-skilling." The re-skilling of workers must be a subtle process of helping them to get comfortable with abstractions and to understand the "significance of intellective skills and how they differ from action-centered skills in this new environment." The vital issue, according to Zuboff, is that "workers feel a stark difference in the forms of knowledge they must now use. Their experience of competence has been radically altered." She quotes one interviewee as saying, "We never got paid to have ideas. We got paid to work" (1988, pp. 74–76). What Zuboff's groundbreaking research revealed is that re-skilling and the character of worker training and retraining will have to take into account the increasingly vital connection between (rather than separation of) abstract knowledge on the one hand and action-centered knowledge on the other.

Continually Educating Professional Practitioners

Close to 20 percent of the American labor force will work in fields categorized as professional by the year 2000. Add to this the projected additional 7 to 8 percent who are expected to work in managerial positions, and more than a quarter of the labor force will possess qualities and expectations we associate with being "a professional."

A number of distinguishing characteristics of professionals are described in the rich literature on the sociology of occupations (Pavalko, 1988). First and foremost, professionals are characterized by their possession of a distinct and often esoteric body of knowledge—a body of concepts, information, and skills that are highly specialized and not easily understood by outsiders. To master this body of knowledge requires a long period of study and usually apprenticeship or practical experience as well. Professionals deliver specialized services to users and thus are governed by standards of quality and codes of ethics, which are generally shared throughout the professional community. Identification with a self-regulating community of practitioners with similar values, language, and practical concerns is another dimension of being a professional. Part of this tradition of self-regulation is an ethic of continued learning and professional updating. This provides a way to assure high standards of professional practice throughout a career and inspire confidence among the beneficiaries of the service that the professional provides. It contributes to the perception that a professional can successfully address problems in his or her area of expertise. The dominant characteristic of professions most relevant to this book is this commitment to lifelong recurrent professional education. As Philip Nowlen notes, "the one unchanging feature of the professional is unceasing movement to new levels of performance. In the achievement of these new levels, inadequacies of performance become clear and better levels of performance possible" (1988, p. 11). With increased performance expectations, the need for recurrent education also increases.

The demands for continuing professional education are increasing exponentially. This is happening for a variety of reasons. Foremost is the growth in the size and variety of professions. Professionals today include not just doctors and lawyers, but engineers and an enormously diverse group of managers; architects/urban planners and interior designers; teachers, nurses, social workers, marriage and family counselors, and clinical psychologists; accountants and certified financial planners; dietitians and health and fitness educators; legal assistants. All these groups possess a sense of professional identity and legitimize their specialness through entry requirements, certification rituals (degrees/certificates/testing), and assurances that practitioners are current and competent through mandatory continuing education and relicensure, usually on an annual basis. Milton Stern, a former dean of the University of California, Berkeley, extension, describes the relicensing requirements of professionals in virtually all of the fifty states as "lifetime education with a vengeance." In effect, our country is in the process of extending compulsory education beyond childhood, beyond adolescence, to the end of professional careers. We may embark upon a second or third career, and second or many marriages, but the continuing certainty of our lives, at least for active professionals, will be lifetime education. It was Benjamin Franklin who said, "in this world there are only two things certain, death and taxes." Stern asserts that "now we can add a third, education" (1983, pp. viii–ix).

Statistics bear this out. In a single year, according to the National Center for Educational Statistics, close to one-half of all the practicing professionals participated in one or more formal educational activities: 43 percent of allied health professionals, 40 percent of physicians, and 35.8 percent of teachers. In addition, approximately 33 percent of middle and upper management participate in at least one formal education program annually (Nowlen, 1988, p. 12). The annual investment of all U.S. employers in executive and professional education is in the multibillion-dollar range.

It is driven in no small part by the fact that close to 27 million people today have four or more years of study beyond the twelfth grade, and the more education people have, the more continual education they need in order to remain current and be occupationally mobile. Continuing education is also a necessity for professionals because of changes in information, techniques and practices, the regulatory environment, and clientele groups. Each year, more and more states mandate continuing education. Figure 2.2 illustrates the pervasiveness of this trend in a number of practitioner areas.

Figure 2.2. Number of States Requiring Continuing Education, by Profession, 1993.

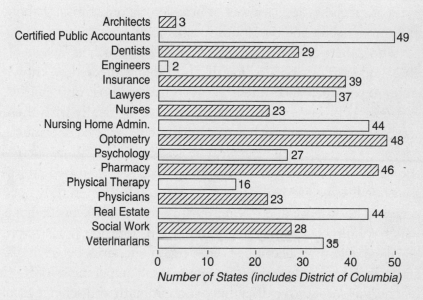

Number of States (includes District of Columbia)

Source: Louis Phillips and Associates. "1993 Mandatory Continuing Education Update." Summer 1993 Newsletter, p. 4. Used by permission.

Differentiating Types of Practitioner Education

It is important when thinking about continuing professional education to recognize that, even though one can work with a very inclusive definition, which includes levels of occupational complexity from real-estate sales through neurosurgery, there is some value to sorting professions. They can be sorted according to the types of knowledge they use, complexity of work, formal educational requirements, screening and testing requirements to qualify for practice, frequency with which competencies are reviewed, and rapidity of change in the core knowledge base. This is one means of assessing the frequency with which recurrent education will be required and the level of specialization and sophistication needed in the knowledge resources with which a given field interacts. For purposes of this discussion, it is also useful to differentiate (1) established, (2) interdisciplinary, and (3) developmental or emerging areas of specialization as a way of broadening our thinking about practitioner skills and continuing professional education.

The more established advanced professions such as law, medicine, and engineering are directly and rapidly affected by knowledge expansion and research activities. Thus universities, particularly professional schools, interact continually with these sorts of professions through the provision of mandated continuing education and close alliances with professional associations such as the AMA and the ABA as accrediting bodies. Established professions are less well served by professional schools when they need access to knowledge and research from other fields. Outside fields may have direct or immediate implications for their practice but may be inaccessible because of often rigid boundaries between disciplines and fields on university campuses. Competencies of K-12 teachers in substantive disciplines such as math and science or of engineers needing management education are examples. Practitioners in developmental and emerging fields to which new research is vital—such as public health nursing or hazardous waste management—often have problems accessing appropriate knowledge vital to practice because it resides outside their immediate field. Practitioners rely primarily on individual professional schools or associations that are often highly specialized and remote from other knowledge sources. Thus opportunities to address important new knowledge needs may be missed. Interdisciplinary issues in professional practice—such as the substance of high school biology instruction or engineering management—are difficult to serve because biologists do not talk with education professionals, and schools of engineering rarely talk to their counterparts in schools of business.

Additionally, established schools and associations are often unable to respond to vital emerging fields of professional practice that do not easily fit the research, teaching, and special interests of the faculty and professionals organized into specializations. Examples of such problematic emerging specializations are not-for-profit management for business schools, or manufacturing management for schools of engineering. Emerging interdisciplinary fields often get lost as well because subjects such as toxic and hazardous waste management or engineering management do not "fit" the existing curricula or research specializations of any single department, much less professional schools. The new emerging economic and social environments require more varieties of competency than can often be found in a single specialization. They require skills and competencies outside conventional approaches. Attorneys need to have knowledge of biology or speak a second language in order to serve new industries or clients; medical doctors need to become informed about finance and management in a managed care environment; designers and graphic artists need to master advanced computers in order to function in a multimedia environment. Research universities, because of their campuswide commitment to new knowledge development and their rich array of knowledge organization and delivery services (such as libraries, extension services, medical resources), have a potentially significant role to play in facilitating curriculum development and outreach in cross-disciplinary fields. However, they need to create offices or programs capable of facilitating such efforts.

This sort of theme is echoed in all the popular media. The

twenty-first century executive is described as having skills and competencies not readily found in current professionals because of the narrow curricular emphases of their earlier professional training. In a 1988 issue of *U.S. News & World Report,* an article titled "The 21st Century Executive" described a person who could "tell time in Bonn and know the exchange rate in Seoul, feel at home with a spreadsheet and mix well with politicians." The piece identified the following as the essential characteristics of "tomorrow's boss":

1. Global strategist: Working as deftly in Tokyo as in Toledo, he sees—then seizes—markets worldwide.

2. Master of technology: A fast-moving manager must use high tech to stay ahead.

3. Politician par excellence: Knowing which buttons to press can often cut red tape.

4. Leader/motivator: Old-time charisma is nice, but execs must coach teams as well as command them [Mar. 7, 1988, p. 49].

The article also emphasized that most U.S. managers will have to change their thinking and retool in order to develop these essential characteristics.

It should be underscored that the demands for more interdisciplinary skills cannot wait on the next generation of professors and researchers who will move into the seldom vacated tenured university positions nor for the next wave of inexperienced graduate students. One of the great contributions of continuing professional education is the way it innovatively responds to these changing knowledge needs in a timely fashion with practitioners positioned to make or influence immediate change. This is done through such things as providing engineers with management skills or managers with foreign language and cultural education or business leaders with more solid grounding in the public policy-making process.

Some of the case studies in Part Two will demonstrate this in far more detail.

Knowledge Relevant to Established Professional Fields

Established fields with roots in science and technology such as medicine have a long tradition of highly developed knowledge linkages. Nonetheless, many fall short of meeting recent challenges. Engineering represents a good example of an established, research-dependent, and rapidly changing field of professional practice with which there is much public dissatisfaction currently. This dissatisfaction derives in part from the fact that the substance of engineering research and undergraduate instruction has increasingly moved away from the basics of design and production into more abstract concerns. In his now thirty-year-old treatise *The Scientific Estate* (1965), Don Price discussed the important manpower and public policy implications of the move in all fields of science and technology away from a preoccupation with "specific objects of everyday experience, in all their complicated and concrete reality" to an increased interest in their abstract qualities that can be measured and related in new ways to other abstractions" (p. 28). The field of engineering has not been immune from this trend. In fact, Price quotes the view of a dean of the MIT School of Engineering (which is still the prevailing view among contemporary deans of engineering) that the "engineer has to be trained in those basic sciences which will give him the greatest degree of competence in facing the unknown future" (p. 32).

Many argue that, despite the creative breakthroughs coming from the more theoretical and basic research emphases, we have paid a price in productivity and competitiveness for this predominantly basic science focus in engineering research and education over recent decades. Of particular concern is the lag in U.S. manufacturing competitiveness attributed to the inattention in universities to applied problems and the education of hands-on engineers.

One antidote to this has been significant growth in programs of continuing education for practicing engineers nationwide. Universities as prestigious as MIT and Stanford, regional state universities, and local community and proprietary colleges are experiencing exponential growth in enrollments in noncredit continuing education programs which have a practical, applied focus. This is both because of the needs among practitioners for skills and competencies not acquired in conventional degree programs and because the rate of change in the engineering knowledge base is so rapid that engineers must continually update. Research universities across the nation are uniquely positioned to do more in this arena, particularly as the sophistication of even the most applied fields like manufacturing is being transformed by advanced technology such as robotics and CAD/CAM systems.

A related knowledge problem in any discussion of continuing professional education is the national concern with the insufficient numbers of young people choosing to study math and science. This has profound consequences for the pipeline of persons qualified to function in an economy that needs more and more highly educated scientists, engineers, and technicians. The growing scarcity of qualified engineers and scientists has three inextricable implications for a knowledge-based economy. There is a present and potential future shortage of college and university faculty in all fields of engineering. There is an increase in demand for engineers, particularly in electronics and computer science. There is a severe pipeline problem, meaning that not enough students entering universities are sufficiently competent in math and science to have either the interest or ability to major in fields such as engineering or the basic sciences. This latter point is further exacerbated by the fact that the curriculum in the public schools until recently underemphasized math and science. Additionally, the math and science skills of the large, tenured public school teaching force are for the most part below acceptable standards, in part because the competency requirements of professional schools of education have emphasized issues of teaching and learning at the expense of knowledge of core fields such as math, physics, or history.

What all this means is that there is a pressing need for new forms of continuing education and even reeducation among America's teachers in order to expand the opportunities for more and better forms of math and science education in the public schools, thereby increasing the number of youngsters well educated in math and science. The 1983 report *A Nation at Risk* triggered an unprecedented awareness of this problem among the general public, and in the last decade significant changes have been taking place that *may* resolve the pipeline problem in the long run. However, in 1991, American thirteen-year-olds still ranked thirteenth among fourteen nations in math and twelfth in science. High school dropout rates have also remained in the 22 to 28 percent range for two decades (National Center for Education Statistics, 1993). Clearly the need to retool and reenergize America's schools and teachers, especially in math and science, has become a significant national priority as numerous reports and studies affirm. Without motivated and competent K-12 teachers in math and science, we cannot address our needs for technological literacy in all work spheres, much less our engineering manpower needs. The urgency of the problem is similar to that in other professional fields as well. We cannot wait five to ten years for the changes in faculty, research, and teaching at the university level that will yield a new crop of differently prepared teachers. Research universities are uniquely qualified to bring teachers back in contact with the newest and most exciting findings and ideas in various fields, thereby helping develop the skills of the already certified and employed teaching cadre to begin addressing the issue of how to enhance math and science competencies *and* enthusiasm for these fields among young people.

The focus of continuing professional education as traditionally structured by universities and the professions may be overly narrow.

It most assuredly should include updates on new findings and applications based on discipline-based research. However, as the examples of teachers and engineers suggest, continuing professional education may also need to expand opportunities for cross-disciplinary and interdisciplinary education suited to the knowledge needs of the well-educated professional in society. This may require research universities to take a more active role in facilitating on-campus collaboration and off-campus links with school districts. Some institutions do this already. Many more need to.

Interdisciplinary Knowledge Needs

The example of teachers ill-prepared in math and science has parallels in other fields. Many professionals have knowledge needs that don't fit the knowledge frameworks of existing professional schools or professional associations. They could be met, however, by the research, information, and educational strengths in other parts of the university. Increasingly, professionals such as teachers, nurses, attorneys, and engineers are being called upon to master knowledge areas and develop competencies in fields outside their original field of certification. As high-technology industries such as computers and pharmaceuticals have become a larger part of our economy, the need for scientists and engineers to develop management skills and strategic-planning abilities has increased. As the demand for earlier and earlier exposure to mathematics and science education has emerged, elementary school teachers need to master basic mathematics and science knowledge in order to be effective in the classroom. As business services such as law, finance, and marketing anticipate the industries and markets of the future, financial analysts need to understand the substance and character of biotechnology development; attorneys need to understand international regulatory issues; marketers need to be responsive to ethnic, cultural, and linguistic diversity. All of these require access to knowledge that typically does not reside within the boundaries of traditional law schools, business schools, schools of engineering, or schools of education. The knowledge is within the university, however, in other academic disciplines. We simply lack institutional mechanisms that easily cross campus-based disciplinary boundaries in order to serve practice-based interdisciplinary knowledge needs. As a consequence, significant knowledge-based practice needs go unmet.

Interdisciplinary knowledge needs are as important within the liberal arts as they are in professional fields such as those just described. Teachers at every level of education—K-12, community college, undergraduate, and graduate—are relating to new constituencies and drawing upon new developments in research and scholarship that critically affect the content of the curriculum. Libraries and museums are continually redefining and expanding the works they should house and the exhibitions and educational programs they should make available. Professionals and service providers are greatly hampered by language and cultural barriers and increasingly need access to knowledge about the histories, practices, and values of people whose roots are in different national heritages. Without access to informed sources of knowledge about the historical and cultural roots of our diverse national population, it is difficult to design and manage systems which not only embrace but value diversity.

Paradoxically, interdisciplinary knowledge needs are growing throughout the society while our approaches to research and formal education are becoming more specialized. This need not be an unsolvable paradox if we conceptualize lifelong learning as a continuous process of information gathering, regrouping, and linking diverse ideas and perspectives at different ages and stages in the life cycle. But we must provide institutional mechanisms that provide citizens with access to appropriate knowledge throughout their lives. Conventional academic departments and schools rarely do this, however. What is required oftentimes is an approach to organizing knowledge resources different from and complementary to earlier forms of knowledge mastered in traditional degree programs. Specialization by academic departments with clear boundaries may be important to providing an educational foundation at the undergraduate level or in focused advanced degree programs. However, in postbaccalaureate programs, more interdisciplinary and cross-disciplinary arrangements may be needed to serve a more elaborate set of knowledge needs common to the dynamics of sophisticated practitioner environments. A number of university programs that do this are described in the chapters making up Part Two.

Emerging Knowledge Needs in the Work World

A final set of equally significant knowledge-based human capacity development needs relate to fields of practice for which advanced educational needs are limited and to fields of practice that are emerging as technological and social conditions require new forms of expertise and competency. In the broadest terms, these represent what Milton Stern (1983) refers to as developmental continuing education. Their focus is human resources development, which can be defined as either (1) noncredit advanced certification—which is more general than may be appropriate or even necessary given the rigors of advanced professional degrees in more established fields such as law, business, medicine, or education; or (2) emerging fields of specialization—that is, practice areas which require knowledge and competencies not yet integrated into the research and teaching programs of the university. Each type deserves some description.

Constituencies seeking non-degree-oriented advanced certification opportunities tend to fall somewhere on the occupational continuum between generalists and specialists. They are composed substantially of liberal arts graduates seeking workplace-relevant conceptual tools and pragmatic skills in a program of study which is less than a full-fledged graduate degree but more than a few on-the-job training workshops. At places such as the University of California and New York University, literally tens of thousands of adults annually pursue further education through certificate programs in fields such as computer programming, advertising and public relations, personnel management, personal financial planning, interior design, purchasing, restaurant management, teaching English as a second language, or microcomputer processing. These programs serve both to qualify people for positions and to advance people who work in such positions. They usually involve a deliberately structured curriculum of four to ten courses, oftentimes taught by practitioners. They create opportunities to reflect on aspects of practice, enhance practitioner skills, and facilitate interaction with peers from other office or industrial settings. Although these programs fall into that regrettable and increasingly meaningless university category of noncredit education (because they do not result in advanced degrees), they are nonetheless a major human capital development resource in a knowledge-dependent economy. Employers recognize that their employees need specialized knowledge as well as new skills. For competencies in accounting and financial management, in computer programming and analysis, in foreign language and culture, in technical management or marketing, employers typically turn to educational institutions for help. Educational institutions help by defining learning objectives, identifying appropriate instructors, and evaluating student progress in a manner not unlike that they use for degree programs.

These sorts of programs are based on the assumption that the students already have an intellectual base and some kind of certification for the world of work. However, the knowledge-dependent character of the work they do requires continual involvement in an educational process. Such a process is characterized by a combination of experiences that encourage reflection, information gathering, and critical discourse, typically in a classroom or seminar context. Such learning opportunities are essential to individuals for whom job currency, retention, elaboration, or mobility is a goal. The National Center for Education Statistics reports that three out of four colleges and universities now offer noncredit study of this type and that as of 1990 more than twelve million registrations in noncredit courses were reported by colleges and universities. These noncredit registrations are not in "basket weaving," but in a variety of knowledge areas directly pertinent to the worlds of work and citizenship. The University of California extension system alone serves more than a quarter of a million people annually with noncredit programs of study in such diverse fields as toxic and hazardous waste management, project management for engineers, professional writing and publishing skills, landscape design, alcohol counseling, and advising. All represent carefully planned programs of study taught by highly qualified faculty and professional practitioners.

Reeducation in response to workplace changes is another impetus for this sort of noncredit developmental continuing education. Until recently educators, especially those in research universities, regarded this form of education as the primary responsibility of the individual student or of the employer. As more and more of the graduates previously certified by our colleges and universities as qualified are no longer so—either because of rapid changes in knowledge or because of an earlier, more limited view of the knowledge and skills needed—universities may have a more central role to play. For example, although the science of nutrition has been with us many decades, an appreciation of the relationship between nutrition, exercise, and health has only recently become appreciated in schools of nursing and medicine. The positive effects of nutrition and exercise on disease prevention and even treatment represent a whole field of knowledge for which previously trained physicians and nurses are now seeking knowledge that can affect their professional practice. The phenomenal changes in the field of biology, as a result of the research breakthroughs in molecular biology and DNA, have made obsolete much of the early biology education K-12 teachers received in previous decades. Changes in mathematics and the introduction of computers as tools for modeling problems and exploring alternative solutions as well as for processing information have resulted in a national effort to bring practicing teachers back into university classrooms—not for degrees or certification but for the essential knowledge they need to educate young people and prepare them for the kind of knowledge they will have to deal with in college and the world of work. Production workers and engineers, be they in the automobile, aerospace, or computer industries, find themselves in need of continual retooling in the face of new products as well as new production processes, most notably robotics.

Developmental continuing education of these types is typically pursued by the products of university degree programs, college alumni who have learned how to learn and who appreciate the economic and social benefits of continuous exposure to new ideas and practices. It is an area of education and knowledge linkages that is growing because of the specializing character of many kinds of work skills on the one hand and the need for broader skills and knowledge on the other. Narrowly educated specialists seek general skills. Broadly educated ones seek specialized skills. In neither case is the education compensatory. Rather, it is a part of a lifelong process of learning, the sequencing and substance of which varies for different people at different stages in the life cycle.

Another dimension of human capacity development tied to the advanced knowledge resources of America's universities has to do with what, for purposes of this volume, we will refer to as emerging fields of specialization. These represent another area of practice-related knowledge needs that are currently underserved. Emerging fields do not represent fully developed areas of professional research and certification, deeply entrenched professional associations, or established interest groups. They generally represent the growing need in society for increasing numbers of people with the specialized skills required to work with an emerging technology, a category of workers, or a new set of organizational responsibilities. In twenty-five years of professional life, I have witnessed the growth of categories of specialized employment that hardly existed while I was in graduate school in the late 1960s: microcomputer specialists, personal financial planners, toxic and hazardous waste management specialists, affirmative action officers, volunteer services coordinators, technical writers, computer graphics specialists, and legal assistants. The incumbents of positions such as these tend to be college graduates with degrees in chemistry, engineering, sociology, or history and no formal education in these practice areas. But as new technologies and social trends give rise to new services and activities, new roles emerge for which education, training, and knowledge exchange are necessary. Research universities as a primary source of the technologies affecting social change *and* the primary center of scholarship and discourse on the changing ethical, cultural, sociological, and geopolitical landscape have unique contributions to make to these efforts. They simply need to provide more responsive mechanisms or programs through which all this potentially useful knowledge can be organized and shared with the larger society. Traditional academic departments are not such mechanisms. The chapters in Part Two provide some examples of innovative university-based programs set up to help practitioners in these emerging fields acquire the knowledge and skill base they need. In these rapidly emerging fields, it is also interesting to note that the very process of curriculum development often contributes to the definition of the field and its requisite competencies.

Professional, interdisciplinary, and developmental continuing education understood in the terms just described represent profound "pushes" in the society for increased access to and interaction with diverse knowledge resources. Universities with established professional schools, as well as established professional associations, represent mechanisms for effectively serving some types of practitioners. However, this remains within certain (and increasingly problematic) disciplinary and accrediting limits. Developmental continuing education and education for emerging fields of specialization have been less central concerns of universities. This is because of the established curriculum of college and university degree programs and the precise certification requirements of established professions and because even schools of continuing education are often just mechanisms for extending on-campus degrees to working adults. What is required is a different approach to organizing knowledge and developing curricula necessitated by the changing knowledge base at the workplace. Knowledge in action is configured and utilized in ways we have yet to master in this rapidly changing world. The growing need for education in new fields of knowledge and competencies is another reason why the publics for America's universities are growing.

If educators were to embrace the broader definition of practitioners being proposed here, analyze the legitimate knowledge needs of each category, and begin to see the reciprocal benefits of responding to constituencies representing each field—established, interdisciplinary, and emerging practice—it would be possible for research universities to see where they can contribute most immediately and meaningfully to the human capital development needs of the society. The case studies in Part Two introduce some promising models of institutions that have developed programs to serve new needs simultaneous with serving more traditional needs in the context of traditional liberal arts and professional degree programs.

Sustaining a Vital Civic Culture

A third and final human activity to which new knowledge is essential relates to the more humanistic sensitivities and skills needed to live harmoniously in an advanced industrial democracy. This has deep connections to broad issues in the liberal arts and humanities as well as aspects of knowledge relevant to public policy. It involves at least three distinct knowledge problems: (1) the development of analytical and critical thinking skills essential to interpretation and the exercise of judgment; (2) the availability of information and opportunities for discourse relevant to citizenship and policy-relevant judgments; and (3) the pursuit of ethical, aesthetic, and humanistic values central to the quality of life in a democratic society. One of the mistakes we often make when thinking about the knowledge needs of mature citizens is to assume their concerns are primarily utilitarian or pragmatic—in other words, job related—rather than intellective, aesthetic, or policy focused—in other words, life related. There is much evidence to the contrary.

The growing constituencies for knowledge are not just hard-driving professionals, business people and industrialists, scientists and engineers, and public officials concerned with economic issues or personal advancement. As the population becomes more educated and complex demographically, constituencies include those for whom the liberal arts and humanities have profound significance. Mature adults bring experiences and live in contexts that differ dramatically from those the conventional undergraduate brings to his or her initial encounters with the arts, literature, history, and philosophy. Most who pursue opportunities for liberal learning or civic education later in life also have already had a number of years of college or university work. Statistics from institutions such as Johns Hopkins, Columbia, Harvard, the University of Chicago, and University of California, for example, indicate the vast majority (numbering in the hundreds of thousands annually) participating in postbaccalaureate liberal arts programs are college graduates and close to half already have some kind of advanced degree. They also have a substantial amount of life experience and action-based knowledge that they bring to the learning experience, which profoundly affects motivation, interpretation, and judgment. Why do they continue to pursue knowledge—especially in the liberal arts? Love of learning may seem like a glib explanation, but it is a very important issue and is one less utilitarian way universities can assess their long-term effects on students—by the fact that they long to return to campus, not to relive the good old days so much as to remain intellectually engaged in important issues and the good new ideas. They also come because they need the ideas, the information, the communities of discourse to help them make sense of the important choices confronting their worlds and their lives lifelong.

Knowledge Needs Relating to Liberal Learning

Knowledge needs connected to sustaining civic culture require critical thinking skills and familiarity with humanistic and intellective knowledge sources as well as opportunities to participate in communities of discourse that can facilitate insight and understanding. For many trained in the sciences or professions, liberal learning can fill knowledge gaps. For persons already well grounded in the liberal arts, there is the need to continue the pleasure of reading, intellectual discourse, and encounters with important ideas. For everyone, there is a need for an opportunity to discover new voices. The transformations in knowledge described in the preceding sections are not limited to the economic, scientific, and technical spheres. The frontiers the liberal arts have forged, coupled with significant demographic and political trends, have shifted many of the central questions of these disciplines and introduced significant new voices into the scholarly literature.

The poetry and literature of Latin America, Africa, and Asia were rarely taught in the 1940s, 1950s, and 1960s in this country, even to literature majors in college. The economics, politics, and history of non-Western nations were rarely studied except among area specialists. The study of culture, the family, gender roles, and child rearing was for the most part within the frame of reference of Western values and experience. And, as the painful sixties and seventies in this nation demonstrated, it was researched primarily within the frame of reference of white, middle-class males. Research and scholarship have been quick to embrace these new voices and to place them in the context of the important intellectual traditions characterizing fields such as history, sociology, and literature.

There is little question that how we think about American history has been enlarged and deepened by important new works of scholarship. Work on pioneer women has greatly added to our understanding of the dynamics of the westward expansion in the United States. In literature, the availability of works of Latin

American literature in translation has introduced U.S. readers to sensibilities and histories totally unique to our own, from the magical realism of Gabriel García Márquez's *One Hundred Years of Solitude* to the probing social and political dialogues of Manuel Puig in *Kiss of the Spider Woman* or Carlos Fuentes in *The Old Gringo*. We can encounter the paradoxes of third-world development so movingly captured by Chinua Achebe in *Things Fall Apart*. Who are these wonderful voices? Where do they come from? How do their voices fit with the way we first learned to appreciate and analyze literature? Do these voices give insight into how to live more harmoniously in a multicultural society or function more effectively in a global community? These are concerns that motivate many.

It is important to reiterate what was stated earlier about the diverse needs of those whom the traditional education literature has too often summarily described as "adult learners." The constituencies seeking out knowledge in the liberal arts and humanities often do so because they desire an intellectually "broadening experience." This is often triggered by the engineer's, the doctor's, or the businessperson's discovery of the limitations of his or her specialized education for dealing with the more humanistic and ethical dimensions of life and work rather than by a desire to be a "cultivated" individual. The recent establishment of major programs of research and teaching in areas such as ethics at the Harvard Business School; peace studies at Notre Dame; global understanding, alcohol and drug studies, and medical ethics at numerous campuses across the country suggests that this knowledge need among citizens and practitioners also represents a serious intellectual concern for the more mainstream worlds of research and teaching.

Businesspeople who find themselves dealing with a primarily Asian or Hispanic workforce or moving into world markets where they know nothing about the language, culture, or folkways are interested in *understanding*, not just in facts that can enhance business strategies. The medical doctor of today must reflect on the social and ethical consequences of new technologies and the problems of providing equitable health care, not just the science and techniques of his or her field. The engineer managing a chemical plant must deal not only with the economic benefits of the uses of the chemicals being produced but also with the potential social consequences of releasing pollutants into the atmosphere and the political problems of disposing of toxic waste. These are issues that call upon forms of discourse and analysis that are value based and political, not just technical.

Finally, it is important to acknowledge that the nature of the intellectual questions with which we approach the study of history, sociology, philosophy, or literature cannot help but be framed by the character and years of life experience we have had. Questions regarding the nature of good and evil or truth and beauty that one encounters in the reading of philosophers such as Plato, Nietzsche, and Sartre are framed and understood differently at ages forty or sixty than at eighteen. The problem of faith wrestled with in Augustine or Tillich is a recurrent issue that may be resolved differently by the young adult than the senior citizen.

Liberal learning in the service of expanding one's critical and analytical thinking skills clearly represents a lifelong developmental process. The assumption that these issues, these literatures, which the public studied as eighteen-to-twenty-one-year-olds in undergraduate programs, have for all intents and purposes been resolved for life is simply wrong. Clearly the "big questions" to which the liberal arts relate mean different things and need to be revisited at different stages in one's life. The case studies in Part Two demonstrate the significant and growing publics which exist for this kind of liberal learning and the types of knowledge linkages and discourse essential to its success.

Knowledge Needs Relating to Public Affairs and Policy

The citizenship and public policy challenges of the day are varied and complex. All have important value and political dimensions.

What contributes most profoundly to their complexity is the fact of continuous social and technological change. Thus, as in the economy and the workplace, the elucidation of citizenship and public policy issues becomes increasingly dependent on new knowledge. The public is inundated with information and data related to personal choices and policy matters but often lacks a critical framework within which to evaluate the "meaning" or implications of all this information for action. The issues with which various publics are confronted fall into broad categories relating to the conduct of personal life, such as drugs, alcohol, and AIDS; challenges facing the contemporary family (in all its forms) such as child care and school curricula; community concerns such as school integration; land use issues such as the location of industrial sites; global challenges such as world hunger, international migration, and global economic interdependence. Added to all these are such cross-cutting issues as the problems of poverty, global ecology, and world peace. The era of specialization within which we live presents unique challenges to our citizens, many of whom were formally educated in a less specialized time and many of whom were quite narrowly educated in recent times. They find themselves making personal decisions and ballot box decisions with a deficit of necessary information and while lacking a critical perspective. This means people may rely too heavily on traditional forms of guidance in decision making: values learned in another era ruled by a different set of social and technological contingencies; opinions of friends and neighbors; prejudices born of misinformation; or the traditional social powers of one group over another or self-interest at the expense of others.

For many, the response to all this complexity is simply to disengage from public issues. Recent voter turnout data suggest this is what is happening. For many, however, the choice is to find a way to understand issues, to become engaged in positive action. It is the rare individual in society today whose life is untouched by one or more of these issues. In fact, most of these issues have become rallying points for organizations and triggers for social mobilization and constituency group coalescence—from the relatively benign and established Sierra Club to the emerging and growing animal rights advocates; from gay rights activists to homophobic AIDS policy activists; from traditional minority rights activists such as blacks and Hispanics to the new concerns about possible new forms of reverse discrimination among Asian groups; from the energy crisis to the anti–nuclear power movement. All tend to be narrow "interest groups," however. The media, special interest groups, books, and community resources such as libraries provide more and more information. However, many citizens are seeking mechanisms and communities of discourse that will do more than just inform. They seek enlightenment and perspective on issues so they can make better decisions that reflect common interests, not just special interests. This requires more than just information; it requires access to forums and settings in which debate and conversation can take place so people can develop clearer points of view and collective judgments. The intellectual and educational resources of research universities and their reputations for "fair-mindedness" uniquely position them to be conveners of forums and community dialogues capable of transforming all this diffuse information into knowledge that can inform judgment and action.

The most pressing public issues of our times cannot be resolved so long as research specialists, expert practitioners, and concerned citizens operate in isolation from one another. The growing information glut and rise of special interest groups has contributed to a civic culture greatly in need of revitalization. Chapter Seven provides a brief analysis of the contemporary forces giving rise to a fragmented democratic process in which the development and exercise of public judgment is becoming ever more difficult. The need for forums and settings in which citizens can move beyond "personal opinion" on issues and develop some form of consensus as to what represents the common good vis-à-vis particular issues is critical. There need to be contexts in which researchers, policy makers, practitioners, and ordinary citizens can become informed, dialogue on points of interpretation, and struggle with alternative approaches to problem solving. Notable programs with this sort of emphasis are in place at the John F. Kennedy School of Government at Harvard, where recently elected mayors and local officials can study government and policy making; through the state legislature–focused California Policy Seminar at University of California at Berkeley; through university-based World Affairs Councils at such places as the University of Wisconsin, Milwaukee, which provide forums for interaction between foreign service professionals, academics, and the general public.

The potential informing and clarifying value of new research and thinking in the humanities and social sciences, as well as the biological and physical sciences, for citizenship and public policy issues has barely been realized in this society, in large part because the institutional mechanisms for organizing essential dialogues and knowledge exchanges are not in place. The case studies in Part Two provide some instructive examples of programs that draw on disparate intellectual resources in ways that enrich citizen participation as well as policy formation.

Knowledge Needs Affecting Quality of Life in a Democratic Society

Education and especially the process of intellectual engagement has profound implications for quality-of-life concerns. This is particularly true in industrialized nations where prolonged life cycles, increased leisure time, and early retirement intersect with increasing levels of educational achievement and affluence. In such a social context, educational and cultural pursuits become strategies for coping with complexity as well as consumer goods pursued purely for pleasure. This happens in part because more people have the time and resources to enjoy the life of the mind but also because it is in the interests of the society to have the mature adults who continue to vote and affect the direction of public policy well informed about new social trends and public issues.

It is important to emphasize the qualitative as opposed to quantitative dimensions of increased free time for intellectual pursuits in the last two to three decades of life in contrast to the incentives for learning in the first two to three decades of life. The meaning of knowledge in later life can be quite different than it is in early life, and knowledge-linking efforts directed to very mature learners need to be designed with that in mind. For increasing numbers of people in democratic societies, one of the animating principles of life— one of the rewards of economic prosperity, stability, and increased free time—is the opportunity to pursue "the good, the true and the beautiful." In Western society, increasing numbers of educated middle-class citizens, not just aristocrats and elites, have been freed to do just that; and they represent a significant part of the increasing numbers of knowledge seekers. It is important to begin delineating the sorts of intellectual concerns and the highly varied older populations—the retired professional, the voluntarily nonemployed (early retirees), the less affluent economically vulnerable retiree— for whom different kinds of knowledge in the latter third of life are meaningful.

As pointed out earlier, these concerns are not just the purview of retirees and the nonemployed. They are also often the preoccupations of professionals' midlives, as they begin to settle into their early achievements and evaluate how and to what purposes they wish to use their energies in the decades ahead. The expansion of programs of study in liberal learning across the nation speak to this phenomenon. Programs have grown from just a dozen in the 1970s to ten times that by the 1990s. Institutions such as Harvard, Johns Hopkins, and UCLA have thousands of adult students involved in programs of serious study in the arts and humanities. No less significant is the important role colleges and universities play in many communities as primary or innovative centers of the visual and performing arts to which large audiences from the community are drawn.

Unique Role of Research Universities as Knowledge Resources

The focus of this chapter has been on the expanding importance of knowledge as a driving societal force. It is the centrality of knowledge in the economy—in the world of work and professional practice, in the life of the community and the individual—that is transforming us into a knowledge society. The unique knowledge needs of various constituencies give rise to an exciting and challenging set of problems. It should be no surprise that the nation's educational institutions, especially research universities, are being called upon to relate to these diverse knowledge needs. With the exception of a very few urban centers, colleges and universities traditionally have been the designated centers of intellectual life for their states and communities, the ivory towers to which young persons are sent to study, reflect, and learn. This is in part due to the fact that in a culture in which individualism, a pioneering spirit, and entrepreneurial activity have been celebrated over intellectual and artistic pursuits, colleges and universities represent safe (and isolated) havens for these pursuits, which until recently were limited primarily to the formative years of life. The absence of an aristocracy in the United States, coupled with the Puritan ethic of good works, has fostered an approach to ideas and education that is highly pragmatic. Nonetheless, educational institutions and especially this nation's colleges and universities, more than any other institutions in American society, have managed to sustain their commitment to the life of the mind, to the dispassionate and rational pursuit of the truth. Thus they represent a unique and invaluable lifelong social resource in the knowledge system, not just a place for young persons.

They represent as well, in a democratic society, the settings in which a vast majority of people have their first encounters with an intellectual community, with an openness to new ideas and a spirit of critical inquiry. Most people still turn to established academic institutions when they wish to engage in study or intellectual pursuits. Finally, the growing complexity and uncertainty of everyday life—at home, at work, and in the community—has given rise to more and more individuals and groups seeking information, guidance, and support as they grapple with uncertainty throughout their lives. For many, the perceptions and experiences they have had with universities reinforce their sense that universities are the proper setting for struggling with new and vexing ideas, which they can ultimately integrate into their everyday lives as workers and citizens. However, too many research universities have been slow to respond to the needs of those concerned citizens who are frequently these universities' own graduates.

At the risk of overstating the case, in a knowledge society, citizens increasingly view colleges and universities as lifelong resources to which they can turn as new knowledge needs arise, much as they relate to other vital social institutions. Like churches, universities are stable and credible institutions which, if responsive to changing human needs, can play a unique and essential social role. The expanding role for universities in meeting society's lifelong knowledge needs is a direct outgrowth of the work universities do—discovering and developing new knowledge. This revolution in knowledge, which over the last century has accelerated with each successive decade, has created a society in which access to learning lifelong is essential to work and citizenship. It is appropriate that research universities find ways to meet these needs.

Research Universities as Centers of Critical Discourse

There is a final word to be offered about why people perceive colleges and universities as appropriate knowledge sources despite their esoteric and specialized preoccupations. The educational and intellectual needs of various publics can be served in the workplace, through cultural organizations, through reading, or even through public television up to a point. However, because they usually lack mechanisms for analysis and discourse, they stop short of aiding the development of judgment. Research universities are more than just centers of information and learning in a material sense—buildings, teachers, computers, labs, and yes, even parking lots. They are communities of values and centers of *conversation* though loosely confederated, as Kerr described so well in *The Uses of the University* (1964). They are continual sources of new information, ideas— knowledge—as well as contexts in which criticism, analysis, and politically unencumbered debate are both possible and celebrated. As such they have a reputation for intellectual fairness and disinterestedness that allows them to function as honest brokers in the increasingly complicated world of expanding information and ideas. Most who participate in the life of our comprehensive universities, from faculty to budget analysts and departmental secretaries, from undergraduates and graduates to community supporters and alumni, have a sense that the primary business of the institution is the unimpeded pursuit of knowledge. There is respect for the intellectual and creative achievements of faculty even though ideologies may differ as may the immediate social implications of faculty work. There is the sense that, however flawed and wasteful at times, the institution's "business" is a good one to be in.

The nature, focus, and quality of that business is largely determined by the faculty, not just in what they do in face-to-face interaction with students but in the environment they make possible through the kind of work they do and resources they represent to the community. This is true not only in the one hundred or so leading research universities committed to developing new knowledge, where "star" faculty can draw large grants, other faculty, promising graduate students, and outstanding leaders from the nonacademic world because of their personal reputations and contacts. It is true in *all* institutions of higher learning. Faculty are the critical resource. They represent the focus of the curriculum, the level of discourse, and the standards of excellence of a place. They can profoundly affect campus resources; the focus, depth, and breadth of campus

libraries; the guest lecturers and special events that enrich the classroom experience; the vitality and heterogeneity of the surrounding
community that develops in part because of the presence of a campus with a unique ambiance. They represent as well a magnet to
diverse off-campus sources of ideas, knowledge, and experience—
the labs, museums, archives, and data sources described in Chapter
One. There is great pleasure in participating in this community,
only part of which is direct classroom interaction with a tenured
faculty member. The faculty imprint is felt even in courses taught
by off-campus instructors or programs of visiting lecturers because
the focus, the tone, the level of these activities occurs within a
framework set by the faculty. The infrastructure the off-campus
publics can draw on—the libraries, the cultural events—exist
because of their primary relationship to the intellectual activities
of faculty.

The harsh criticism of contemporary research university faculty
by many advocates of society's unmet education and training needs
derives in part, as suggested earlier, from an overly utilitarian view—
a view dominated by the conviction that we should educate people
for the workplace and solve vital social problems. And well we
should. But that is not all universities should do, as I hope this
chapter clarifies. Liberal learning and citizenship skills, as well as
economic development and education for the workplace and professional practice represent the knowledge needs of the American
public. In order to serve these needs, research universities must
expand their sense of mission and their institutional capacity for
fostering knowledge exchange and discourse among diverse constituencies across the life span. Networking and programmatic initiatives, both within the academy and with institutions in society,
must become a more integral part of the structure of research universities if the knowledge needs of society are to be adequately
served in the twenty-first century.

In Part Two, a number of college- and university-based programs
which respond to the sorts of knowledge needs just described are

profiled. However, that discussion cannot proceed without a brief look at some of the major social and demographic forces that are shaping the knowledge revolution in the United States. Demographic and social forces, not just technical developments, give rise to different types of constituencies within each action sphere affected by knowledge. These constituencies have different levels of sophistication. Their varied knowledge needs have to be served in different ways by different educational strategies, all in the service of the same broad social outcomes.

Chapter Three

Assessing the Knowledge Needs
of Diverse Populations

The previous chapter sought to provide a framework for describing the increasing social significance of knowledge by discussing three distinct spheres of human activity—the economy, the workplace, and civic life—which are continuously changing as a result of new knowledge. It also suggested the unique contributions research universities have to make to help communities, organizations, and individuals understand and adapt to the changes and implications of increasingly advanced knowledge. This chapter seeks to provide a more sociological context for understanding the specific publics for knowledge—markets, niches, constituencies—which are proliferating in modern society. The chapter's intent is not so much to provide new data or insights as it is an effort to select a few well-known social and demographic trends and discuss them in terms of the knowledge needs to which they give rise—some of which can be addressed appropriately by research universities. As a result, this discussion will be selective rather than comprehensive and derivative rather than original. It involves a general overview of two levels of sociological "trends," or developments, which affect society's shifting knowledge needs. Macro-level trends, such as *technological transformations* and *demographic shifts*, affect the character and the organization of social action and economic growth. A review of such trends can help elucidate both the supply and the demand sides for new knowledge. Micro-level trends, such as housing patterns, regional life styles, family values, and voting behavior, also give rise to knowledge gaps previously filled in different ways. Trends at both the macro and micro level of society contribute to the character of knowledge needs and to the development of constituencies for knowledge in the economy generally, in the workplace specifically, and in civic life. By differentiating trends and publics along these social and demographic lines, it is possible to begin identifying the ways in which research universities are uniquely qualified to serve the expanding knowledge needs of specific groups concerned with economic vitality, practitioner competencies, and civic participation.

Macro-Level Trends

A number of significant works have emerged in recent years that describe the changing economic landscape internationally and the shifting international distribution of invention, technological innovation, financing, manufacturing, marketing, and the problem of the national debt. (See especially the works by Reich, Dertouzos, Peterson, and Halberstam in the references.) The central themes of these studies are extremely relevant to any discussion of the emergence of new knowledge needs and new constituencies for learning in American society. Three broad trends are common to all such works: (1) the changing sources of economic vitality given international economic trends; (2) the transformational character of technological innovations for all aspects of economic and social life; and (3) worldwide demographic trends affecting social relations and core institutions.

The Global Economy

In his book *Unheard Voices* (1987), labor economist Ray Marshall summarizes the view of a cross section of social commentators:

> Although the United States remains the world's strongest economy, the productive potential of the United States is being eroded, its companies are losing their competitiveness and the gap between

our economy's potential and its actual performance is growing. These developments have ominous implications for America's national power and for the welfare of its people. The United States is losing its ability to project its values and defend its global interest. Poor economic performance means, in addition, declining real incomes for American families, increasing joblessness, serious social pathologies and a diminished standard of living for most Americans. These problems are camouflaged by the rising incomes of the wealthy, who get most of their income from property and not from work, and by the fact that so much of our current consumption is financed by heavy borrowing, much of it from abroad [pp. 282–283].

Marshall goes on to suggest that it is internationalization, especially competition with the Japanese, that has exposed weaknesses in American management, industrial relations, and public policy making, all of which need to be changed if we are to transform the American system to assure economic vitality in the future.

Peter G. Peterson, former chairman of Lehman Brothers, offers similar themes in a probing essay for the October 1987 issue of the *Atlantic Monthly,* which in 1993 was integrated into his book *Facing Up.* In the earlier piece, "The Morning After," he argues that our preoccupation with "competitiveness" tends to focus popular and political attention on trade policy issues rather than on the more profound issues of a crumbling infrastructure, out-of-control budgets, burgeoning borrowing from foreign sources to finance both government and consumer spending, and declining productivity as well as a declining share of foreign markets for American goods and services. Whereas Marshall's critique focuses on industrial policy and management issues, Peterson emphasizes shifts in financial policy including (1) how we legislate the federal budget with the shift from discretionary allocations based on projected tax revenues to inflation-proof entitlements simultaneous with limiting taxation; and (2) the move away from fixed exchange rates in international currency to floating currency rates, which make it much easier for nations to borrow currency from one another. In describing the increasing federal deficit, Peterson points out that the reviled "Tax and spend" motto of the 1970s was replaced with a new motto, "Borrow and spend," in the 1980s: "In every previous decade we consumed slightly less than 90 percent of our increase in production; since the beginning of the 1980s we have consumed 325 percent of it—the extra 235 percent being reflected in an unprecedented increase in per-worker debt abroad and a decline in per-worker investment at home. This is how we have managed to create a make-believe 1980s—a decade of 'feeling good' and 'having it all'—without the bother of producing a real one" (Peterson, 1987, p. 48).

Peterson goes on to point out that in the 1980s the U.S. investment rate was the second lowest in the industrialized world, the rate of growth of output per worker was the lowest, and our level of borrowing from abroad for purposes of consumption rather than investment was high. Growth in indebtedness in all sectors of the economy over the last decade is summarized in Figure 3.1. The Clinton administration forecasts a reduction in the total annual deficit as of the mid 1990s. However, large deficits continue to be expected through this decade.

Recently, in spite of the positive reductions in the total size of the federal deficit, the continuation of deficit spending in all sectors of the economy gives rise to a lack of investment in the future, which could yield dire consequences. Thus it is a matter of continuing concern for political economists and policy analysts.

Peterson's point is that the strategic problems confronting the United States in the global marketplace are far more complex than merely trade policy, or the need for accelerated innovation in industry, or more competitive products internationally. They reside more accurately, in his view, in the very fabric of American life. Peterson's concern is that after decades of prosperity and a sense of near invincibility economically, we have let our factories, roads, bridges,

Figure 3.1. Debt Continues to Grow
in All Sectors of the Economy.

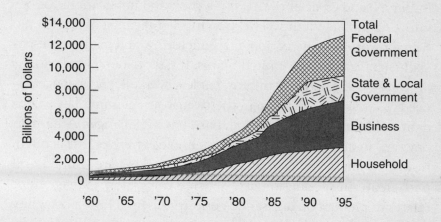

Source: The Conference Board, 1986; reprinted in United Way of America, 1987, p. 40. Used by permission.

and laboratories run down. We have allowed the skills of our workers to decline. We have accepted the erosion of the educational attainment of our citizens. We have substituted consumer spending for savings and investments in the future.

The most important investment we have been shirking, Peterson asserts, as does Ray Marshall and virtually every other social scientist or economist writing on this topic, is an investment in that most "precious of our assets: the skills, intellect, work habits, health, and character of our children" (p. 60). The problems of disadvantaged children, of ineffectual schools, and of a lack of investment in human resources during the early years of life, coupled with the enormous investments we currently make in retirement and health benefits for the later years of life, portend a grim economic future for a United States competing in a world in which knowledge and "working smarter" are the keys to prosperity. This argument is similar to that made by Marshall and Tucker (1992) and Drucker (1993).

The changing fiscal policies of the United States, coupled with a decline in productivity relative to many still-growing economies in Europe and especially Asia, have profound implications for our future economic vitality. The growing significance of the Pacific Rim for worldwide invention, manufacturing, and markets is especially significant to the United States. It has profound implications for what we as a nation—citizens, leaders, workers, and managers—need to know to be effective in the twenty-first century. The ascendant Asian nations, especially Japan, have challenged American practices in important ways—how technology transfer is structured, how manufacturing is organized, how workers are trained and participate in production and service roles, how management relates to production and service enterprises, and how a company penetrates potential markets linguistically and culturally (Halberstam, 1991).

In the 1990s, the policies of the Clinton administration, particularly vis-à-vis balancing the federal budget, supporting technology development, and expanded support for education and retraining, represent attempts to reverse the trends emerging from the 1970s and 1980s. However, the continued competitive advantage enjoyed by countries such as Japan, Sweden, and Germany means the United States must evaluate many traditional assumptions and practices. In particular, the United States has begun to seriously evaluate traditional approaches to technology transfer, manufacturing, industrial management, and labor force education and training. We also are beginning to focus on the need for foreign language and cultural skills in our population, as well as on the need for more scientific and technological literacy generally. These transformations in the international marketplace, and the variety of new and diverse knowledge needs to which they have given rise, challenge research universities in profound ways. Increased technology commercialization, improved manufacturing technologies, midcareer education in languages and culture, and a major focus on the developmental needs of children are potential ways to relate to these issues. All represent areas where research universities can (and many argue should) be doing more.

Technological Innovations

In addition to changing global trends in finance and trade, continual changes in technology give rise to new products and new manufacturing techniques, as well as to constant change in communications, transportation, marketing, and distribution systems. In the early 1980s, American citizens began to grasp the pervasive effects of technology, in part because of books such as Drucker's *Managing in Turbulent Times* (1980), Naisbitt's *Megatrends* (1982), Reich's *The Next American Frontier* (1983), and Botkin, Dimancescu, Stata, and McClellan's *Global Stakes* (1982). These accessible treatises on challenges to the American economy found large audiences and made important points about the challenges of technology in the workplace and for the overall economy. Technology represents a significant "macro" level influence on knowledge needs because of its profound effects on industry and the nature of work, the nature of products, the content of work, the forms of production, the organization of the workplace, the terms of employment, and the skills and attitudes of workers.

There is significant debate at a more theoretical level about the social and human consequences of technology. Some classic work by social scientists, such as Braverman (1974) and Bluestone and Harrison (1982), projects an increased trend toward the de-skilling and degrading of previously well-paid, more complex jobs. They are concerned that autonomous high-paid manufacturing jobs slowly are being replaced by low-paid less skilled jobs. Similar concerns have been expressed by policy analysts working on contemporary labor force trends who are currently involved in the Clinton administration, such as Magaziner and Patinkin (1989) and Cohen and Zysman (1987). On the other side of the argument sit many economists and business leaders who worry about the scarcity of skilled workers in the future, caused by both a declining birthrate and an expanding minority representation in the labor force. (See Johnston and Packer, *Workforce 2000*, 1987, and Boyett and Conn, *Workplace 2000*, 1991).

Clearly technology's impact on the occupational structure, in terms of declining, expanding, and emerging occupations, is profound. It affects the specific skills and competencies needed in the labor force, the character of the workplace itself, and the changes in the terms of employment in many industries. These trends have implications not only for the knowledge needs of workers and employees. They have implications for the management challenges of the future; for the legal frameworks affecting labor law and industrial policy; for occupational health and safety issues. They affect, as well, a variety of workplace-related issues such as child care, training needs, and retirement policies. These transformations give rise to new functions, new categories of need, new job descriptions, and new demands for education and training. Business, industry, and government keep insisting that the curriculum and central concerns of universities are more and more out of step with the day-to-day experiences and challenges facing their enterprises, but their concerns are too often dismissed.

Industrial technology, for example, like agricultural technology between the nineteenth and twentieth centuries, has advanced to such an extent over recent decades that manufacturing employment, which represented nearly 50 percent of the U.S. labor force at midcentury, will likely decline to as little as 10 percent of the labor force by early in the twenty-first century. Simultaneously, technology has been responsible for the growth of new employment sectors: telecommunications; computer and medical products industries; business, retail, and personal services. There are rapid changes in the goods and services being produced and in the ways they are being produced and delivered to customers and clients. For example, computer-aided design, fax, and real time transactions through computer networking are different ways of conducting business.

This has implications for the organizational capacities and individual skills of workers. Technology also has implications for the kinds of professionals and managers needed to get jobs done.

More and more managers manage socially diverse, highly skilled professionals, databases, and information systems rather than assembly lines and sales forces made up of "All-American" white males. These rapid transformations also mean that the technology transfer process—the means by which new inventions or research discoveries get applied as processes or products—may need to be accelerated. Cycles of new business development are different from what they were in the recent past. They have been accelerated and complicated, particularly as larger numbers of enterprises are knowledge based and seek global markets. This means new jobs continuously arise from these new developments—diverse jobs for computer operators, programmers, and maintenance and repair workers exist today that twenty-five years ago were hardly imagined. This means jobs get displaced and become obsolete. Aerospace engineers are no longer in demand, but toxic and hazardous waste management specialists are needed everywhere. This means the emergence of new kinds of services in diverse professional fields such as accounting, law, education, and health as well as in clerical, cashiering, maintenance, and food service fields.

Department of Labor projections indicate that workers will change jobs five to six times during their lifetimes. It can no longer be said once an autoworker, always an autoworker; once an aerospace engineer, always an aerospace engineer; once an executive secretary or elementary school teacher or appliance salesperson, always such a person. Technological changes coupled with demographic changes disrupt the orderly transitions we used to expect in the world of work. Instead we have shorter and often chaotic cycles of change. We no longer wait for a new generation to come along to change the ways business is conducted. Biotechnology and wireless communications are examples of growing industries barely visible a decade ago when aerospace (now declining) seemed to dominate the industrial landscape. Current generations are being called upon to constantly adapt and change, given that the half-life of most new technologies is less than five years. It is expected, for example, that over a single decade, an estimated five to fifteen million manufacturing jobs will require different skills, while an equal number of service jobs will become obsolete. Approximately 1.5 million workers are permanently displaced each year and require retraining or assistance to reenter the workforce (National Alliance for Business, 1987, p. 1). As a nation, we are faced with profound economic, occupational, and workplace changes that will call upon our education and training resources in new and challenging ways, primarily because of the shifts in the distribution of jobs and the content of work.

Types of Jobs and Their Distribution

Technology is eliminating many jobs, transforming others, and giving rise to heretofore unimagined jobs. What is critical is the process of continual change. In addition to changing jobs five or six times in a lifetime, the typical professional worker can expect to continually integrate new skills and competencies in order to remain up-to-date and respond to changing conditions in existing jobs. The changing character of the occupational structure over the next decade is described in the Hudson Institute's report *Workforce 2000*, which suggests that "job prospects for professional and technical, managerial, sales, and service jobs will far outstrip the opportunities in other fields. In contrast to the average gain of about 25 percent across all occupational categories, the fastest growing fields—lawyers, scientists, and health professionals—will grow two to three times as fast. On the other hand, jobs for machine tenders, assemblers, miners, and farmers actually decline" (Johnston and Packer, 1987, pp. 96–97).

The list reproduced in Table 3.1 provides a more detailed picture of where occupational expansion and contraction have been taking place.

Table 3.1. The Changing Occupational Structure: 1984–2000.

Occupation	Current Jobs (Thousands)	New Jobs (Thousands)	Rate of Growth (Percentage)
Total	105,008	25,952	25
Service occupations	16,059	5,957	37
Managerial and management-related	10,893	4,280	39
Marketing & sales	10,656	4,150	39
Administrative support	18,483	3,620	20
Technicians	3,146	1,389	44
Health diagnosing & training occupations	2,478	1,384	53
Teachers, librarians, & counselors	4,437	1,381	31
Mechanics, installers, & repairers	4,264	966	23
Transportation & heavy equipment operators	4,604	752	16
Engineers, architects, & surveyors	1,447	600	41
Construction trades	3,127	595	19
Natural, computer, & mathematical scientists	647	442	68
Writers, artists, entertainers, & athletes	1,092	425	39
Other professions & paraprofessionals	825	355	43
Lawyers & judges	457	326	71
Social, recreational, & religious workers	759	235	31
Helpers & laborers	4,168	205	5
Social scientists	173	70	40
Precision production workers	2,790	61	2
Plant & system workers	275	36	13
Blue-collar supervisors	1,442	–6	0
Miners	175	–28	–16
Hand workers, assemblers, & fabricators	2,604	–179	–7
Machine setters, operators, & tenders	5,527	–448	–8
Agriculture, forestry, & fisheries	4,480	–538	–12

Source: Johnston and Packer, 1987, p. 97. Copyright, Hudson Institute, 1987. Used by permission.

Workforce 2000 also points out that "among the fastest-growing jobs, the trend toward higher educational requirements is striking. Of all the new jobs that will be created over the 1984–2000 period, more than half will require some education beyond high school, and almost a third will be filled by college graduates. Today, only 22 percent of all occupations require a college degree. The median years of education required by the new jobs created between 1984 and 2000 will be 13.5, compared to 12.8 for the current workforce" (Johnston and Packer, 1987, pp. 97–98).

In Figure 3.2, the fastest growing occupations identified by the U.S. Bureau of Labor Statistics provide a summary of the importance of education.

The requirement of more education at every level of the labor force is a direct consequence of technology, of the move away from

Figure 3.2. Fastest Growing Occupations Requiring at Least a College Degree: 1992–2005.

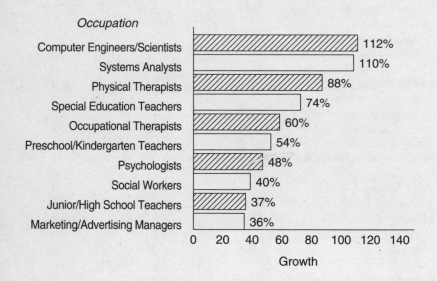

Source: Johnston and Packer, 1987, p. 98. Data taken from U.S. Bureau of Labor Statistics, *Occupational Outlook Quarterly, 37*(3). Used by permission.

brawn to brain power, whether it is the use of robots in manufacturing, computerized inventory systems in retail sales, or complex diagnostic equipment in the routine delivery of health care. The labor force will remain largely traditional in the range of jobs available. There will be high demand for cashiers, nurses, and salespeople, for example. However, the skill requirements of even very traditional jobs will increase. *American Demographics* reports that the fastest rate of growth will be in fields requiring high levels of education, such as computer programmers, systems analysts, paralegals, electrical engineers, and electronic data processing ("Fastest Growing Jobs," 1986). Nonetheless, the service sector will continue to see the most growth, with nine out of every ten new jobs created in the 1990s being in service industries—jobs ranging from janitors and bank clerks to lawyers and doctors to computer repairers and programmers (United Way of America, 1987, p. 46).

In fact, *Workforce 2000* projects significant gains in service areas such as wholesale and retail trade as well as health care and business services. The trade and service sectors are expected to add more jobs between 1985 and the year 2000 than now exist in all manufacturing categories. However, all these long-range forecasts and planning documents raise serious questions about the wage and general economic productivity implications of the fact that 80 percent of new jobs are being generated by service businesses. The United Way points out that "as manufacturers restructure to be more cost-effective and productive, they are eliminating jobs. The U.S. steel industry, for example, accounted for 400,000 production workers in 1979, but only 200,000 in 1986. Employee layoffs, union wage concessions, closure of marginal plants, transfer of more production overseas, and investment in new technology typify the changing industrial sector. Some industries, such as electrical machinery and printing, are prospering. Unless U.S. productivity picks up quickly, however, America's previous international supremacy will be matched and then surpassed by other industrialized nations by 1990 (United Way of America, 1987, p. 40).

The enormous reductions in manufacturing jobs as a result of defense cuts in the 1990s have displaced hundreds of thousands of engineering, technical, and skilled manufacturing workers. With such reductions comes not only employment at potentially lower wages in less skilled jobs but also the potential for an overall reduction in standard of living, unless new industries appear that can generate demands for high-wage skilled workers. This is in large part why new enterprise development productive of job creation and new manufacturing opportunities is becoming so critical in the mid 1990s. In a knowledge-based economy, there is great promise in the potential of composite materials science to create whole new industries in construction materials, of environmental research to yield industries that can manufacture and sell worldwide abatement and monitoring devices, of biomedical research to yield enterprises that design, manufacture, and globally distribute such things as prosthetics. Research universities can and must play a vital role in the early research and technology commercialization stages of these new industries.

The growth in services also clearly raises serious questions about potential productivity gains to offset declines in other sectors. *Workforce 2000*, for example, argues that productivity gains in services are one of the keys to future economic growth in the United States and even identifies four potential service industries that are ripe for such changes. The authors describe an array of organizational, managerial, and skill-building initiatives that could improve the service sector. They advocate such things as the development of self-diagnostic health clinics and automated nursing homes in the health care industry. They describe the potential for direct sales manufacturing and automated checkout counters throughout retailing. They suggest the desirability of more computerized approaches to education and training as a way to increase productivity in the expanding education system. Home banking or electronic fund transfers could streamline financial services. Initiatives such as these require the adaptation and utilization of advanced technologies and the education of managers and workers about how to do familiar things in new, more productive ways. Research universities have a role to play in analyzing what can be done and, where appropriate, in delivering research findings, consulting, and educational services that can assist in achieving productivity gains.

Content of Jobs

Proposals for increasing service sector productivity, such as those outlined in *Workforce 2000*, are also controversial because they imply further de-skilling and fewer jobs in each of these sectors. The question that has to be addressed simultaneously with the efficiency one is whether or not we can sufficiently enhance our systems of education and employment tracking so as to redirect workers displaced by productivity increases in one sector into fields where labor scarcity, higher compensation, and greater job security are likely. Such fields include public school teaching, nursing, engineering, and computer services.

It is also unclear what will be the precise nature and content of many new jobs of the future. Many argue that technology can free us to do a great deal of work that is necessary but not currently done. Gail Garfield Schwartz and William Neikirk describe this sort of potential new work as "jobs for the common welfare" in their 1983 book, *The Work Revolution*. The ideas they introduced more than a decade ago are today a central part of the national discourse on work, community service, and the new technology needed to rebuild our core infrastructure. Schwartz and Neikirk state,

> Technology will make it possible to do much useful work that is not now done, financed through productivity gains in the private sector. For want of a better phrase, we need "quality of life" workers who can build and repair roads, railroads, airports, water systems, waste treatment plants, parks, and recreational facilities. They can renovate historic buildings. They can monitor power plants and toxic

waste disposal and air and water quality. Undersupplied services—
day care, health services, mental health care, geriatric care, rehabil-
itation of criminals and the physically and mentally handicapped,
beautification, and arts and cultural projects all can be provided in
abundance. That is the promise of the work revolution [p. 228].

They argue, as do many in Washington, D.C., today, for an
increasing number of publicly funded jobs which would capture
those who are regularly unemployed but willing to work and thus to
become productive citizens. Potentially, as many as 76 million citizens could be employed in areas of high social need, for example, as
public works construction and maintenance employees or as nursing home attendants or toxic waste inspectors. Such individuals
would also be taxpayers and contribute to the overall economy as
consumers. Setting up the systems that would identify, organize,
train, and manage this "quality of life workforce" is a formidable task.
The idea is also a controversial one because of the expansion of publicly supported jobs. The larger point for our purposes is simply that
were the national will there, the capacity to sustain high employment in the face of technological efficiencies is there in the form of
jobs in the undersupported quality-of-life sectors. Mobilizing to
develop those sectors would require new knowledge services as well.

One additional significant economic trend occurring simultaneously with rapid technological change and the growth of the service sector is the accelerated growth in small business and industrial
enterprises. Most of the *new* employers are small enterprises and
most employment growth is in small enterprises, while downsizing
is occurring throughout large national and multinational enterprises
such as the steel, automobile, aerospace, and computer industries
(see Figure 3.3).

Part of the reason for this shift to smaller business is that service industries, the sector of greatest growth, tend to be smaller than
manufacturing industries, the sector of greatest decline. In fact, the
average service industry employs one hundred or fewer persons. The

Figure 3.3. The Shift to Smaller Businesses: Growing Percentage of Private-Industry Workforce.

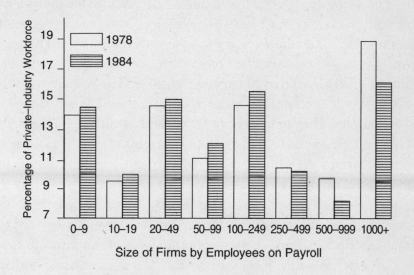

Source: *Wall Street Journal*, July 25, 1986, p. 23; reprinted in United Way of America, 1987, p. 40. Used by permission.

decline in overall employment in large enterprises also is a result of the precipitous increase of corporate restructurings even in so venerable a corporation as IBM in the last decade. Such restructurings tend to result in company closings and job losses, which are hard on communities as well as individuals. The industrial and economic restructuring of the 1990s, precipitated by the end of the Cold War defense industry wind-down and military base closures, has been another reason for rapid downsizing. California has lost more than 200,000 jobs in defense-related industries such as Hughes, Lockheed, and General Dynamics in recent years, and those industries (especially aerospace) are not likely to rebuild their employment base with the shifts in defense spending.

These well-known trends—corporate restructuring, defense conversion, plant closings, growth of service industries, and increased employment in small businesses—represent important factors affecting productivity increases, economic development, and human resources development strategies. They raise important public policy questions as well as challenge traditional assumptions regarding such important issues as technology transfer, management preparation, and employee training and development. The way small businesses organize their productive activities and communications differs from that of larger enterprises. The resources available to smaller enterprises are different from those of multinational corporations. They tend to have fewer funds available for research and development, as well as for in-house training and development of their labor force. They are also less able to be major donors to universities or joint venturers in collaborative research initiatives. Nonetheless, they need to be connected to vital knowledge centers. Colleges, universities, and independent research labs need to establish mechanisms to better serve the needs of this growing economic sector as well as meet the research, management, and human resources development needs of big corporations. Part Two provides two case studies of university programs that do just that.

Demography: Changing Population Characteristics

Demographic trends have a profound effect on a variety of issues relevant to knowledge needs and emerging constituencies for learning. The knowledge needs of American society are being largely influenced and framed by worldwide population shifts as well as by important national population trends. We are only beginning to come to grips with the character and significance of these trends. Increasingly we need to mobilize our research and teaching capabilities in the direction of discovering and disseminating knowledge that equips people to understand, make informed judgments, and perform effectively in a daily context framed by the needs and interests of highly heterogeneous social groups. Otherwise, we will not be serving essential work, citizenship, and family needs. Research universities are responding to many of these changes through the establishment of international business programs, Pacific Rim study centers, and ethnic studies programs. However, these efforts, while having a strong component of research and scholarship, combined with degree programs for undergraduate and graduate students, have been less effective than they might be in connecting with the organizations and constituencies in society who need and can contribute to the new knowledge they are developing.

As pointed out in Chapter One, the nature of these changes and the rapidity with which they take place means that knowledge needs extend beyond the preparation of children and young adults. They extend into virtually every area of professional practice, business, and citizenship. All sectors of the society are being confronted with new needs for knowledge as a result of demographic shifts. The discussion of these changes of necessity will be brief rather than comprehensive and will focus on distribution and growth issues with reference to age, race, social class, education, ethnicity, and density, both nationally and worldwide. Of special significance for our purposes are the shifting age, ethnic, and regional distributions of the population across the United States and the effects these have on the worlds of education, work, and citizenship.

Age.   One very dramatic fact is the extent to which the United States population is aging. With the maturing of baby boomers and recent low birthrates, there has been a substantial increase in adults. The United Way of America has described the status of the elderly over the next two decades:

> The graying of America may be the most significant demographic change facing the U.S. in the next 50 years. The 1980s marked the first time in U.S. history that elderly persons outnumbered teenagers. The elderly population is expected to grow steadily until 2010. At that time, it will increase sharply as members of the baby boom begin reaching 65 years of age. The oldest old—those aged 85 and over—will be the fastest-growing segment of the elderly population

for the next 30 years. The number of persons in this age group is expected to double by the year 2000.

Today's elderly are generally healthier, happier, and better off financially than ever before. In fact, today's elderly have the highest per-capita discretionary income available, more than any other age group in America. The prosperity of the elderly, however, may be exaggerated. Although the poverty rate for the elderly (12.4 percent) is now lower than for the population as a whole (14.4 percent), there is a large cluster of the elderly just above the poverty line—a cluster known as the near-poor [United Way of America, 1987, p. 13].

Figure 3.4. More Elderly and Fewer Children to Support.

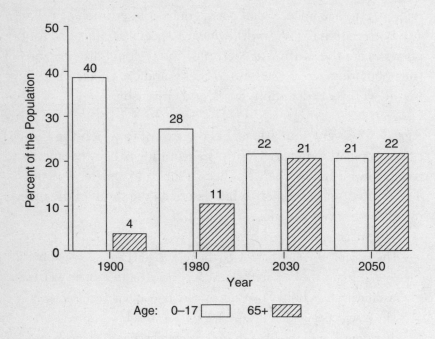

Source: U.S. Senate Special Committee on Aging, 1988, p. 13.

At the beginning of this century, the ratio of elderly to young was one to eight. By the end of this century, it will be one to two. However, in that two will be a large percentage of minority persons who may or may not be equipped to function effectively in a highly technological economy, providing the tax base and medical and social services needed for a large elderly population (see Figure 3.4).

Race and Ethnicity.   The shift in ethnic composition of the United States population and its attendant sociocultural characteristics is one of the greatest challenges we as a nation face in the decades ahead. The proportion of minorities in the United States is rapidly approaching 33 percent; among children and young adults in states such as California, New York, and Texas, it is already 50 percent.

Overall, the racial and ethnic diversification of the nation as a whole will continue (see Figure 3.5). Population projections into the year 2050 indicate that it is likely that this nation, originally

Figure 3.5. Percentage of the Population, by Race and Hispanic Origin: 1990, 2000, 2025, and 2050.

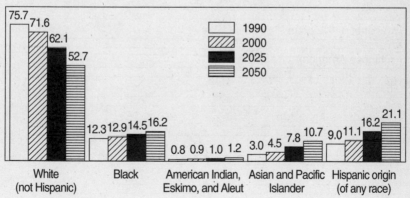

Source: U.S. Department of Commerce, 1993, p. 5.

founded by white Europeans on the principles of openness and equality for all, will be just a little more than 50 percent white.

Race and ethnicity continue to carry with them significant socioeconomic characteristics affecting the life chances of individuals and the human resource challenges facing the society. Of special significance are the disproportionate levels of poverty among ethnic groups in the United States and the low rates of school completion. The socioeconomic characteristics of most minorities in the United States are quite different from those of most elementary and secondary school-aged whites, as well as those of traditional college-going students. High school dropout rates are much higher, especially for Hispanics and blacks (college completion rates are also much lower), as Figure 3.6 illustrates.

The overall economic and social hazards of being a black or Hispanic youth in the United States are startling when one looks at the figures (Bennett, 1992). As pointed out in the previous section, one child in five lives in poverty today, and children in poverty

Figure 3.6. U.S. High School Completion Rates: 1984.

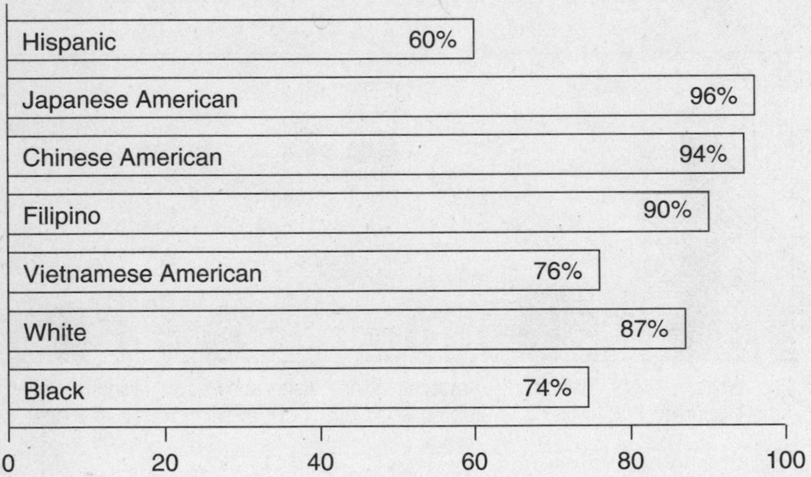

Hispanic — 60%
Japanese American — 96%
Chinese American — 94%
Filipino — 90%
Vietnamese American — 76%
White — 87%
Black — 74%

Source: Hodgkinson, 1986.

are one-third less likely to graduate from high school; 50 percent of all black females are pregnant by age twenty, and the percentages for white and Hispanic females are rising. The high school dropout rates are close to 25 percent nationally and as much as 50 percent in some cities. In contrast, as pointed out earlier, one of the effects of technology and the increasing workplace skill requirements is that 50 percent of all new jobs will require education beyond high school and 30 percent will require a college degree. The data on the educational attainment of the poor and minorities provide little about which to be optimistic and are characterized by high illiteracy, high dropout rates, and increasing teen pregnancy (National Alliance for Business, 1987).

The changing racial and ethnic composition of the population is an increasingly significant social and economic development issue. This is because of the increasingly important connection between literacy, school completion, and economic self-sufficiency for the individual. Even though the overall birthrate in the United States is declining, high birth rates continue among the poor. The demand is high for skilled workers to keep the American economy competitive amid a declining supply of qualified workers. Our human resources are our most valuable resources as we enter the twenty-first century. More than 30 percent of the pool of future workers is made up of immigrants and minorities, an increasing proportion of whom are not native English speakers. Ronald Kutscher, who writes on major employment trends and issues in the decade ahead, reinforces the significance of the trends.

The more promising growth rates for occupations requiring relatively more education also have significant implication for Hispanics and blacks, who taken together will account for more than a fourth of all entrants to the labor force between 1990 and 2005. Attainment of high school education is significantly lower than average for Hispanics. It is also somewhat lower than average for blacks. And both of these groups are also more likely to be currently

employed in occupations for which growth is projected to be significantly less and for which earnings are currently lower. These two
groups will be better able to compete in the future labor force if the
challenge of achieving greater education is met [Kutscher, 1993,
p. 5].

The increased reliance on minorities and immigrants in the
future labor force raises other important issues. Given the knowledge-based nature of so many occupations and the need for basic
reading and computational skills even for the least demanding jobs,
assuring even basic literacy has become a national concern. The
National Alliance for Business regularly reports sobering statistics
on the lack of fit between job requirements and the qualifications
of large numbers of minorities and immigrants. Of particular concern are difficult-to-reverse high school dropout rates, which
approach 50 percent among inner-city blacks and Hispanics; a 50
percent pregnancy rate among black females by age twenty; and the
fact that one in five children born today lives in poverty, with children in poverty one-third less likely to graduate from high school.
Lester Thurow, dean of the Sloan School of Management at MIT,
has frequently been quoted for pointing out that the appropriate
measure of a society's economic competitiveness is the skills and
competencies of the lower rather than the upper 50 percent of its
labor force. The lack of basic education and workplace skills among
significant numbers of poor and minority groups needing to find useful work in a fast-paced, technology-driven economy is sobering
indeed. Transformations in both the distribution and content of
jobs, along with poor education, have precipitated a major crisis
requiring creative responses from all types of institutions concerned
with the knowledge system.

These trends represent significant new demands for knowledge
development through research, teaching, and service and require
approaches that go far beyond traditional university approaches
to teaching and learning in undergraduate classrooms. Cultural

sensitivities and competencies will be increasingly important in the delivery of basic human services such as health and education. Alternative economic development strategies sensitive to the histories and the distinct character of inner-city and ethnic groups need research and evaluation. Expanded research on the relative effectiveness of culturally sensitive approaches to teaching and learning may be in order. Retooling is needed to develop the skills of practitioners grappling in their day-to-day lives with how to be effective in a multicultural/multiethnic society. All of these represent immediate challenges to which the knowledge resources of research universities, properly organized, could potentially be very useful.

Gender.   Related to the discussion of race and ethnicity is the increasing significance of gender. Only 15 percent of the net addi-

Figure 3.7. Labor Force Components: 1985 and 2000.

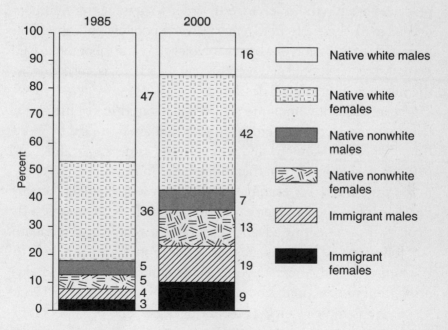

Source: Johnston and Packer, 1987, p. 95. Copyright, Hudson Institute, 1987. Used by permission.

tions to the labor force between 1985 and 2000 are to be white males. Rather, labor force growth has been dominated by women, blacks, and immigrants, as Figure 3.7 illustrates.

As noted previously, related statistics on the small numbers of women and minorities studying math and science at the secondary school and college levels suggest a potential skill shortage of substantial magnitude in this country. As more and more fields require more and more scientific literacy and technical competency, fewer and fewer graduates possess the needed skills.

Until very recently, demographic trends and intergenerational supports in fields such as medicine, science, and engineering at the professional level, and mechanical and technical specialists in the manufacturing and trades sectors, assumed new recruits would be white males. White male dominance was further aided by recruitment, training, retention, and benefits practices reflective of the sociocultural preoccupations of white males. These policies and practices are having to change in order to attract the numbers needed to fill these jobs from a more diverse pool of applicants. The increased participation of women at all levels of the labor force, particularly the managerial and professional since 1970, is staggering, as the numbers in Figure 3.8 demonstrate.

Even though women are still concentrated in traditionally female occupations (32 percent in jobs that are occupied by more than 90 percent women) and still earn full-time wages about 70 percent of what men earn, there is much to indicate improvement in the years ahead. For example, women represent a rapidly increasing share of workers in many traditionally male occupations, particularly those requiring advanced education, as indicated in Figure 3.8. Johnston and Packer state that "these proportions are likely to rise further over the next 15 years, as the number of women graduating from professional schools increases. For example, in 1983, 45 percent of those receiving accounting degrees, 36 percent of new lawyers, 36 percent of computer science majors, and 42 percent of business majors were women. And although women's wages

Figure 3.8. Women Hold a Growing Share of Managerial and Professional Jobs.

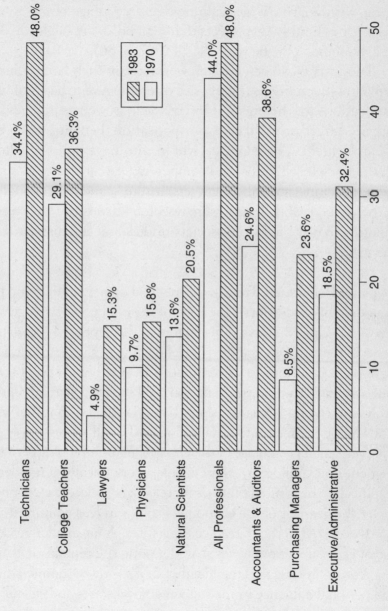

Source: U.S. Bureau of the Census, *1980 Census of the Population, Supplementary Reports;* U.S. Department of Labor, Bureau of Labor Statistics, *Handbook of Labor Statistics,* 1985, Table 18.

relative to men's have shown little improvement when looked at over two decades, the pattern of the last five years is more encouraging, with relative wages gaining five percentage points in five years. One Rand study projects that women's wages will equal 74 percent of men's by the year 2000" (1987, p. 86).

The entry of women into the workforce in such large numbers and across such diverse categories of employment has profound implications for the organization of work, as well as policies and supports affecting child care, compensation, benefits, and terms of employment. These impacts will in turn have profound effects on the knowledge, skills, and competencies required of management, personnel specialists, lawyers, insurers, and budget analysts in the world of work. Once again, research universities have a contribution to make in helping society understand and manage these changes.

Regional Population Trends.   One final demographic trend pertinent to this discussion is the issue of regional population growth across the United States. This relates to the supposed population boom in the Sun Belt and the parallel decline in the Rust Belt. Population data continue to suggest that the United States will be very much an Eastern-dominated nation well past the year 2000; that decline in the mid-Atlantic states has slowed; and that the West, while still experiencing substantial growth, still represents only a relatively small percentage of the U.S. population (and most of that segment is in California). Nonetheless, economically, if not demographically, the United States is increasingly a bicoastal economy. By far the greatest of the economic growth in this country in the 1980s occurred in the sixteen coastal states. A far smaller percentage of economic growth was shared among the remaining thirty-four states. This suggests the likelihood of strong economic growth and personal affluence in the sixteen coastal states and stagnant if not declining economic vitality in the other thirty-four in the years ahead, unless these states initiate economic development activities and federal lobbying efforts to accelerate resource development productive of more active participation in the knowledge-based economy. As research, knowledge, and technology development are increasingly tied to economic development, more and more formerly agricultural and industrial states are increasing their investments in research and education, giving the coastal states new competition for research grants and business development.

Demographic characteristics also vary significantly from region to region. It is clear that in twelve of the Sun Belt states, there will be more than a 25 percent decline in school-age children. In addition, the regional distribution of persons aged sixty-five and over is heavily concentrated in states such as California, Texas, Illinois, and New York (U.S. Department of Commerce, 1993). All of these regional demographic differences suggest that demands for services and human resources needs and potential will vary regionally. This in turn suggests that the publics looking to state universities for services will vary regionally, and the demands in states like New York, Iowa, Texas, and California may be regionally distinct. Even though all areas will be concerned with the broad categories of economic development, practitioner needs, and enhancement of the common good, the ways in which universities express and ultimately respond to these concerns are likely to vary regionally.

In sum, these macro-level trends give rise to important changes in the overall economy and in specific workplaces that call upon knowledge resources and educational institutions in ways not before experienced. The authors of *Workforce 2000* introduce six key policy areas that may require rethinking and revision in order to face the new contingencies. Each policy area represents new types of knowledge needs among specific constituencies. Each in turn has implications for the research, teaching, and service activities of universities. The challenges they identify can be summarized as follows:

- *Stimulating balanced world growth:* The United States must pay less attention to its share of world trade and more to the growth of the economies of the other nations of the world, including those nations in Europe, Latin America, and Asia with whom the United States competes.

- *Accelerating productivity increases in service industries:* Prosperity will depend much more on how fast output per worker increases in health care, education, retailing, government, and other services, than on gains in manufacturing.

- *Maintaining the dynamism of an aging workforce:* As the average age of American workers climbs toward forty, the nation must insure that its workforce does not lose its adaptability and willingness to learn.

- *Reconciling the conflicting needs of women, work, and families:* Despite the huge increases in the numbers of women in the workforce, many of the policies and institutions that cover pay, fringe benefits, time away from work, pensions, welfare, and other issues have not yet been adjusted to the new realities.

- *Integrating black and Hispanic workers fully into the economy:* The shrinking numbers of young people, the rapid pace of industrial change, and the rising skill requirements of the emerging economy make the task of fully utilizing minority workers particularly urgent between now and 2000.

- *Improving the education and skills of all workers:* Human capital—knowledge, skills, organization, and leadership—is the key to economic growth and competitiveness (pp. 105–106).

Micro-Level Trends

The changing context for education and the emergence of new knowledge needs are also affected by micro-level trends and changes—changes in the more immediate content of everyday life and values. Having looked briefly at key macro trends—internationalism, technology, demography—it is important to take a moment to examine a few examples of micro trends that affect knowledge needs and learning constituencies. Many micro effects evolve out of macro trends. Nonetheless, they can have independent power and influence on the character of knowledge required or the profile of the constituency for learning. They include such things as changing family organization and function, changing character of housing and neighborhoods, new forms of community and patterns of relating to government, as well as evolving ethical and religious values. Such changes create the context out of which new knowledge needs develop, as well as the parameters within which knowledge resources can be mobilized. These trends may be more cyclical and transitory perhaps than the issues identified as macro level. Nonetheless, they affect the daily needs for knowledge and issues clarification increasingly felt by America's population.

Marriage and Family Patterns

The distinguished sociologist Amitai Etzioni (1983) points out that even though 92 percent of all Americans will marry at some point in their lives, the amount of time they will spend as married persons is decreasing in the United States. Marriages last a shorter time than they used to, and a higher percentage of marriages end in divorce. Second marriages end in divorce even more often than first ones. People are also living longer today than ever before. There is increased acceptance of single status and delayed marriage among young adults. (The United Way reports that 54 percent of eighteen-to-twenty-four-year-olds live with their parents and 11 percent of twenty-five-to-thirty-four-year-olds do [1987, p. 19].) All these trends result in a lower proportion of husband-wife households, highly mobile households, and ultimately fragmented communities. The data in Figure 3.9 summarize the changes over the last twenty years.

Figure 3.9. Household Composition: 1970–1992.

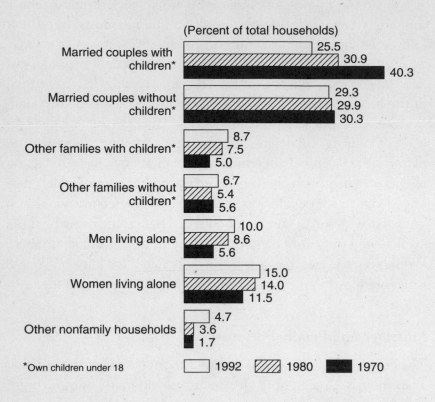

(Percent of total households)

Married couples with children*
25.5
30.9
40.3

Married couples without children*
29.3
29.9
30.3

Other families with children*
8.7
7.5
5.0

Other families without children*
6.7
5.4
5.6

Men living alone
10.0
8.6
5.6

Women living alone
15.0
14.0
11.5

Other nonfamily households
4.7
3.6
1.7

*Own children under 18   ☐ 1992   ▨ 1980   ■ 1970

Source: U.S. Department of Commerce, 1993, p. 16.

Etzioni's work over the last decade reflects concern about this trend. He asserts it has profound implications for the development of long-term social relationships and even more importantly, the rearing of children. According to Etzioni, the downside of the increased social acceptance of single status and diverse or multiple relationships is the tendency to ignore the positive effects of a stable family context. The family has a vital influence on the development of patterns of mutuality. The family also serves an educational mission in the character formation of future generations (1983, p. 111). Etzioni suggests that the essentially anti-family attitude characteristic of the pop psychology, which emphasizes the "natural" development of children, minimizes the need for structure, direction, and support among even very young children. This theme is echoed in a variety of more recent publications—conservative and liberal—in which the importance of "values" and the family as the center of values formation are emphasized (Wilson, 1993; Bennett, 1992; Aaron and Schultze, 1992).

Even within husband and wife families, patterns are changing due largely to the labor force participation of women (more than 63 percent among mothers of children under six years of age) and their increased economic power in the family. As a consequence, the ways women and men use time are converging, even though working women still carry a larger burden of household tasks. All the pressures are in the direction of an increase in child care services, use of convenience foods, new domestic technologies, and new and expanded forms of personal service (housecleaning, gardening, catering, pet tending) to support the equal participation of men and women in the paid labor force by the year 2000. The American family is becoming much more a "partnership" than a unit of specialized roles such as breadwinner and homemaker.

These changing characteristics of the American family have profound implications for employment policies (as, for example, families want increased corporate sponsorship of child care); management strategies (as, for example, two-income households show less willingness to be geographically mobile); and education and training strategies (as, for example, families juggle Saturday soccer games with career-related meetings and travel). These changes also affect the economy by accelerating the reliance on services for numerous functions previously performed by homemakers as well as by increasing the buying power of women for such durable goods as cars or housing. Additionally, they encourage the development of products and services that enhance the life styles of employed men and women. Changing family patterns also affect the community. Voluntary associations and the schools, traditionally dependent on nonemployed women, must find new ways to deliver service, given that they can no longer rely on women's contributed labor. Changing work and family patterns also make it more difficult for people to give time to traditional forms of civic participation. All of these result in a restructuring of vital social services. Vital social institutions are changing the content of their day-to-day activities. The competencies of those who plan, manage, and deliver services through them are also changing. Much of the new knowledge we need to understand and to adapt to these changes is inside our great research universities, where women's studies, family studies, and child development programs are elucidating issues previously not even researched. This work needs to be better connected to the policy and practitioner communities.

The role of education and training is a critical one in this process. Many of the new knowledge needs in our society flow from this refocusing and restructuring of work and family life. These are important issues vis-à-vis the integration of women into the "for pay" economy but also vis-à-vis the declining labor force participation of women in the "not-for-pay economy" of voluntary service to schools, hospitals, community, social, and cultural organizations. Both sectors are changing the ways they do business, and with those changes come new education and training needs.

Housing Patterns

One of the more significant trends growing out of the demographic and family changes described above is the changing character of the American household, particularly its size. This is in large part attributable to the effects of technology, particularly birth control, on family planning and family size. It is also a result of an expanding demand in the labor force for workers, particularly in the growing office work and service categories over the last three decades. This has drawn millions of women, including young mothers, into the labor force. However, women's increased labor force participation is only part of the reason for household changes.

The increased life expectancy and improved health of persons over fifty-five has resulted in a major growth in small or single-person households in that age group. In addition, significant changes in social values resulting in fewer marriages in the population as a whole, later marriages, and an increased divorce rate also contribute to the larger number of smaller households than previously. Finally, in a geographically highly mobile society, people move in and out of neighborhoods with great regularity. In a region of nearly two million people such as San Diego, California, 25 percent of the population moves annually. Thus the types of households that are forming and will be formed in the future are far more varied than in the past. The Bureau of the Census projects that by the year 2000, married couples will represent 52 percent of households. Of the remaining 48 percent, the vast majority will be one-parent and single-person households. The data in Figure 3.10 show the changes in household composition in the direction of smaller units based on increases in single-person households rather than married-couple households.

Income levels of households are also changing. Mature households, those headed by persons fifty-five and older, are showing faster than average growth, and this will continue over the next fifteen years. Reflecting the move of upper-level professionals and other well-paid people through the life cycle, the median incomes of the mature market continue to be nearly 80 percent of the median of all households. In fact, the fastest household growth will occur among those with the highest incomes. Projections developed by *American Demographics*, Census Bureau staff, and economic consultants indicate that by the year 2000, there will be 5.9 million households with incomes of $50,000 or more, a 70 percent increase from the 1986 level of 3.5 million. Within the mature population, approximately 16 percent will be among the less affluent households in 2000. Thus, in addition to becoming smaller, households are

Figure 3.10. Today's Changing Family.

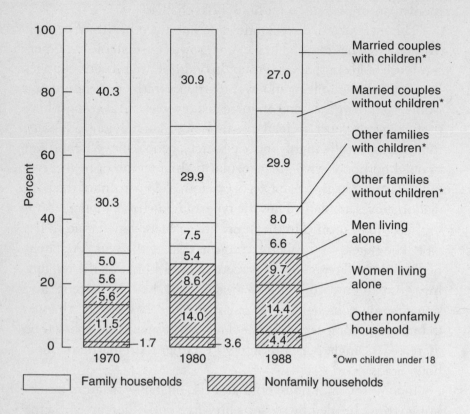

Source: U.S. Bureau of the Census. Current Population Reports (1988), Fig. 1, p. 3.

becoming more affluent among older and less affluent among younger populations. For example, by the year 2000, most fore-casters predict a doubling of households headed by persons fifty-five or older in the $75,000 and over category compared to 1986. The under $20,000 category for this age, in contrast, is expected to decrease by about 5 percent. This change will occur because of cross-cutting factors such as divorce, lower educational achievement among minorities, and changing economic realities for younger cohorts—meaning older people are likely to be better off than younger people in the decades ahead.

Why are these trends relevant to knowledge and the work of universities? Demographic shifts such as these give rise to general social and economic changes, which are relevant to the types of knowledge people need to function, and to the characteristics of the constituencies needing access to knowledge. For example, the substantive dimensions of urban planning and real estate development are affected by these sociological shifts, as are a variety of public policy matters. How buildings, neighborhoods, and communities are designed, proximity to vital services, and new issues of affordable housing emerge because of these shifts. This means the knowledge needs of practitioners as well as citizens are changing and refocusing in order to deal with these new contingencies. At a more cultural and sociological level, these new patterns of living say something about why populations increasingly look to neutral institutions such as museums, universities, and cultural associations as centers of social and intellectual activity. For persons not otherwise linked to a neighborhood or community through children or family ties, finding a "community" is not always easy.

It is interesting to observe the large numbers of single professionals, early retirees, and voluntarily unemployed who spend time on U.S. campuses in degree programs, in extension courses, or at special lectures and performing arts events. (Data are provided on participation levels in Part Two.) Such high numbers were unlikely twenty-five years ago when families and neighborhoods were less fluid. People today not only have the discretionary time and income to pursue learning but they are drawn to colleges, universities, and parallel institutions because many of the traditional ties to family, neighborhood, and community no longer bind. The proliferation of college and university programs for senior citizens are an excellent example of this. People have moved from the homes and communities in which they lived during their working lives; their old neighborhoods have been changed by new populations; children and grandchildren live at distances and are highly independent; affordable and efficient housing for retired persons may be in new developments or neighborhoods. They seek out a new community, often by affiliating with the educational and cultural organizations in the towns in which they retire.

This is not to suggest that these institutions are becoming the recreation centers of the elderly nor the meeting places of single young professionals, although they do serve some of these functions. What is being suggested is that the pattern of contemporary family life, housing, and neighborhoods increases the probabilities that certain kinds of public institutions—churches, libraries, museums, and universities—will become centers of community life, and a very meaningful community life at that—one that is based on shared values and interests rather than simply residential proximity or small children. Educational and cultural institutions can choose to close their doors to such constituencies, or they can—as have places such as the University of Chicago, Harvard University, the University of California, and most major campuses around the country—set up institutional mechanisms which make it possible for such constituencies to participate in the life of the campus through learning communities based on annual memberships and frequent interaction. Done properly, such programs also provide the opportunity for full-time students and faculty to benefit directly or indirectly from the presence of such constituencies on campus. The discussion of programs for retired persons in Part Two points out some of the reciprocal benefits of such activities.

Changing Values

Of the many publications over the last decade reflecting on cultural values, social change, and public attitudes, two are particularly relevant to our concern with the role of knowledge in society: *An Immodest Agenda*, by Amitai Etzioni (1983), and *Habits of the Heart*, by Robert N. Bellah and Associates (1985). Alan Wolfe (1989),

William Bennett (1992), James Q. Wilson (1993), and Aaron and Schultze (1992) offered more recent discussions of value issues and their implications for public policy. However, Bellah's work provided such an original and thoughtful analysis of the tension between individualism and commitment in American life that it struck a responsive chord in a variety of communities, finding its way onto the *New York Times* bestseller list for a number of months in the late 1980s and enjoying lively sales well into the 1990s. What Etzioni refers to as the "hollowing of America" and Bellah describes as "the culture of separation" represent social phenomena that they assert threaten the democratic traditions of this great nation as well as our potential economic viability in a worldwide economy. *Habits of the Heart* looks at the role of family life, religious and ethical traditions, and participation in local politics as activities that contribute to a "morally coherent life." It examines how changes in the character of each of these social institutions and their growing lack of integration in contemporary society are giving rise to changes in American character. This theme is introduced early in the book:

> The most distinctive aspect of twentieth-century American society is the division of life into a number of separate functional sectors: home and workplace, work and leisure, white collar and blue collar, public and private. Such division suited the needs of the bureaucratic industrial corporations that provided the model for our preferred means of organizing society by the balancing and linking of sectors as "departments" in a functional whole, as in the great business enterprise. Particularly powerful in molding our contemporary sense of things has been the division between the various "tracks" to achievement laid out in schools, corporation, government, and the professions on the one hand, and the balancing life-sectors of home, personal ties, and "leisure" on the other. All this is in strong contrast to the widespread nineteenth-century pattern in which, as on the often-sentimentalized family farm, these functions had only

indistinct boundaries. Domesticity, love, and intimacy increasingly become "havens" against the competitive culture of work [1985, p. 43].

Habits of the Heart describes the results of four parallel investigations into the contemporary way of life of white middle-class Americans in four separate communities. Members of the middle class traditionally have been central participants in the public life of America. From their in-depth analyses of love and marriage, psychotherapy, voluntary associations, and local politics and political action organizations, the five authors conclude that American life is being threatened by an excessive individualism, which places personal good above the "common good."

This theme of growing self-interest, a lack of integrative social vision, and the relentless pursuit of individual self-interest results in what the Oxford Analytica research group describes as a "strident individualism lacking in the idealism or moral conviction necessary to do more than muddle through." Oxford Analytica describes a kind of moral schizophrenia in contemporary American society. Based on the data that group members have amassed in their study, *America in Perspective* (1986), they point out that

While many Americans want the society to seek the rewards of traditional morality and values, they do not want to pay for those rewards personally by pursuing traditional patterns of work, family life, sexual behavior, religious devotion, and so on. They want what they believe are the benefits of the good old ways, while at the same time they want to keep their new-won freedoms. . . . What seems to be emerging is a culture of compromise. As the suburb, the prevailing American way of life, is a compromise between city and country, so what we are seeing is a "suburbanization" of values. The philosophy is pragmatic; the style eschews conviction; the criterion is, does it work for me? [p. 369].

At the conclusion of their study, the members of the Oxford Analytica group offer this further observation on America:

> This picture reflects not only the values of technological life but also its progeny, which in turn foster a pervasively manipulative approach to the problems of society. The public's need to believe in the system creates a tension with its perception of economic, political and social malfunction. In turn this puts a premium on the political leader who is *seen* to be doing something, almost regardless of the substance or the success of what he does. Of course, this is not a new approach to politics. Machiavelli argued in the sixteenth century that the appearance of possessing good qualities was more important than their possession in reality. But what is new is that the skillful exploitation of modern media technology can give those in power an unprecedented capacity to determine how they will appear [p. 369].

One possible effect of this strident individualism may be in the declining participation in local and regional politics, based in part on a growing cynicism within the electorate about the capacity of the individual to make a difference. Politics, like everything else, has become careerist, leaving the country with little visionary leadership to call upon at the local, regional, or national level.

In Etzioni's work, this theme of "strident individualism," of an absence of "integration," is articulated in terms of an absence of "commitment to shared concerns" as exemplified by a decreased willingness to "play by a shared set of rules, to commit resources (including psychic energy and time) to the public realm, and to attend to some commonweal matters." Etzioni ascribes this decline in activities in support of shared concerns to the erosion throughout the society of a sense of civility and mutuality, qualities which require the individual to forego self-interest for the sake of some larger social group, or social as opposed to individual values. In

and Associates, 1985, p. 287). The fundamentals Bellah and his colleagues would want addressed include: (1) changing the meaning of work back to the idea of work as a contribution to the good of all and not merely as a means to one's personal advancement; (2) reintroducing the notion of "vocation or calling"; and (3) reducing the inordinate social "punishments of failure and rewards of success" (p. 287).

What is significant in all this, for the purposes of this discussion, is that it suggests the potential relevance of programs that foster the sorts of knowledge connections and informed discourse on broad intellectual and value concerns essential to sustaining civility and our democratic traditions. Expanded knowledge connections are critical to enriching civic culture, not only to supporting new forms of economic development. Such connections relate to the renewed importance of liberal learning in the society and the need for expanded institutional mechanisms to assure public discourse and citizen education. (In Part Two, programs at the University of Wisconsin and the University of California that bring citizens, policy makers, and academics together to address regional, national, and international issues in a spirit of open inquiry are described.) Bellah states the issue well:

> It should be clear that we are not arguing, as some of those we criticized . . . have done, that a few new twists in the organization of the economy would solve all our problems. It is true that a change in the meaning of work and the relation of work and reward is at the heart of any recovery of our social ecology. But such a change involves a deep cultural, social, and even psychological transformation that is not to be brought about by expert fine-tuning of economic institutions alone. On the contrary, at every point, institutional changes, educational changes, and motivational changes would go hand in hand [p. 289].

Finally, the Oxford Analytica group emphasizes (as does Bellah;

as did Tocqueville in the nineteenth century for that matter) an additional central factor. That is the special importance of religion in American history and the unusual articulation of religion with both our personal and national values and vision (p. 120). As the institution closest to the creation and preservation of American values, organized religion has been and will continue to be a significant element in the "crisis of Americanism" and the American claim to exceptionalism (p. 128). The philosophical, ethical, and increasingly social and political forces linked to formal religious institutions represent significant topics of research and public discourse in modern America. They play a central role in the struggle of ordinary citizens for values clarification and reaffirmation of community. How new forms of knowledge can intersect with traditional religious perspectives is an important issue in an advanced society such as ours. The current public controversies surrounding creation theology and the abortion issue dramatically demonstrate the need for informed discourse and community consensus building. Universities are potentially the developers of contexts in which such informed public discourse can take place.

Any discussion of constituencies for learning in our postindustrial landscape must be framed by an appreciation of the significance of continuous and oftentimes revolutionary change. Change affects the central questions of research and scholarship, the curriculum of undergraduate and graduate degree programs. It also affects the substance and form of the knowledge connections which must be forged between universities and the larger society that is attempting to understand, respond to, and integrate change as individuals and communities. This chapter has selectively described a number of the well-known structural changes—economic, technological, and demographic—and sociological shifts—in family, life styles, and values—taking place in American society. This selection is based on the need to establish such well-known trends relating specifically to the expanding demand for knowledge services throughout the society. We also need to understand how these trends might shape the ways in which various institutions of higher learning can and should relate to specific subsets of their growing publics. In the next chapter, distinct publics, with particular knowledge needs arising in large part because of these important social, economic, and technological changes, are described in detail; and where research universities can best have an effect will become much clearer.

Chapter Four

Matching Knowledge Needs with University Resources: A Matrix Approach

The focus in Chapters Two and Three has been on some of the major social, economic, and technological forces giving rise to transformations in all forms of knowledge, which in turn give rise to new and distinct publics with a potential stake in the core capabilities of research universities. Out of this apparently complex jumble of forces it is possible to (1) begin sorting the types and dimensions of knowledge needs within particular areas of activity as well as (2) sociologically profile the various potential constituencies for knowledge and their levels of experience and intellectual sophistication. Out of such a sorting process, what began as a highly complex set of needs within a seemingly large and heterogeneous public starts to assume manageable dimensions. It then becomes possible for various providers of knowledge and educational service to identify for what issues and for which publics they most appropriately can be a resource.

Taking the three increasingly knowledge-based areas of human activity discussed in Chapter Two—the economy, the workplace, and civic life—and matching them to specific constituencies for new knowledge shaped by the macro- and micro-level trends discussed in Chapter Three, a summative matrix of needs emerges. Clearly no single institution can serve all of the diverse knowledge needs described in the matrix. Colleges, universities, professional associations, and proprietary institutions all have potential roles to play, based on the strengths and capabilities they have vis-à-vis specific types and levels of knowledge needs. The matrix is meant to be suggestive, not directive, a heuristic device rather than a rigid typology. Research universities, for example, can relate to only some of the needs and services described in the matrix. Other constituencies are better served by providers of education and training with a more central commitment to basic or compensatory education, such as community colleges.

The various types of critical knowledge connections arrayed in the matrix suggest a far greater range of needs in the public as well as a richer range of potential knowledge services than is typically understood within traditional institutions of higher education. Rather than categorizing knowledge needs in the conventional way, which is by level or type of academic degree or credentialing, the matrix offers a more generic definition of knowledge needs. Such a rendering is based on the relationship of types of knowledge mastery to the different kinds of social or workplace outcomes needed in society. Degrees and credentials are means to a knowledge mastery end not an end themselves. Following this approach yields a matrix of knowledge needs around nine key outcomes essential in postindustrial democratic societies.

1. Basic skills and literacy among a socially, economically, and culturally diverse population

2. General education in the social traditions, cultural values, and the building blocks of specific disciplines essential to the development of critical thinking and lifelong learning skills

3. Credentialing and certification for the world of work and professional practice

4. Professional/work-related updates for specific specializations (such as accounting, neurosurgery, landscape architecture, or electrical engineering) for purposes of job effectiveness, retention, mobility, expansion, and career transitions

5. Technology updates across all areas of practice for individuals, organizations, and communities through technology diffusion, transfer, and exchange

6. Reeducation in response to economic, social, environmental, and workplace changes

7. Knowledge exchanges across specialized fields and industries

8. Access to new knowledge and developmental skills essential to informed participation in communities and civic culture at local, regional, national, and international levels.

9. Intellectual enrichment of the quality of life for individuals, communities, and society as a whole

What these nine general categories represent in sum is a range of social outcomes that need to be addressed in order to sustain the social and economic viability of a modern democratic society in a global context. The categories underscore the diverse sorts of institutional mechanisms needed in order to assure that all citizens, organizations, and communities throughout the life span have access to opportunities to acquire:

- Knowledge for basic functioning in a postindustrial economy (matrix items 1–3)

- Knowledge that facilitates individuals, organizations, and communities adapting to and integrating continuous change (items 4–7)

- Knowledge that enhances citizenship skills and quality of life in a continuously changing environment (items 8–9)

Although there are growing expressions of concern coming from business, industry, and government leaders about many of the unmet needs arrayed in the matrix, there is still relatively little serious research or discussion of these knowledge needs in the scholarly and academic literature. Only recently have research universities included these concerns in their discussions of institutional mission. In contrast, educational institutions with a primary interest in teaching and training have been extremely responsive to many of these issues over the past decade. However, despite often superb curriculum content and teaching abilities in many proprietary, community college, and regional state university programs, most are not also involved in the creation, evaluation, and organization of new knowledge. Few have readily available databases, archives, and advanced libraries, or the labs and facilities essential to the verification and application of knowledge. Thus they cannot be the single resource in addressing society's continuing knowledge needs. Research universities have a vital role to play within the increasingly differentiated knowledge "marketplace." The matrix that follows can help to identify where research universities can have the greatest impact. The case studies provided in Part Two similarly elucidate the ways many fine research institutions are connecting the work they do with these growing constituencies for new knowledge.

The growing chasm between the main preoccupations of our more traditional centers of knowledge production and development and the users and public beneficiaries of that knowledge is a gap that cannot be bridged without a serious concern within the academy for the increasing knowledge needs of external constituencies and an expanded commitment to institutional mechanisms which serve critical knowledge needs across the life span. The modern research university must adapt its structure in order to be fully capable of fulfilling its commitments to the public simultaneously with its traditional commitment to knowledge development and the credentialing of citizens through undergraduate and graduate degree programs (see Table 4.1).

The items in Table 4.1 will be familiar to every reader. They embrace the virtually universal programs and institutions we invest in to meet the fundamental knowledge needs of children and young adults in this society to prepare them for the worlds of work and citizenship. However, there is less universality and uniformity when it comes to other clusters of knowledge needs, around which centers so much debate inside the higher education establishment.

Table 4.1. Matrix of Knowledge Needs and Knowledge Resources: Basic and Fundamental Knowledge.

Knowledge Needs	Knowledge Resources	Potential Providers
1. Basic education for a socially, economically, and culturally diverse population	Traditional K-12 education	Public/private K-12 schools
	Compensatory adult education for dropouts and the passed over	GED and community college adult education
	Adult basic literacy for the underprepared	Local/regional literacy programs
	English language and cultural education for immigrants seeking skills for work and citizenship	Tutorials/classes through social service agencies
2. General education in social traditions, cultural values, and building blocks of knowledge essential to the development of learning skills and critical thinking	College- and university-validated associate and baccalaureate degree programs	Public/private/proprietary institutions of postsecondary education including research universities
	Part-time postsecondary degree programs for working people of all ages	Corporate/company-based degree programs
	Programs of degree study organized specifically for adults "returning" for first or second degrees	Media/telecommunications enterprises for degree programs
		Contract degree programs with public/private higher education providers

Table 4.1. (Cont.)

Knowledge Needs	Knowledge Resources	Potential Providers
3. Credentialing and certification for the world of work	Vocational, apprenticeship, and on-the-job training programs for skilled and semiskilled technical service and paraprofessional workers	Licensed vocational/technical schools and institutes
		Professional associations and state licensing boards
	Specialized business, management, technical training through proprietary school programs, cooperative education, or traditional colleges and universities offering accredited undergraduate degrees	Accredited company-based programs
		Accredited proprietary/for-profit degree providers
	University, college, and specialized institute advanced degree programs in such fields as law, medicine, business, human service, engineering, and so on	Public/private/proprietary institutions for postsecondary education including research universities

Nonetheless, in the eyes of many policy makers and increasing numbers of business and government leaders, meeting the underserved needs is essential to sustaining prosperity and democracy in a postindustrial society. All of society's institutions concerned with knowledge may need more connections to their publics in order to assure regular and easy interchange between the users and producers of knowledge. Modern society depends upon a continuous infusion of new knowledge across the life span and the continuing development of informed publics capable of considered judgments and humanistic values. Thus all institutions concerned with knowledge are likely to discover expanding audiences for the work they do and the resources they represent. It is important to briefly discuss the less traditional categories of knowledge needs (Tables 4.2 and 4.3) in an attempt to make the case that universities may be neglecting important knowledge needs to which their capabilities are essential.

Underserved Knowledge Needs

Traditionally, what colleges and universities have defined as noncredit education often has been seen as a trivial adjunct to the more serious and demanding credit- and degree-related programs: classes taught in conventional formats leading to a terminal degree such as a baccalaureate or master's. The proliferation of outreach and continuing education programs over the last decade, as well as the renewed interest in public service and campuswide attention to service, suggests an increased interest in the potential value of providing recurrent and developmental continuing education (Table 4.2, item 4). This type of education is not just continuing professional education for relicensure such as that needed by doctors or accountants. As described in Chapter Two, it is a type of education that serves the individual who already has a firm intellectual base and some kind of certification for the world of work, but nonetheless requires continuous involvement in education for purposes of

Table 4.2. Matrix of Knowledge Needs and Knowledge Resources: Advanced and Developing Knowledge.

Knowledge Needs	Knowledge Resources	Potential Providers
4. Professional/work-related updates for purposes of on-the-job currency, retention, upward mobility, or job expansion and reeducation and reskilling in response to economic, social, environmental, and workplace changes	Workplace training through on-site programs, and off-site consultants	Independent trainers/consulting firms/contractors
	Mandatory professional continuing education for relicensure through proprietary schools, colleges, universities, professional associations in fields such as law, accountancy, counseling, teaching, nursing, and medicine	Professional associations
		Media/telecommunications enterprises
	Developmental continuing education in new skill areas or interdisciplinary fields through institutes, colleges, and universities	Specialized institutes and research centers
	Provision of new technical skills in response to declining, changing, or emerging job requirements, such as CAD/CAM in manufacturing; new diagnostic/treatment modalities in medicine; new paradigms in fields such as molecular biology	Public, private, and proprietary institutions of postsecondary education including research universities

Table 4.2. (Cont.)

Knowledge Needs	Knowledge Resources	Potential Providers
	Provision of crossover skills for expanding assignments, such as management for engineers, international business practices for attorneys	
	Provision of transition counseling/education for displaced workers/professionals due to industry layoffs/obsolescence/no further demands for services, such as homemakers reentering employment; laid-off aerospace, computer, and banking executives and professionals; early retirees from downsizing military and multinational corporations such as GM, IBM	
	Home-based freelance independent workers seeking market-valued skills and competencies	
5. Knowledge brokering across fields and industries	Provision of interdisciplinary knowledge and skills to practitioners and problem solvers in technical, social, economic, and community contexts, such as occupational health and safety workers, people such as not-for-profit association managers and administrators, journalists, and public administrators	Independent consultants and brokers Industrial/governmental researchers and laboratories Professional associations and schools

Table 4.2. (Cont.)

Knowledge Needs	Knowledge Resources	Potential Providers
	Provision of assistance on complex interdisciplinary social problems to alliances of individuals or social groups, problems such as regional economic development, alcohol and drug use, intergroup and race relations, urban poverty	Major knowledge centers such as research universities
	Interactions between researchers and practitioners in areas of research-affected practice undergoing rapid changes, such as molecular biology in agriculture or pharmaceuticals, magnetic recording in computers, signal processing in telecommunications, scholarly work in women's history or black history for K-12 teaching	
6. Technological updates through technology diffusion, transfer, and exchange	Provision of knowledge for consumers and users of basic research interested in the application of findings for new services, processes, or products, people such as technical, research, and development specialists in fields such as aerospace, computers, pharmaceuticals, medicine, computers	Industrial/governmental researchers and laboratories Major knowledge centers such as research universities

Table 4.2. (Cont.)

Knowledge Needs	Knowledge Resources	Potential Providers
	Provision of knowledge to constituencies interested in new business formation, such as venture capitalists, bankers, attorneys	Independent consultants and brokers
	Provision of knowledge to professionals and laypeople whose work requires technological literacy, such as journalists, politicians, voters	

job currency, retention, elaboration, or mobility. The reader is reminded that the National Center for Education Statistics reports that three out of four colleges and universities now offer "noncredit" study, and that as of 1990, more than 12 million registrations in noncredit courses were reported by colleges and universities.

The noncredit registrations reported by these many colleges and universities are in nontrivial fields of study. For the most part, they represent knowledge areas directly pertinent to the worlds of work and citizenship. As pointed out in Chapter Two, the University of California extension system alone serves a half a million people annually, primarily college graduates, with noncredit programs of study in fields that rarely overlap campus degree programs—fields such as toxic and hazardous waste management, publishing skills, and alcohol counseling. All represent carefully planned programs of study taught by highly qualified faculty and professional practitioners.

Reeducation in response to workplace changes is another emphasis with which university leadership has concerned itself little until recently (with the exception of established professional schools). Faculty are slowly recognizing that many previously certified graduates and professionals no longer are qualified to meet the challenges confronting them, either because of rapid changes in knowledge or because of expanding views of the knowledge and skills needed in an area of practice. As noted in Chapter Two, the positive effects of nutrition and exercise on disease prevention and even treatment represent a field of knowledge about which previously trained physicians and nurses are now returning to universities to learn more. Teachers are returning to universities to learn about changes in the fields of biology, mathematics, and computer science. They are not earning new degrees but are acquiring the essential knowledge they need to continue to be effective professionals. Production workers and engineers, be they in the automobile, aerospace, or computer industries, find themselves in need of continual retooling in the face of new products as well as new production processes, most notably CAD/CAM and robotics. Colleges and universities have an important and lifelong role to play in all these sorts of educational challenges.

Knowledge exchanges and technology transfer (Table 4.2, items 5 and 6) may seem more obscure. Yet for those industries, institutes, colleges, and universities that are engaged in research and are operating in states and regions where economic development is a central concern of the community, these items have increasingly significant implications. Oftentimes, knowledge and skills from one area of endeavor cannot be catalyzed for social and economic good without making a connection with knowledge and skills in another vital sector. For example, more and more new business start-ups are tied to the development of innovative ideas and new technologies. However, the commercialization process requires accelerating technology transfer and the development of the relationships between ideas, capital, and markets. Technology flows out of engineering and science fields, but it depends on principles and expertise from finance and marketing fields to be transformed into a viable enterprise.

The modern research university can play a very important role in the development and growth of high technology industries, by linking programmatically ideas, expertise, and practitioners across these fields. This role is much like the one it has played through agricultural extension, which has served so effectively the complex economic development needs of the agricultural sector of our economy. Universities across the nation are establishing industrial liaison programs with their schools of engineering and biology; technology transfer centers which provide research seminars and technical briefings for industry-based scientists and engineers; entrepreneurial development programs to brief and educate leaders of start-up enterprises on vital financing, marketing, personnel, and legal issues necessary to making a commercial success of their technology. All these activities are knowledge based. They involve lectures, panels, and exchanges of papers between professors and practitioners. They involve books, labs, and directed learning, and yet few relate directly to the undergraduate curriculum or the awarding of college degrees. None can be comfortably linked to a single discipline because these activities require not just updates but information sharing across disciplines, professions, industries, and oftentimes, social and cultural communities. Programs of this nature draw upon the unique capabilities of research universities.

Knowledge needs related to issues of civic culture are identified in Table 4.3 (items 7 and 8) because, as discussed in Chapter Two, the knowledge and skill requirements for informed participation in civic life are constantly shifting with changes in technology and global relations. The tradition of research and scholarship characterizing most American colleges and universities uniquely equips them to be ongoing centers of citizen education or to work collaboratively with organizations committed to citizen education. Research universities bring to these efforts resources not easily duplicated by other potential providers, particularly if the goal is issues forums based on high levels of expertise, competing points of view, ongoing dialogue, and analysis, as well as the development of archival or reference materials. So many contemporary public issues cannot be elucidated without reference to new knowledge and comparative perspectives. The intellectual breadth and depth of research universities gives them the potential to provide community forums of substantial richness and value. A single lecture, news show, or panel discussion is not a substitute for centers of ongoing study, discourse, and analysis that draw upon both public experience and academic expertise. One or two examples may be useful.

The effects of technology on the military capacities of modern nations and their storehouse of arms raises important questions about war and peace, the need for deterrence, the potential for nuclear annihilation, the desirability of nuclear disarmament, the level of defense spending and related issues. The discussion of such issues has significant scientific, economic, historical, ethical, and moral dimensions. The very complexity and interdisciplinary character of the issue suggests a role for colleges and universities. Centers

Table 4.3. Matrix of Knowledge Needs and Knowledge Resources: Knowledge Enhancing Citizenship and Quality of Life.

Knowledge Needs	Knowledge Resources	Potential Providers
7. Basic and developmental skills for informed participation in civic culture on neighborhood, local, regional, national, and international issues	Provision of comprehensive and timely civics education for children and young adults through recurrent teacher education	Voluntary associations, religious institutions
	Provision of timely humanistic and policy science perspectives on issues for key influentials, such as officials and government workers, teachers and journalists, voters and community leaders	Museums/libraries, civic groups, and special interest groups
	Provision of issues-oriented discourse and education for the general public and special interest groups, such as labor, environmentalists, retirees	Private, public, and proprietary institutions of secondary and post-secondary education including research universities
8. Enhancement of the quality of life for individuals, communities, and regions	Provision of enrichment opportunities for adults and families with interests in the arts, culture, history, and the environment	Voluntary associations, religious institutions
	Provision of opportunities to encounter new ideas and "voices" in the arts, humanities, and sciences	Museums/libraries, civic groups, and special interest groups
	Provision of learning communities for special interest groups such as writers or specialized constituencies such as retirees	Private, public, and proprietary institutions of secondary and postsecondary education including research universities

of research and dialogue on issues of national security and global conflict and cooperation and on peace studies are springing up on American campuses across the nation; many of these centers have a citizen education mission. Such a public service mission can be served through campus-based lectures and events but also can be achieved through the design of instructional materials that can become the basis for community discussion groups. One example is the civic forums on university campuses in collaboration with groups such as the Domestic Policy Association operated by the Kettering Foundation. Many educational institutions are also involved in targeted programs on topical issues for journalists, legislators, and community leaders. New research findings and the rapidly changing socioeconomic landscape allow for fresh approaches to issues, exposure to new information, and exploration of strategic solutions to real world problems. Programs in alcohol and substance abuse education and environmental issues also come to mind.

Finally, the expansion of quality-of-life-enhancing education, which was once regarded as the exclusive purview of the idle rich or the putative "bored housewife," will become a more important part of the educational missions of institutions of higher learning as demographic changes and transformations in the workplace result in larger constituencies of retirees and the voluntarily unemployed as well as educated adults with discretionary time. Mature and older adults represent vital members of the community as well as an increasing percentage of the total population. As healthy and intellectually alert citizens, they are likely to increase their demand for educational services. Here again, the interest is in liberal studies options rather than degrees and programs of study which certify one for the world of work. Programs already in place at institutions such as the New School for Social Research, the University of Chicago, and the University of California suggest that this cohort is vitally interested in education focused on history, current affairs, the humanities, and the arts. In fact, they are a virtually untapped group of advocates for the value of the arts and humanities in an increasingly technological society.

On the surface, none of these shifting knowledge needs or potential program initiatives appears particularly new or startling. What is of primary concern is the minimal attention that leadership in higher education continues to give to these critical knowledge needs. We must begin thinking comprehensively about the lifelong educational needs of all citizens, and the institutional initiatives required to meet them in a postindustrial economy. Given the knowledge-based character of contemporary social, political, and economic life, we must consider all the needs in the matrix displayed in Tables 4.1, 4.2, and 4.3. Our failure until recently to grasp the size and complexity of the various constituencies for knowledge—beyond those interested in conventional K-12 education and traditional credit and degree-oriented programs in colleges and universities—has resulted in vital areas of national economic and social concern being underserved. Most notable recently have been the problems of unprepared teachers in science and math, or the slowness of the technology transfer process in vital internationally competitive fields such as pharmaceuticals and robotics.

As we move through the 1990s, there are increasing incentives for colleges and universities to become involved in these knowledge problems by making better use of their knowledge resources through diverse and innovative forms of "out" reach and "in" reach. Defense conversion, global technology competitiveness, and overall economic restructuring at the state and federal levels have resulted in financial and programmatic initiatives as well as explicit political concern with better developing our human and intellectual capital societywide. In such a context, universities that continue to question the necessity and validity of an expanding role for fear that traditional functions such as basic research, scholarship, and the intellectual development of young people through undergraduate and graduate degree programs will be slighted risk the loss of public support for these essential traditional functions. The matrix of knowledge needs argues not for a *substitution* of new functions for old but for the *addition* of new functions to traditional ones in order to relate effectively to society's complex knowledge needs well into the twenty-first century.

Leveraging Existing Resources to Serve New Knowledge Needs

Embracing the broadened definition being advocated here does not automatically imply a quantum increase in the costs of delivering knowledge services. The secret lies rather in the leveraging of existing resources and in calling upon existing faculty and university, college or industry-based programs to develop institutional mechanisms for broadening their service base. It also suggests the need for a new metaphor or way of describing the university's mission and role that better represents this comprehensive view of knowledge in modern society. A new framing of mission and role might also acknowledge how, increasingly, what were once treated as distinct functions—teaching, research, and service—are inextricably linked in advanced industrial economies. Rather than defining the mission of the university as we have for more than fifty years as research, teaching, and service, we may need to restate it more in terms of the critical knowledge resource it represents in advanced societies, with something like the following:

> The mission of the American research university is the discovery, development, organization, application, diffusion, and exchange of all forms of knowledge in ways which continuously serve the economic and social development needs of individuals, organizations, and the community.

Such a statement could yield a very different conceptualization of goals and institutional initiatives to serve those goals than currently frames the organizational structure, fiscal practices, and faculty reward systems on most university campuses. Once again a matrix is useful in describing the relationship between knowledge mission on the one hand and institutional activities in the service of that mission on the other (see Table 4.4).

Rather than force specific activities to one category or another—research versus service, for example—the matrix in Table 4.4 demonstrates how permeable the boundaries between research, teaching, and service are. Such a rendering offers the possibility of getting out of the conundrum posed by the current tensions on campus about what "public service" is and what the relative values of research versus teaching versus service are. It underscores that the most important thing about universities is their vital role vis-à-vis *knowledge* in all its diverse forms and for all its essential uses. Knowledge, after all, is what universities are about first and foremost and why they represent such a unique resource in American society.

What Lies Ahead for Research Universities

The management choices and decisions that will have to be made in order to respond to these diversifying and expanding knowledge needs and opportunities will be discussed in more detail subsequent to the discussion in Part Two of exemplary programs addressing these needs at many of the most distinguished research universities in this country. It is also clear that the ways in which knowledge is organized will become more varied. To respond to such a far-reaching and continuous set of educational needs through reliance on existing classrooms, tenured faculty, and on-campus schedules is neither feasible, economical, nor intellectually appropriate. Traditional institutions of learning may need to broaden their concept of who (or what) can do the teaching in what contexts and for what constituencies. For example, the provision of basic education in science and math, of university-based foundation courses, and even of professional degree work by traditional means with full-time science

Table 4.4. Matrix of Key Institutional Activities of the Research University in the Twenty-First Century.

Key Knowledge Missions	Basic Research	Applied Clinical Research	Collaborative Research	Expert Interactions & Consultations	Undergraduate Graduate Degrees	Professional Degrees	Continuing Education/ Lifelong Learning	Information Media, Public Libraries, Friends Groups	Direct Service
Discovering new knowledge	X		X	X				X	X
Developing knowledge		X	X	X			X	X	X
Collecting, organizing, and preserving knowledge		X	X	X			X	X	X
Applying and testing knowledge		X	X	X	X	X	X		X
Transmitting and diffusing knowledge		X	X	X	X	X	X	X	X
Dialoguing and interacting with knowledge stakeholders	X	X	X	X	X	X	X	X	X

and engineering faculty may represent the essential launch for an electrical engineer. But updates in the field may be more efficiently provided through courses taught by practitioners or delivered to the worksite through electronic networks and distance learning technologies. Well-designed and self-paced computer packages in new applications in a given field could be utilized. Management education could be organized into interdisciplinary sequences of courses and seminars taught by a combination of practitioners and faculty reinforced through electronic networks of enrollees at a variety of locations, across a variety of industries. The acquisition of new knowledge of the history and culture of the peoples that a professional will be working with could be elucidated through a carefully designed self-paced program of reading and interactive video. A single individual or organization over time may be linked into knowledge networks in a variety of ways for a variety of purposes.

The educational needs outlined in Part One are *recurrent* in an information age and *vital* to a participatory democracy and healthy economy functioning in a global geopolitical context. University leadership must evaluate the role universities can play and whether we as a nation can afford our current heavy reliance on the financial resources of the oftentimes short-term training concerns of industry or the upward mobility concerns of self-paying middle-class professionals. In the face of a teaching labor force sorely in need of retooling, of a manufacturing core sorely in need of revitalization, of an engineering and scientific labor pool substantially smaller than that of many of our international competitors, we need to make a broader *social* investment in building knowledge linkages. For such far-reaching social and economic ends a substantial, but not prohibitive, investment in new personnel, in new methodologies, and in innovative delivery systems may be called for, not at the expense of existing programs but in addition to them.

Part Two of this work presents descriptions of a number of programs that have been selected because they are superb examples of university-based knowledge-focused programs that serve diverse constituencies for learning in the spheres of activity introduced in Chapter Two. One goal of the program descriptions is to demonstrate that despite regional economic and social diversity, despite variability in institutional strengths and preoccupations, research universities can effectively relate to publics in reciprocally beneficial ways. The knowledge needs relevant to supporting economic development, enhancing practitioner skills, and sustaining civic culture can be met by America's research universities. Institutions are idiosyncratic. Exogenous factors vary from place to place, and so responses vary. Nonetheless, the capacity to respond in ways which are reciprocally beneficial is clearly possible as the program description in Part Two demonstrates.

Part Two offers a chapter on each sphere of activity—the economy, workplace, citizenship—and the various dimensions of knowledge described within each of the major categories introduced in Chapter Two. Each chapter also focuses on programs for constituencies whose profile and sophistication fit the profile of the undergraduates and graduates served by the research universities sponsoring them. They may, therefore, be criticized for having an "elitist" cast to the extent that the publics served already have some, or even a great deal of, higher education and tend to be primarily middle class. However, the issues addressed, the diversity of social and economic needs served, are not elitist, because they directly relate to some of the most vital issues and trends affecting the future of this nation.

Any program of community outreach and public access must reflect the overall academic mission of the campus and will, of necessity, be affected by the characteristics of the knowledge and skills being shared, the characteristics of the learner, and the characteristics of the institutional context in which the learner and the knowledge are brought together. Thus different types of institutions serve different constituencies. The publics served by the programs described in Part Two emerge from a highly differentiated adult population. Just like undergraduates, adults are highly differentiated in terms of their needs, abilities, and motivations. They can also be differentiated by such factors as age, gender, prior education, occupation, income, religion, social and ethnic status, formal and informal peer group expectations, family status, economic resources, and what sociologists refer to as their share of "cultural capital." These factors are relevant to how a program is planned and executed.

Universities also vary in their missions and functions, in the relative priorities they place on liberal and professional education, in their relative emphases on teaching and research, in their dependence on state, federal, or private funding, on the economic and political realities of their immediate context. For programs to effectively serve the broader knowledge needs and social trends we have been discussing, there needs to be a "proper fit" between institutional capacities and constituency needs and capabilities. Research universities in particular have significant contributions to make to technology transfer, small business development, and continuing professional and developmental education. They also have much to contribute to dialogues on public policy, citizen education, and cultural values exploration. The program descriptions in Chapters Five, Six, and Seven provide a glimpse into each of these necessary and valuable knowledge connections in the context of some of America's finest research universities.

Part Two

Organizing and Disseminating Knowledge to Serve Public Needs

Chapter Five

Supporting Economic Development

Contributing to national economic growth and development has been a central animating principle of America's universities since the Civil War. This principle was first clearly expressed in the combined federal, state, and regional support provided to build the great land-grant universities of this nation in the last quarter of the nineteenth century. Simultaneously, federal investments in regionally based research programs aimed at expanding the agricultural and mechanical arts created a relationship between the university and the farmer that assured effective knowledge transfer. Contributions to economic growth were further expanded with the infusion of federal dollars into basic scientific research in nonagricultural areas, triggered by Vannevar Bush's 1945 Report to the President on a Program for Postwar Scientific Research, *Science, the Endless Frontier.* As described in Chapter One, in the years since World War II, our basic research investment has grown exponentially and the expanding economic prosperity of the entire nation can be linked to the inventions and innovations coming out of that research and new knowledge. The increasing importance of new knowledge to industrial developments means an even greater role for higher education in economic development. The role universities play in the development, organization, transmission, and application of all forms of knowledge in the United States is becoming central to more and more industries.

An earlier version of this chapter appeared in the March 1994 issue of *Industry and Higher Education.*

If we understand economic development to mean the expansion of a region's or nation's productive capacity through improving resources generally (human resources, material resources, capital, and technology), then the research university's primary focus on the indirect economic benefits of basic research is too narrow. Research universities must also emphasize activities that facilitate the application and utilization of all their promising basic research throughout society. To do this, they need to embrace an expanded definition of the factors and interrelationships essential to economic development in a knowledge-driven high-tech economy. This definition must be one that recognizes the growing interdependencies between scientific, technical, and managerial competencies; the importance of political supports; and issues relevant to capital formation and infrastructure development.

Knowledge Linkages Needed for New Forms of Economic Development

In a 1988 paper prepared for the State of California Economic Development Corporation, higher education's role in the economy of the state was described in terms common to numerous similar state-based and national studies.

Problem Statement: New Economic Challenges and Higher Education

California has an extraordinary system of higher education, which has made a number of historic contributions to the development of the state's economy—as evidenced in such areas as agriculture, aerospace, and the development of Silicon Valley. Today, however, the state faces a new set of economic challenges brought about by international competition, fast-moving technology, rapidly changing human resource requirements, changing markets and demographics. In this new context, the state needs to consider how capable, responsive, and well-positioned its higher education system is to help the state, its communities, its people, and its large and small firms compete in the new economy [State of California Economic Development Corporation, 1988].

According to the California report, the key economic competitiveness challenges facing the state include:

- *Enhancing human resources development* to meet the changing human resource requirements of industry in an increasingly knowledge-based economy and the significant demographic shifts in the state's population and workforce.

- *Promoting international relations and trade in the Pacific Rim* to deal with the increasing globalization of the economy and enable the state to take full advantage of its strategic opportunities in the Pacific Rim.

- *Improving technology development and transfer* to support research in areas of strategic economic importance to the state and to help ensure that the economic benefits of the state's vast research programs are being "captured" in California.

- *Strengthening manufacturing* to provide the science and technology base, skilled managers, and trained workers needed to implement the more flexible, technologically advanced manufacturing concepts required for competitiveness.

- *Supporting entrepreneurship and small business development* to ensure that the sector of the state economy that produces most new employment opportunities has access to the technology, human resources, and management and technical support it needs to grow and flourish.

- *Addressing regional economic development issues* to strengthen higher education links with surrounding communities and regions, particularly to help economically depressed areas such as the resource-dependent counties and inner-city neighborhoods.

In spite of its academic strengths and a variety of initiatives in each of these areas, California's higher education system as a whole is charged by the report with not being as well linked as it could be and needs to be to many of the key issues of economic competitiveness facing the state today.

The report argues further that "the emergence of a knowledge-based economy requires the development of a new kind of economic infrastructure emphasizing access to technology, skilled and adaptable labor, risk capital, an entrepreneurial climate, and a high quality of life. Higher education needs to explicitly add economic competitiveness to its agenda today because it is a critical contributor to virtually all of the elements of this new infrastructure." Research universities have a unique contribution to make in assuring that inventions, basic research, and innovative ideas get into society in the form of new and improved products and practices that can enhance our competitiveness worldwide and provide the basis for new industry formation at home. What these institutions need are more varied and responsive institutional mechanisms and resources committed to the dissemination and application of knowledge useful to economic development as well as continued support for important basic research. Accomplishing such expanded postindustrial economic development objectives requires innovative institutional mechanisms linking appropriate knowledge producers and users in ways that assure frequent and meaningful interactions. Lynn Johnson, in a monograph prepared for the American Association for Higher Education, presented two tables describing the sorts of interactions that are required in order to serve such major economic goals. They are excellent summaries of what is required (see Tables 5.1 and 5.2).

In Chapter Six, attention will focus on the university's role in

Table 5.1. Academic/Industrial Relationships in Relation to Economic Development Goals and Strategies.

Economic Goals	Developmental Strategies	Academic/Industrial Relationships
Generation and application of scientific technological knowledge	Strengthen basic and applied research in colleges and universities	Research and development relationships
	Increase interaction among basic research, applied research, and development processes as they occur in academia and industry.	
Trained manpower at all levels for technological employment	Strengthen scientific, engineering, business, and other professional and technical programs in higher education	Human resource development relationships
	Strengthen training and retraining in technology skills	
	Improve labor market information and occupational forecasting	
Effectiveness and innovativeness in new and existing industries	Support technology transfer mechanisms to increase innovation among larger, established firms and small entrepreneurs	Entrepreneurial development relationships
	Encourage a variety of services to help entrepreneurs in creating and expanding new industries	

Source: Johnson, 1984, p. 79. Used by permission.

Table 5.2. Academic/Industrial Relationships by Type and Level of Interaction.

	Major Types of Interaction		
Level of Interaction	Research and Development Relationships	Human Resource Development Relationships	Entrepreneurial Development Relationships
Academic/industrial partnership	Cooperative research centers	Cooperative planning and program councils	Cooperative entrepreneurial development
Academic activity in collaboration with industry	Research consortia Personnel exchange programs Special research agreements Contract research	Industrial adjunct faculty Nontraditional credit programs Extended degree programs Continuing education courses Cooperative education Business industry advisory committees	Industrial incubators and parks Extension services Industrial associates programs Consulting relationships
Academic activity oriented toward industry	Research centers and institutes	Scientific, engineering, business, and other professional and technical degree programs	Seminars, speakers, and publications
	Generation/Application of Knowledge	Trained Manpower	Industrial Innovativeness

Major Economic Goals

Source: Johnson, 1984, p. 81. Used by permission.

meeting the human resources challenges vital to economic prosperity. In this chapter, our attention will be on the sorts of knowledge connections that not only assure technical assistance, research partnerships, and technology transfer but also (1) serve the unique needs of small and medium-sized enterprises, particularly in areas of expanding high technology, and (2) are productive of business formation and growth that can enhance regional economic development.

Economic development in knowledge-driven economies arises out of a confluence of technical, sociological, economic, and political forces. In an era of rapidly changing technology, worldwide markets, production and distribution centers, and highly mobile sources of capital, juggling simultaneously the opportunities and obstacles in each of these sectors is critical to successful business formations productive of broad-based regional economic development. University-industry partnerships established over the past decades to address technical and engineering issues have been valuable but are limited in their relevance to the new challenges. Such initiatives cannot achieve their intended consequences without a parallel and reinforcing set of knowledge linkages, which assure a policy environment supportive of economic growth, a regional infrastructure ready to support new and renewing industries, and an appropriately competent, informed professional and technical labor force.

The university mechanisms currently in place to link research and application are often based on a model of economic development that assumes less technically complex problems and less globally interdependent business development opportunities. Assuring economic development into the twenty-first century will be based less on buoying up traditional industries than it will be on developing industries that are based on new technologies, provide new products and services, and continuously re-skill the people who lead and work in those industries. Examples of just this sort of technology-driven economic development are increasing worldwide. The word *technopolis* has been brought into play to describe such geographic centers of innovation and economic dynamism.

Technopolis refers to the types of metropolitan regions developing across the globe that are experiencing dynamic economic growth because of their ability to link technology commercialization with the public and private sector support essential to spurring broad-based economic development and promoting technology diversification (Smilor, Kozmetsky, and Gibson, 1988). This pattern is beginning to represent the dominant form of economic development and has profound implications for the sorts of knowledge linkages that will be needed to enhance economic vitality in the future. The concept of technopolis contains within it a variety of dimensions suggestive of what types of knowledge connections may need to be developed.

The Concept of Technopolis

Ray Smilor, in his introduction to the collection of case studies that makes up *Creating the Technopolis* (Smilor, Kozmetsky, and Gibson, 1988), notes that technology is dramatically altering the shape and direction of society. With that alteration, the nature of economic development has fundamentally and permanently changed (p. xii). Many argue that the modern university is to the information age what the factory was to the industrial revolution—the center of production from which markets, jobs, and individual wealth emanate. Well-known political economist Walt Rostow has often referred to the "new knowledge" coming from the university as a form of "capital" which, if properly leveraged, can give rise to whole new enterprises resulting in new jobs, tax revenues, and sources of wealth. The linkage of basic research, technology development, and economic development is a worldwide phenomenon and the articles in Smilor's collection provide fascinating analyses of this phenomenon in the United Kingdom, France, Japan, and China and in the United States in metropolitan areas such as Troy, New York;

Austin, Texas; Silicon Valley in Northern California; and the Route 128 corridor in Boston. According to Smilor, the characteristics that bind these various centers around the world can be reduced to two, each of which represents important principles: the existence of a major center of research and a network of social and infrastructure supports. Each merits brief discussion.

The presence of a research center, usually a research university, is critical to the development of centers of economic innovation in postmodern society. Segal (1988), in describing the growth of new enterprises in the Cambridge University region of the United Kingdom, talks about the culture of excellence and individualism characterizing the region due to the presence of a research university. He describes three key dimensions of this culture: (1) sizable numbers of research scientists living and working in an area, giving rise to a culture of quality and individualism essential to entrepreneurship as well as a collegiate structure conducive to interdisciplinary discourse, collaborations, and networking activities; (2) a center of international (rather than local or regional) scholarly and research prominence, which assures the ability to attract worldwide talent as well as attention from worldwide industries and financiers; and (3) the university's essentially "hands-off" view of intellectual property in terms of the ownership and exploitation of ideas for commercial purposes, which allows new ideas to be researched free of marketplace criteria. (As new discoveries find their way into commercialization under the auspices of nonuniversity entities, the university can continue to push the frontiers of knowledge with new basic research questions. It is this sort of synergy between research and industry that spawns innovation, according to Segal.) Combining these three factors assures the presence of the necessary talent and a climate of openness essential to innovation.

Segal, along with numerous other students of the economic development process in postindustrial society, points out a second set of essential factors if the growth of new industries and the expansion of jobs are to occur. The research center needs to be situated in an urban, frequently industrial context, which assures the talent, know-how, networks, and access to capital essential for turning ideas into industries. Such a context typically represents five critical ingredients for business development: proximity to effectively operating market systems; flexible, adaptable labor markets; a dispersed, essentially unstratified metropolitan context conducive to the growth of interlocking networks of talented, influential, and accessible individuals, which in turn is conducive to informal, congenial, and efficient business dealings; land to accommodate growth of such things as industrial parks and housing for new professionals and workers in geographically hospitable and affordable regions; and investment in communications infrastructure conducive to the conduct of worldwide information exchange and markets—roads, airports, and the like.

This broader-based conceptualization of the technopolis provides a more integrated view of the factors influencing future economic growth and development. It suggests a need for crosscutting and interlocking knowledge linkages of a more complex order than can currently be provided by the linear models of technology transfer characterizing most university-industry relations vis-à-vis technology transfer and business support. The Technopolis Wheel in Figure 5.1, developed by Smilor and Kozmetsky, summarizes the essential elements for technology-driven regional economic development.

If the thrust of postindustrial economic development is truly tied to technological innovation and commercialization in a global economy, then the knowledge linkages established by universities to assist in this process need to incorporate mechanisms that can facilitate the sort of intrainstitutional collaborations and interinstitutional alliances represented in the Technopolis Wheel. Empirical research on the history and current dynamics of such economic centers reinforces this multiple factors model and emphasizes the importance, in addition, of a particular kind of social dynamic that can support and sustain the networking and collaborations neces-

Figure 5.1. The Technopolis Wheel.

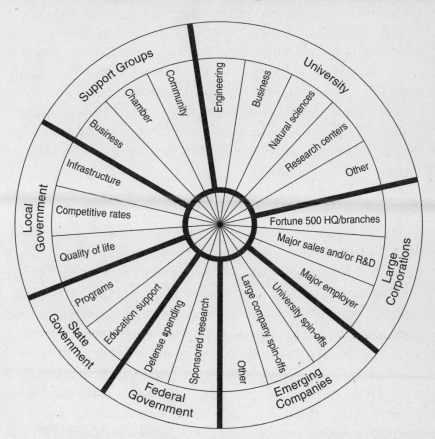

Source: "The Technopolis Wheel" from *Creating the Technopolis*, edited by Raymond W. Smilor, George Kozmetsky, and David V. Gibson. Copyright © 1988 by Ballinger Publishing Company. Reprinted by permission of HarperCollins Publishers, Inc., p. 146.

sary to such a complex economic development process. Allen J. Scott's analysis (1993) of how these factors interacted to produce the large base of aerospace and high-technology industries in Southern California is the most recent affirmation of the multiple factors model.

This social dynamic was first presented in Rogers and Larsen's comprehensive analysis (1984) of the birth and evolution of the Silicon Valley in Northern California. Their work places enormous emphasis on informal intra- and interorganizational communications networks as crucial to success. It describes the critical significance of social as well as informational networking both within and between the academic/research community and the business community. They also describe a network of "influencers," who function as the visionaries and champions for economic development within these communities.

The importance of these informal interlocking networks and intersectoral interactions cannot be overestimated when thinking about the nature of economic development driven by research breakthroughs and technological innovations. These networks of talent and support represent a "readiness" to develop new industries, rather than a focused or studied community economic planning process, according to Rogers and Larsen. Readiness rather than planning is the key to high-tech economic development because it is difficult to be certain which of the myriad basic and applied research programs will yield results or implications that can then be adapted for useful and profitable, individual, social, or industrial purposes. Such an orientation does not represent an anti-planning position but rather a recognition that adaptability and flexibility in the face of uncertainty is essential. It parallels the development of alternative scenarios and response capacities historically found in strategic defense planning, for example. Defense development also has a significant component of technology and uncertainty, making definitive planning difficult. The way we think about how to positively influence future economic development thus may require a higher component of building a knowledge-based readiness to respond to emerging opportunities, rather than developing long-range plans for specific markets or technologies.

The early work of such students of technology development as Smilor and Rogers and Larsen is echoed in more recent research by urban planners, geographers, and economists interested in technology-based regional economic development, such as Bingham and Mier through their collection of essays *Theories of Local Economic Development* (1993). Julia Melkers and Associates, in writing about the process, emphasize the cross-discipline, cross-industry, and cross-professional character of high-tech development, suggesting it is a cultural and organizational process as much as a technical one (Melkers, Bugler, and Bozeman, 1993, pp. 233–234). Allen Scott (1993) makes similar points. He emphasizes the importance of interestablishment interactions to innovation and the importance of a dense mixture of science, engineering, business services, and government support to regional high-tech business development. Ed Blakely's extensively used primer, *Planning Local Economic Development* (1989), emphasizes the importance of a shared vision, civic and government involvement, marketing, and financial support as well as specific technologies.

CONNECT: A University-Initiated Program to Foster Economic Development Through High-Tech Entrepreneurship

The CONNECT Program at the University of California, San Diego (UCSD), a burgeoning technopolis in the United States, is an excellent example of a university program that links the various actors and capabilities essential to the type of economic development discussed so far. It does this through the sponsorship of continuous informal and educational programs and events supportive of developing competencies needed within existing enterprises, as well as through readiness to respond to new opportunities. CONNECT has become a critical regional resource in getting new ideas and research findings into the marketplace, in new enterprise formation, and in small company growth and diversification. How does it do this?

Started in 1986, the mission of CONNECT from the beginning

was to leverage the multiple advantages of the San Diego region—world-class research institutions, an urban business-industrial context, available land, and hospitable geography—for purposes of growing and supporting locally based enterprises capable of contributing to the long-term economic health and prosperity of the region. It developed out of early interactions between the chancellor at the university, the director of San Diego's Economic Development Corporation (EDC), and the dean of the university's Extension Division. These interactions focused on the region's unsuccessful efforts to attract headquarters, companies, or important high-tech consortia such as the MicroComputer Consortium, a major national research and development initiative. The board of the EDC, on which the chancellor sat, determined it needed to stimulate some initiatives that encouraged and supported the development and growth of regional industries, particularly those growing out of university- and institute-based research. A small advisory group of university and community leaders was formed, which (1) crafted a concept for providing educational and informational support services to entrepreneurial high-tech companies; (2) assisted in the identification of an appropriate director for the program; and (3) identified a list of initial financial backers for the program from whom group members personally solicited seed capital. The members of the community advisory group included the director of the Economic Development Corporation, the dean of the university's Extension Division, the dean of the Division of Engineering, a locally prominent venture capitalist, the CEO of a large successful telecommunications company, the CEO of a large successful biotechnology company, and a managing partner of a major accounting firm. With the exception of the director of the EDC, none of these had an "official" role in regional economic development, but each represented a sector with interest in community economic issues and points of access into networks vital to the establishment and ultimate success of the initiative—government, business, and higher education.

Mission and Structure

From the beginning, the mix of advisers assured an agenda that would be multidimensional. The group agreed that effective support for expanding the growing high-tech sector and supporting existing high-tech enterprises required a program of briefings, lectures, courses, and technical and social support useful for

- Providing financial skills and management supports to high-tech entrepreneurs, typically scientists and engineers
- Increasing interaction between campus-based researchers and industry scientists on important research issues as a way of accelerating the technology exchange and transfer process
- Providing technical briefings and education about the unique characteristics of high-tech products, financing, R&D, manufacturing, and marketing, designed for service providers accustomed to working in traditional industries, as a way of building the knowledge base and competencies of regional attorneys, bankers, accountants, and marketing professionals
- Creating opportunities for high-tech entrepreneurs, research scientists, and business service providers to interact on a regular and informal basis as well as through structured informational and educational activities
- Providing one-on-one technical and managerial assistance to individual entrepreneurs and companies
- Increasing local companies' access to national and international sources of R&D funding and capitalization
- Increasing community awareness of the issues affecting the development of high-tech enterprises and the potential economic returns of that development through a program of community education and media relations
- Providing a community resource for data and information on

the status of research activities and business development in the high-tech sector

In addition to defining the program's mission, the advisory group contributed to thinking through the appropriate structure, the financing, and the staffing of such a program. The university was an obvious home for the program because of its recognized research strengths in basic science, computers, medicine, and engineering, and its credibility among high-tech professionals (in spite of the absence of a business school or school of management). The Extension Division took a lead in developing the program because of its institutional capabilities in program delivery, its academic neutrality, and its experience in administering other successful self-supporting academic programs in engineering and technology management. The decision to seek private financing to start up the program was based on a desire to move quickly and build a core of local stakeholders and investors and on a long tradition of self-support public service programs through the University of California. A group of thirty-five founding sponsors, most of them local service providers such as law and accounting firms, provided an initial $70,000 in "seed capital."

Finally, the consensus of the group was that the director of this program had to be a person with credibility in the entrepreneurial community, not just the established business community, because of the need to be responsive to the unique problems and issues facing high-tech entrepreneurs. In addition, the person had to be sufficiently accepted within the academic and research community to be able to work with faculty and university administrators and with a sufficient record of success in the business world to command their respect as a peer. After more than six months of talking with many well-respected but inappropriately experienced business leaders, the program was able to recruit an engineer educated at University of California, Berkeley, and with a Stanford M.B.A., who had successfully built in the San Diego community a computer disk drive company, which had recently been sold to a larger company. He was a respected entrepreneur and philanthropist in his mid fifties and was committed to remaining in the community. He had also been very active in the affairs of the university's medical school and had served as the president of the UCSD Cancer Center foundation board. An energetic, likable person, this individual brought to the program the type of credibility, vision, and charisma Rogers and Larsen maintain is so critical to high-tech–led regional economic development. Over a five-year period, he was able to build the CONNECT program into a highly effective, visible, and influential organization committed to regional economic development through networking and education. It is fully funded by fees, memberships, and underwriting, with a budget as of 1994 of $1 million.

Specific Programs and Services

It is important to examine the specific networks and knowledge linkages facilitated by a program like CONNECT because they are so critical to the kind of future economic development under discussion. They are more far-reaching and interorganizational than those found in more typical knowledge linkage activities currently pursued by college and university industrial extension and entrepreneurial education programs, for example. The narrower focus in most universities on issues that are primarily internal to business formation or relevant to technical upgrading means they may be less effective in contributing to the gains in regional economic development that are so needed in the United States. Technical solutions, apart from new business development support activities, have more limited payoffs, according to the research cited earlier. Focusing on new business development strategies apart from the wider technical and political context affecting business formation is also too narrow a focus when economic development is the goal. The attractiveness of the CONNECT program is its simultaneous focus on knowledge linkages that enhance competencies across a

variety of sectors relevant to supporting and enhancing the formation and growth of enterprises. With this multiple focus, it represents a valuable resource to the broader regional social and
economic agenda as well as an invaluable high-tech business
resource.

The knowledge-linking and social-networking activities of the
CONNECT program can be described along four key dimensions:
ideas and research issues, financial and technical assistance, the
development of professional and technical competencies, and creating a supportive environment for high-technology-based regional
economic development. (The following summary of these various
dimensions of CONNECT is indebted to a recent program
overview developed for CONNECT members and sponsors by
Bryna Kranzler.)

A number of activities facilitate linkages on the dimension of
research and ideas. These activities include regular research briefings by university-based researchers for industry representatives,
much like those provided by industrial liaison programs organized
by science and engineering departments across the nation. CON-
NECT goes further, however, because of its commitment to the
notion of technology "exchange" rather than just technology transfer. The exchange model encourages a two-way interactive process
between researchers in the university and researchers in industry
and nonacademic research settings. It is based on the assumption
that off-campus research can often inform on-campus research questions in the same way that applied research questions can be
enhanced by insights into the directions being taken in basic
research. It is also the case that in emerging areas of technology
development, particularly biotechnology, the long cycle of research
and clinical trials required before a marketable product can be
developed gives rise to a research culture in industry very like that
in the university. Thus a climate of collegiality and reciprocity is
easier to develop between the two sectors.

In light of these factors, CONNECT sponsors an ongoing
"Meet the Researchers" series, which brings together scientists and

business people from various sectors to learn more about the various technologies and technological developments reflected within both sectors, as well as more about how technology transfer can be enhanced. Unlike typical university-sponsored research presentations, this program pairs one researcher from academia and one from industry, both of whom are focusing on the same scientific problem. The program has made it possible to highlight research taking place at the university, of which local companies may not be aware, as well as inform the university of exciting research taking place in industry. Topics have included advances in biomedical engineering, with an assistant research bioengineer from the School of Medicine and a director of science, technology, and business development from a local biomedical company talking about vascular research; advances in communications technology, with a professor of electrical and computer engineering from the Center for Magnetic Recording and Research at UCSD presenting with the chief technical officer and vice chairman of a wireless communications company on the evolution of digital communications and storage; and advances in medicine and biotechnology, with the director of the Molecular Neurobiology Laboratory at the Salk Institute and the director of research for a major pharmaceutical company presenting on advanced receptor technology and CNS discoveries.

In addition to the ongoing research briefing programs, CONNECT maintains an active Scientific Advisory Board in order to offer scientific services in the following areas:

- Building linkages between UCSD researchers and industry scientists
- Providing CONNECT with an outreach capability to other UCSD faculty to promote the benefits and concept of CONNECT
- Helping identify and recruit faculty to provide consulting services or to serve on member companies' scientific advisory boards

- Providing scientific evaluations of business plans presented to CONNECT for the San Diego Technology Financial Forum, Biotechnology/Biomedical Corporate Partnership Forum, and Most Innovative New Products Awards Competition

The members of this scientific advisory committee include distinguished professors from biology, chemistry, cognitive science, the School of Medicine, Scripps Institute of Oceanography, and a variety of organized research units on the campus, such as the Center for Molecular Genetics.

Another way in which CONNECT attempts to enrich the research capabilities of the region is through working collaboratively with the campus Office of Technology Transfer in facilitating the patenting and licensing activities of the campus. CONNECT does not manage the negotiation and legal process but serves instead as a point of access to industries potentially interested in faculty work. It also often serves faculty research objectives by introducing faculty to off-campus sources of "arm's length" research funding through the many informal events and research briefings it sponsors.

Finally, the CONNECT program identifies promising areas of technology development within industry and often brokers relationships among industry-based researchers as well as between industry and the university. It goes to great pains to highlight and showcase research breakthroughs and technology advances as well. Through ongoing interactions with the business and science writers of all the major Southern California newspapers and trade publications, as well as its own quarterly newsletter, which reaches five thousand people, it provides a service to smaller companies that typically cannot afford a public relations function. Particularly successful at showcasing is the annual innovative new products award competition sponsored by CONNECT with underwriting from local sponsors. The awards focus attention on the tremendous amount of technological innovation taking place within San Diego's high-tech community and recognize the leaders of technological innovation. Awards are given in up to four categories: biotechnology/biomedical, high-tech electronics, software, and the open-ended category of "other." A special advisory committee made up of community and university people seeks nominations through local newspapers and professional networks and then judges the entries based on criteria such as the following: Does the product represent a significant advance over previously available technology? Are there barriers to entry? Does the product have significant market potential? Dozens of nominations are submitted annually, and typically five hundred persons attend the luncheon at which the awards are announced and the products of finalists demonstrated.

These are but three examples of the connections the UCSD program is making to contribute to the vitality, expansion, and growth of research and technology development in the San Diego region. An equally important dimension of the CONNECT program is its efforts to help companies secure capital and attract capital to the region in order to increase investment in start-up and developing companies. It does this in a variety of ways: courses on how to write a business plan, pro bono one-on-one advisement on financial and capitalization issues, and two very successful annual conferences, which are organized to attract national and international sources of capital to the San Diego region. The first of these conferences is the San Diego Technology Financial Forum, which was organized with the intention of bringing together venture capital investors interested in high-technology with entrepreneurs seeking financial support to fund their innovations. The goal is, through this formal mechanism, to narrow the more than $25 million gap between venture capital needed to support San Diego's growing number of high-tech start-ups and the amount of locally available financing.

The San Diego Technology Financial Forum stands apart from other venture capital forums for a variety of reasons, notably the screening of potential presenters to ensure that venture capital investors make the best use of their time and the extent of community support in the selection and preparation of presenters. A selection committee composed of senior executives and professionals involved with development-stage high-tech companies in San Diego evaluates companies to identify the ones most likely to be successful after an infusion of cash. Evaluation criteria include an assessment of the skill of personnel, company capabilities, marketing opportunities, and barriers to entry, as well as the viability of the technology. CONNECT's Scientific Advisory Board contributes technical expertise to the evaluation process. On average, sixty to seventy firms vie for between twenty-five to thirty presentation slots in front of over one hundred venture capitalists. The facts indicate that the process works. Historically, 30 percent of all companies selected to present at the financial forum have subsequently received financing, and the financial forum points with pride to the many companies its process has highlighted and helped.

The second program supportive of increasing access to capital is the annual San Diego Corporate Partnership Forum, which initially focused on biotechnology/biomedical firms. As the fourth largest center of biotechnology companies in the United States, San Diego is home to 150 biotechnology and biomedical companies. These companies are making significant contributions to the industry through scientific discoveries and progression to successive stages in clinical trials and ultimately through receipt of federal approval to sell their products. The international pharmaceutical, chemical, and diagnostic communities have become increasingly aware of the significance of these San Diego companies and have been entering into strategic alliances with them at an exponential rate. In 1991 alone, major companies entered into partnerships valued at over $200 million with San Diego–based enterprises. The prolific progress created the environment in which it was appropriate to develop the San Diego Biotechnology/Biomedical Corporate Partnership Forum. Held for the first time in 1989, the forum has been credited with introducing several partners to each other since the first year of its existence. Typically, two dozen San Diego biotechnology and biomedical companies make presentations of their technologies and partnership opportunities over two days to a group of international pharmaceutical, chemical, and diagnostic companies. Over 125 international pharmaceutical, chemical, diagnostic, and biotechnology companies have attended the forum. Major pharmaceutical companies from around the world have sent representatives to this meeting, which attracts more than two hundred people.

What could be described as the continuing education component of the CONNECT program is its extensive offering of seminars and courses geared to developing the managerial, professional, and general workplace competencies of people working in or providing services to the growing high-tech sector. This represents the third critical dimension of CONNECT's knowledge service activity. It includes "Meet the Entrepreneur," late-afternoon lectures by the region's best-known and most successful entrepreneurs; periodic breakfast meetings of representatives of special industry groups such as telecommunications on topics of mutual concern; periodic meetings of women entrepreneurs and black high-tech entrepreneurs on topics of mutual interest; and groups organized around special functions across industries such as human resources. Low-fee half-day seminars taught by experts and practitioners focus on issues such as "Marketing Your High-Tech Products," "Translating Patents into Products," "Working with the Japanese," and "Attracting and Retaining Key Talent." All of these programs are designed and marketed in a way that assures a mix of attendance from a variety of sectors. They typically attract 100 to 150 participants who are attorneys, accountants, marketing professionals, and public administrators, as well as scientists, engineers, and internal management staff from high-tech companies.

Assuring readiness to respond to high-tech-led economic development includes adequate infrastructure, an informed community, and a supportive public policy environment. These elements represent the final type of knowledge linkages CONNECT makes. It makes them in a variety of ways. As a program based at a publicly funded research university, CONNECT cannot engage in advocacy and lobbying activities. Its broad economic development mission also means that it must look at the diffuse social benefits as well as potential costs of high-tech enterprise development for the region. Therefore, it cannot be merely an advocate for business. It can be an important linking, educational, and facilitating entity; but it must always resist the temptation to take positions on public policy issues that may pit one set of interests against another. It does, however, create an awareness within the entrepreneurial community of the broader social, political, and environmental concerns affecting how citizens and leadership view high technology. It also provides data, analyses, and briefing sessions for community groups and political leadership on the character of high technology and what is required to support regional economic development driven by the development and commercialization of new technologies. As such, it plays a vital linking role between research, business, government, and the public at large.

CONNECT engages in the following sorts of activities to support intersectoral communication and understanding of issues relevant to the environment for high-tech business development:

- Assuring a stream of information and analysis about research and high-technology developments, directed to the media and community groups, as well as an information stream on the nature of high-tech enterprise development, its current status, and its future prospects.

- Elucidating the factors that enhance or inhibit the growth of this sector—that is, the implications of various regulatory requirements, housing issues, transportation, water costs, toxic waste, and the like—to government leaders.

- Building various business-governmental linkages at the

regional, state, and national level for communication and education purposes.

- Monitoring, through ongoing research, economic and work-force trends in the high-tech sector and releasing reports to the media and community leadership on a regular basis. (Studies have focused on such things as assessment of viable toxic waste sites for radioactive waste derived from research; alternative strategies for smog reduction and their costs and benefits to small business; and an assessment of the procedures for securing FDA approvals for new products.)

- Interacting with organizations, spokespersons, and champions of related economic and business sectors to assure mutual understanding, mutual support, and synergies where possible.

The sorts of activities outlined above allow the interests of otherwise separate spheres to be linked where appropriate to increase the likelihood of broad-based community benefits from economic development initiatives, which in their early stages can be unfamiliar and even threatening. A simple example may be useful here: the business development cycle in biotechnology, especially pharmaceuticals, is highly protracted. An ideas that has been researched in university labs for as much as ten years begins to suggest some possible applications—the usefulness of cloning to insulin production for diabetics, for example—and it may take two years to patent the idea. It then becomes an applied research question in an industry lab staffed by Ph.D.'s examining alternative ways to develop, for example, a drug. Once a process or application is identified, the firm must secure permission to conduct clinical trials on human subjects. Once the clinical trial research is finished, the product can then be produced and marketed through the existing company or licensed to another producer. Each stage of this business development process takes time, money, and talent, and outcomes cannot be guaranteed. However, if a company is successful, as is Hybritech, a

San Diego start-up, which now manufactures and distributes world-wide diagnostic products utilizing monoclonal antibodies, it can represent hundreds of jobs and tens of millions of dollars annually to a region, as Hybritech does. Three hundred companies like this can represent a workforce, tax base, and ripple effect on an economy equal to many of the traditional manufacturing industries currently in decline across the United States.

What is needed to nurture and grow these emerging industries is a set of technical and professional competencies and a type of community support different from that required for the development of more traditional industries. This difference can represent a significant knowledge gap in many communities. A lack of adequate understanding of the technology, the business formation and development processes, and the global interdependencies affecting contemporary new business development can slow down or even stop regional economic growth. Knowledge linkages such as CONNECT are attempts to close that gap on the public policy side and increase sophistication about the importance of public policy concerns among the scientific and technical leaders of these new enterprises.

Essential Lessons from the CONNECT Experience

The aim of this chapter has been to suggest a somewhat different way of thinking about future economic development and the likely forces shaping economic development at the century's end. Knowledge in the form of research breakthroughs and technological innovations is the central engine for economic development in postmodern society. Thus the way in which a community or a nation chooses to organize, manage, and leverage its continuously renewable knowledge resources for social and economic good becomes a critical issue. How this issue is resolved is influenced by five conditions about which most students of economic growth in postmodern economies agree.

- Research-derived technological innovations will give rise to the industries of the future.

- The development of these technologies into productive industries is dependent upon interlocking networks of talent and support from academia, business, and government.

- Regional economic development capabilities will be more affected by a readiness to take advantage of technological breakthroughs than by conventional approaches to planning.

- This readiness must include a policy environment, organizational capabilities, and professional and workforce competencies and knowledge adequate to respond to technology development opportunities in a collaborative and timely fashion.

- The enterprises of the future are likely to be small and medium-sized and characterized by continuous transformations in the nature of the products or services they deliver, the competencies of the workers they employ, and the clients or customers they serve.

The implication of all of this is that successful economic development increasingly will depend upon informed, flexible, and adaptable communities and individuals capable of moving quickly and intelligently to leverage new economic opportunities. Thus information, mutual understanding between separate sectors of expertise and competence, and the capacity for continual learning to assure the upgrading and refocusing of skills are all essential to any community's economic development strategy. This means the need for knowledge-linking mechanisms that simultaneously address these varied knowledge needs. Bridges, pathways, or social contexts need to be established in which learning, information exchange, and networking can take place on a regular basis.

The CONNECT program at UCSD is an example of one such

linking mechanism that can greatly facilitate this process. It is clearly the case that all across the country communities with universities already possess important linking mechanisms—industrial liaison programs, co-op extension programs, small business development centers, schools of continuing education—each of which may already perform one or more of these functions. The point of the CONNECT example is to demonstrate how varied activities need to be to address an issue as large and complex as regional economic development in a postindustrial world. In-place single purpose knowledge-linking programs such as industrial extension services or centers of urban studies and policy analysis could take on these broader linking roles. They could add to their current missions the role of on-campus interdisciplinary broker as well as that of convener of off-campus collaborators for purposes of providing more comprehensive knowledge services. Who takes the lead may be less significant than assuring that such activities are operated by an entity with service delivery capabilities and talented teams of professionals capable of bridging the various cultural, political, and knowledge boundaries, which typically serve as barriers to these sorts of comprehensive efforts.

The "bottom line" based on the CONNECT experience in San Diego and the various research reports identified at the beginning of this chapter is that future economic development can be greatly enhanced if the following four things happen:

1. Regions look to their centers of knowledge creation and technological innovation (typically their research universities) as major players, catalysts, even leaders of their economic development efforts.

2. Knowledge-linking mechanisms, which inform and connect resources and sources of expertise across sectors, professional disciplines, and special interests, are established to build regional readiness.

3. Convenient and regular opportunities for information-rich and socially meaningful interaction exist.

4. An institutionalized mechanism is in place, guided by a cadre of credible and visionary champions whose mission and governance reflect the diverse constituencies with a stake in the direction of economic development.

It can be further argued that the nation's network of its top one hundred research universities may be the most capable and credible convener and organizer of these sorts of activities. What is being proposed is that universities become not the instruments of regional economic development nor the advocates of certain forms of economic development but rather the conveners and organizers of broad-based community efforts which draw on their knowledge resources. What is being suggested is that the directions and strategies for economic development that a community ultimately will pursue depend on a wealth of knowledge and perspectives, which need to be considered in addition to the important political and value-based factors that influence the public policy-making process. Universities typically represent vital knowledge resources in their communities because of the multidisciplinary fields and expertise upon which they can draw and because of their reputations for neutrality. The CONNECT example represents a relatively low-cost, high-payoff way for a research university to provide the knowledge connections needed to enhance the forms of regional economic development likely to characterize all communities in the twenty-first century. It is an approach that celebrates and supports the basic research activities of the university as well as a university commitment to assist in making knowledge useful and productive in society.

Chapter Six

Enhancing Human Capacities
Across the Life Span

In the emerging economy of the twenty-first century, only one asset
is growing more valuable as it is used. That asset is the "problem-
solving, problem-identifying and strategic brokering skills of this
nation's citizens." This assertion by Harvard University political
economist and U.S. Secretary of Labor Robert Reich, in a 1991
piece in *Atlantic Monthly* (1991a, p. 37), is an appropriate starting
point for a chapter focusing on renewing lifelong the human
resources of our postindustrial society. In the preceding chapter, it
was argued that one of the most renewable economic development
resources we as a nation have is the new knowledge and innovation coming out of research and development settings. An equally
significant resource is the *cumulative* experience and continuously
renewable intelligence of our people. Reich in fact argues that it is
the cumulative skills and insights of our people upon which future
innovations are based, and thus people represent a key "technological" asset, not just an organizational one. Equipment, technology, and facilities deteriorate and become obsolete over time while
the skills and competencies of our citizens can become more valuable over time because of the cumulative "value added" character
of experience and continuous learning (p. 37). Increasing the value
of our human resources means finding ways to harness cumulative
experience and to link it to new skills and knowledge for purposes
of more effective and productive workplace performance. This
means a societywide commitment to lifelong learning.

Research universities must develop knowledge linkages that
contribute to the continuous renewal of human resources, which

focus on those jobs and occupations in which skills and competencies are related to advanced research and teaching programs. Prebaccalaureate or preprofessional general, technical, and vocational educations, concern universities only indirectly. To the extent that many of the teachers, trainers, managers, policy and decision makers influencing the work experiences of this component of our human resource pool are products of university-based degree and certification programs, their knowledge needs merit discussion here. However, as research universities rarely provide *direct* education and training services in preprofessional, technical, and vocational fields, the focus of this chapter will be that sector of the American labor force—25 to 30 percent currently—for whom a bachelor's degree is the typical minimum educational requirement for employment and for whom advanced certification, credentialing, and lifelong continuing education are increasingly required. A list of such workers includes schoolteachers, engineers, computer programmers, accountants, doctors, attorneys, nurses, social workers, health professionals, pharmacists, veterinarians, agricultural economists, and urban planners. It also includes hundreds of other current knowledge-rich occupations and professions, as well as dozens of new and emerging occupational specialties resulting from the knowledge transformations and changing work environment described in Part One. These professionals are critical to our nationwide human resources development concerns, in large part because of how they affect broad societal constituencies. K-12 teachers affect the competencies and self-esteem of the nation's children; doctors and nurses the personal health care practices and social "costs" of evolving health care systems; engineers and planners the materials, costs, and social responsiveness of infrastructure developments in transportation, telecommunications, land-use planning, and building design; managers and administrators the cost effectiveness and social responsiveness of industries and bureaucracies serving a society in constant flux.

Three distinct types of workforce-related knowledge needs merit discussion—professional updates, interdisciplinary knowledge needs, and preparation for work in emerging fields of specialized practice. Each must be treated differently because of the nature of the experience and knowledge "mix" needed in programs to enhance competency and the distinct resources essential to making effective educational linkages with practitioners. This means that lifelong learning in different occupational spheres may be organized differently in order to factor in differing sources of expertise and differing players in the linkage process. For example, professional certification and updates in established occupational fields such as business, electrical engineering, or marriage and family counseling tend to rely heavily on established academic programs and leading professionals. In contrast, interdisciplinary and cross-disciplinary knowledge needs frequently necessitate institutional mechanisms capable of crossing the often rigid boundaries between specific academic programs on the one hand and well-defined professional fields on the other—for example, engineering and business or Latin American studies and law. Finally, in the more developmental and emerging fields of occupational specialization or professional practice, institutions may have to rely more on hands-on practitioners to give shape and substance to what the critical knowledge needs are in the absence of directly pertinent academic disciplines or established professional groups. New fields such as toxic and hazardous waste management, for example, face this problem.

Differentiating Types of Professions by Stage of Development

As innovation cycles shrink from twenty-five years to five years, the internal structure of university academic departments and their new program development and curriculum approval cycles become problematic. They are slow and fragmented and suggest a need for more responsive institutional mechanisms that can serve lifelong learning needs more immediately. In time, universities do innovate,

incorporating interdisciplinary topics such as technology management into degree-related teaching and research programs, accom-
modating as well new fields, such as environmental management.
Increasingly, degree programs only appear when there is a clear (and
large) demand for competencies. However, in addition to requiring
new forms of credentialing, rapid innovation cycles result in society's
need to have much of its *current* credentialed workforce reeducated
in these knowledge areas. In order to innovate and be competitive,
society can no longer rely on fresh young recruits emerging from
degree programs with competencies in new fields. This is the social
knowledge "gap" that universities are uniquely qualified to fill
through initiatives outside traditional degree programs.

The important work of Cyril Houle from the University of
Chicago in defining and describing the character of professions and
continuing professional education is particularly pertinent here.
Houle suggests that the use of the concept of *professionalization*
might be a better way to capture the dynamic process characterizing most modern occupations than the use of the more static concept of profession. Donna Queeney does a superb job of
summarizing Houle's development of this idea in a way that is very
useful for our purposes (1987, pp. 12–13). Houle defines fourteen
characteristics broadly associated with the professionalization
process as the basis or goals of lifelong professional education. They
include the *conceptual characteristic*: (1) as many members as possible of a professionalizing vocation should be concerned with clarifying its defining function(s). *Performance characteristics* include such
things as (2) mastery of theoretical knowledge or at least the rudi-
ments of information and theory; (3) capacity to solve problems—
ability to use theoretical bodies of knowledge to deal confidently
with the category of specific problems; and (4) use of practical
knowledge based on history and experience.

The fifth characteristic described by Queeney refers to a *personal
attribute* of the practitioner: (5) self-enhancement—practitioners
of a vocation should, throughout their years of preservice learning

and work, seek new personal dimensions of knowledge, skill, and sensitiveness by the arduous study of topics not directly related to their occupation. The remainder of Houle's list of fourteen comprises *collective identity characteristics*, which distinguish professionalizing occupations from other vocations on the basis of an occupation's leaders encouraging and enforcing standards of practice based on a profound central mission and on advanced esoteric bodies of knowledge. Collective identity characteristics include such things as (6) formal training; (7) credentialing; (8) creation of a subculture; (9) legal reinforcement; (10) public acceptance; (11) ethical practice; (12) penalties; (13) relations to other vocations; and (14) relations to users of service. None of these characteristics can be completely and finally achieved, Houle says. Hence the "race for professional accomplishment" has "no finish line," says Queeney, quoting Houle's 1980 work (Queeney, 1987, pp. 12–13).

To the extent that there is an increasing need in society for advanced continuing education that takes into account this dynamic process of professionalizing, a broader conceptualization of professions and their variable knowledge needs clearly is appropriate. Some way of categorizing occupations that can also take into account different stages in the professionalization process as described by Houle would be useful. Looking at the knowledge needs of professional practitioners in the somewhat broader terms suggested throughout this work is one approach that may be helpful in suggesting how to organize more effective institutional approaches to the knowledge needs of practitioners.

This conceptualization process can be further aided by thinking through the essential components in the knowledge-linking process. What must be present to assure the development of effective educational programs and supports for technical and professional workers in fields where skills and knowledge requirements are continually changing? This question must be answered by differentiating three general categories: (1) skill requirements in established specialized fields of practice; (2) skills needed in interdisciplinary fields of practice; and (3) skills essential to developmental and emerging fields of practice. The matrix in Table 6.1 is an effort to describe the critical differentiators between these three general types by characterizing their varied sources of knowledge, legitimacy, and credentialing. The categories in the matrix are derived from a number of things we know about the nature of professional fields.

Table 6.1. Matrix of Variable Sources of Knowledge for Enhancing Competencies in Advanced Fields of Practice.

	Fields of Practice		
Sources of Knowledge Legitimacy	Established Specialized Fields (for example, medicine)	Interdisciplinary Fields (for example, engineering management)	Emerging Fields (for example, toxic waste)
Higher Education			
Accredited professional school or department program	yes	maybe	unlikely
Single academic department	yes	maybe	maybe
Multiple academic units	yes	yes	maybe
External Agencies and Bodies			
Professional associations	yes	maybe	unlikely
State/federal government agencies	yes	maybe	unlikely
Accrediting bodies	yes	maybe	unlikely
Practice Environment			
Employers/workplace leaders/policy	yes	yes	yes
Hands-on practitioners	yes	yes	yes
Socio/Economic Environment			
Technological developments	yes	yes	yes
Economic transformations	yes	yes	yes
Trends	yes	yes	yes

What the matrix in Table 6.1 clearly demonstrates is that the uncertainty about who has the knowledge and resources necessary to address the lifelong learning needs of advanced practitioners increases the more interdisciplinary or emergent the field is. In established specialized fields of practice, it is possible to secure some form of consensus as to what is required and what is a proper standard of competency for practice. It is much more difficult to do this in interdisciplinary and emerging fields of practice. Universities, research universities in particular, do very well in the first column but shy away from the second two. The dilemma is that increasingly the knowledge needs of advanced practitioners fall into the latter two columns, not just the first, and universities (with a few notable exceptions) have yet to determine if, much less how, they can institutionally address these expanding needs for knowledge in the workplace.

As noted in Part One, established fields of professional practice such as law, medicine, and architecture represent fields with high standards of performance, self-regulation, and strong traditions of continuous learning and competency improvement. Such a professional culture creates incentives lifelong to be associated with schools or professional associations providing the knowledge resources and networks essential to successful professional practice. What society needs for the decades ahead are institutional mechanisms as effective at serving the knowledge needs of interdisciplinary and emerging fields of practice as the mechanisms developed in support of established fields of practice over the decades past.

It is clear that in established fields of practice, the focus of continuing professional education is not simply individual learning activities, but the development of learning agendas specifically designed to meet professionals' practice-oriented needs (Nowlen and Queeney, 1988). Such continuing education is conducted at advanced levels for skilled professionals and usually has its own set of pedagogical, organizational, political, and fiscal characteristics according to Stern (1983). Queeney (1990) further notes that because of its practice orientation, continuing professional education is highly dependent on a variety of knowledge resources from universities, as well as from the professional field. Nonetheless, because it represents an advanced educational function, it has typically fallen to "higher education to assume leadership in bringing interested and responsible parties together to forge an agenda for action for continuing professional education" (p. 3). However, most of the work universities do in this regard is in updating established fields rather than in providing knowledge for the interdisciplinary and emerging fields of professional practice. The professional continuing education agenda has to become broader than our typical professional school programs are currently capable of addressing. New institutional mechanisms may be needed to accomplish this agenda. What the character of these institutional mechanisms should be can be determined by identifying the sources of knowledge that can be tapped and the linkages that must be established in order to transform new information needs into effective educational programs and supports for technical and professional workers facing new challenges.

The matrix of variable sources of knowledge may be a springboard for such a discussion. It summarizes the variable sources of knowledge and legitimacy relevant to the three types of occupational groupings just discussed. What the matrix suggests is that the more established and specialized a field of professional practice is, the broader and more overlapping will be the consensus as to the minimum entry criteria and standards of performance. There will also be a wider consensus with regard to what forms of expertise and sources of knowledge are essential and valid in assuring competency lifelong. In Houle's terms (1980), there is an agreed-upon canon. Interdisciplinary fields of practice must rely on a wider range of knowledge resources—higher education and practice based—but often face problems getting started or gaining legitimacy because of interdepartmental turf wars in universities on the one hand or the bureaucratic inflexibility of many governmental and accrediting agencies on the other. The absence of existing institutional mechanisms to champion needs and deliver resources to these occupations without a permanent home is a major human resources development problem. The best example in this country is the relative absence of technical and engineering management programs in spite of widespread industry demand. This is due in no small part to the inability of schools of business and engineering to work collaboratively on many university campuses.

Emerging fields of practice, such as environmental engineering, digital publishing, and genetic counseling, are even less likely to find much direction or assistance from the established curriculum of university departments or schools, or from professional associations for that matter. This is largely because they do not comfortably fit within familiar knowledge boundaries or workplace competencies. Thus they are often orphaned. Emerging fields of professional practice must of necessity rely less on established sources of expertise and knowledge, such as specialized faculty and academic degree-granting programs, and much more on the creation of new curriculum, on new sources of expertise and teaching, and on the drawing upon but not mirroring of the "establishment." This means a heavy reliance on workplace leadership and professionals, as well as on environmental trend analysis. Universities are often remiss when it comes to these emerging fields, which, despite the absence of an established body of knowledge and direct faculty expertise, could benefit enormously from the concern with standards and learning objectives, as well as from the theoretical knowledge base and instructional resources of the campus.

The virtual abandonment of these emerging fields by many research universities means they are often appropriated by market-driven proprietary enterprises, which can compromise long-term quality and legitimacy objectives. On the other hand, to measure the "quality" of advanced continuing professional education programs primarily by the amount of on-campus faculty involvement in the design and instruction of such programs is a mistake made by many of America's finest universities. If the demands for advanced professional competencies are as varied and changeable as is being described here, then the knowledge linkages needed will have to draw upon *multiple* sources of expertise and information. Universities need to get better at identifying, harvesting, and synthesizing expertise from many places—inside the academy and within the practice environment.

Clearly all forms of contemporary knowledge, expertise, and experience do not reside primarily in the university. Many surely do, particularly in long-standing fields such as law and medicine. However, if the university is going to continue to be a central knowledge resource, it must find ways not only to extend the knowledge that resides in its professors and research programs but also to harvest and organize the increasingly complex forms of new knowledge and expertise developing outside the halls of the academy. The matrix presented here is an effort to array these potential resources across distinguishable types of practice. Examples of programs serving each category of practice field can provide insight into the knowledge linkages required to provide more effectively something as putatively "familiar" as continuing professional education. There are excellent examples nationwide, which can be found for each type of practice—established, interdisciplinary, and emerging. A few are described briefly in the remainder of this chapter.

Knowledge Needed in Established Fields of Practice

Pennsylvania State University has earned a strong reputation as a center not only of exemplary programs but of research and leadership in thinking through the issues pertinent to continuing professional education. Over the last twenty years, the statewide institution has developed focused continuing professional education curricula in over seventy practice fields as varied as athletic coaching, architecture, nursing home administration, optometry, urban and regional planning, and veterinary medicine. All represent fields for which the state of Pennsylvania has legal requirements for practitioners; organizations or associations exist that certify competency requirements; higher education is generally required; and the field is one in which the campus has a curriculum in which faculty teach and research. The program at Pennsylvania State has grown as the list of organized professions and occupational associations within the state has grown. This in turn reflects the trend toward ever more specialized workplace competency requirements and a concern with assuring competency lifelong. To this end, more states are instituting requirements in more and more fields for individuals who wish to enter these fields and to continue practice in them.

The continuing education programs of Pennsylvania State University are based on interaction and collaboration and thus reflect the collective wisdom of faculty members, regulatory agencies, professional associations, and practitioners themselves. For the most part, these programs reflect competencies required by the various forms of regulation imposed by state agencies or professional associations, typically referred to as mandatory continuing education. Queeney (1987) points out that this mandatory continuing education is in response to three types of practice regulation—licensure, usually from a government agency; certification, usually by a professional association; and registration, usually with a nongovernmental agency that maintains a list of legitimate practitioners. The notion of mandatoriness is important here because of its implications for how programs are designed and delivered as well as why people participate. An attorney, a doctor, a personal financial planner, a teacher of high school English, a radiologist, a marriage and family counselor, or a civil engineer cannot continue in their professional practice without completing regular externally mandated educational updates.

This mandatory character of much continuing professional education in established fields of practice requires a set of institutional capabilities for establishing successful knowledge linkages that may be very different from those required in the other fields we will be discussing. First and foremost are the broad-based knowledge resources a program can draw upon in setting up curricula and the consensus across sectors about what is needed and what expertise is appropriate. These requirements mean that the person developing the program has less need to be an expert himself or herself in the content area than in settings where content needs are less clear. They mean that familiarity with specific practice issues may be less significant to effective high-quality program implementation. They may also explain why the focus in many school of education graduate programs for professional continuing educators is on form and process issues rather than content. Adult education degrees often focus on psychological and pedagogical issues such as how adults learn, how to market, and how to evaluate student satisfaction rather than on mastery of more traditional knowledge areas such as history, economics, or physics. In well-established fields of practice such as medicine, one can rely on the professor of medicine, the head of cardiology from a regional hospital, or the professional from an accrediting agency to define content and standards of performance. However, in interdisciplinary and emerging fields, the program developer is called upon to be not only a facilitator and "meeting planner" but also a knowledge synthesizer with sufficient background and capability in both substance and practice issues to make content judgments and to create and innovate new curricula for new constituencies.

Thus it is not uncommon to find a large number of professionals with degrees in adult and continuing education working in continuing education institutions where the knowledge linkages being developed are primarily in established fields and where content direction comes right out of faculty or professional association expertise. In contrast, in many research institutions emphasizing new knowledge and innovation, the professionals responsible for building and maintaining programs typically have credentials in content areas such as medicine, law, literature, or applied physics.

This is not only because of the commonly assumed elitism of many research universities, but because academic degrees and achievements can lend credibility to the person's role both on campus and off. It is also important because the possession of content knowledge is essential to the design and development process when the linkages being developed are in new and emerging fields. Judgments about the quality of information, expertise, and experience need to be made in addition to judgments about pedagogy and program delivery.

It is instructive to take a closer look at the types of continuing professional education programs at Pennsylvania State. They represent an example of a highly respected and effective set of activities linking the university and established fields of professional practice. Pennsylvania State is known nationwide for its fine industrial extension activities and the ongoing support it provides industry through applied research and business development programs. It also offers a comprehensive statewide program of professional updates in more than a dozen engineering specialties licensed under the general designation "professional engineer" in the state of Pennsylvania. The institutional mechanism through which Pennsylvania State serves professional continuing education needs is the centralized Office of Continuing Education whose function is implementing programs originating out of the offices of associate deans for continuing education located in all the schools. The associate deans have degrees in the fields for which they are responsible and have faculty rank. The professionals in the centralized delivery unit focus on the delivery of academic programs, which have evolved out of the intellectual and professional links of the school deans.

This model has been enormously effective in assuring high-quality professional continuing education tied closely to on-campus academic programs delivered in a manner which is responsive to the special needs of adult practitioners. Similarly, at many land-grant university campuses, for example, conference and institute divisions have been established for the primary purpose of assisting faculty in the implementation of seminars, institutes, and workshops on topical scientific and professional issues for practitioners. Many also operate elaborate conference facilities with overnight and food services for residential conferences. At Pennsylvania State, for example, the School of Engineering has made a substantial investment in developing a center for the engineering of composite materials and structures. Testing, processing, and computational equipment in the center allow people to engage in areas of research of particular interest to fields like aeronautics and astronautics. Faculty from the school develop programs of potential interest to practicing engineers, which are offered at the central campus conference center and administered through the continuing education unit.

The seminar "Design and Fabrication of Composites" is an example of what the school offers. It was a three-day residential course covering the whole spectrum of composites technology, ranging from materials selection to final fabrication. Course presenters included a mix of Pennsylvania State faculty and industry professionals in lectures and lab sessions, for a fee of approximately $1,000. Similar programs are offered every year by the College of Earth and Mineral Sciences, the College of Health and Human Development, the College of Arts and Architecture, the College of Liberal Arts, and a dozen more. In each instance the institutionalized mechanism for assuring knowledge linkages is the partnership between an associate dean for continuing education in each college and the well-staffed centralized administrative unit known as the Office of Continuing Professional Education.

Thousands of courses are offered annually by hundreds of professional schools around the country out of a commitment to serving the lifelong education needs of practitioners initially certified by university degree programs and professional schools. These sorts of programs are familiar to all of us. Judged from employer and student reactions, they are also highly effective. For many institutions, they are also extremely profitable, representing millions of dollars in discretionary monies for a school or campus in any given year. They represent an excellent example of successful interactions between researchers and practitioners, in which collaboration and shared expertise result in high-quality professional updating.

The limits of a continuing education program focused exclusively on updates have already been discussed. Such programs tend to stay within often narrow disciplinary boundaries. For purposes of strict updating, such programs are highly effective, but for purposes of serving the growing need in society for interdisciplinary and emerging practice-related knowledge, they may not be the best model of how universities should organize and deliver lifelong learning.

Knowledge Needed to Serve Interdisciplinary Practice Needs

The work of Donna Queeney once again provides a useful way of thinking about interdisciplinary education. In an article published with Casto in 1990 on interprofessional collaborations, Queeney distinguished among the terms "multidisciplinary," "interdisciplinary," and "interprofessional" in a way that is clarifying for program developers. *Multidisciplinary* implies "the sharing of information and skills between and among persons from different disciplinary perspectives," and it involves no particular commitment to developing a collaborative plan of action or reaching a common understanding of professional standards. "Continuing professional education designed to enhance multi-disciplinary work focuses on developing skills in networking and accessing information from a variety of sources" (p. 58). *Interdisciplinary*, in contrast, suggests not only sharing but an exchange or interactive process, which gives rise to a new way of defining issues or solving problems. Interdisciplinary work requires persons skilled in leadership and group process so that consensus and coordination happen. *Interprofessional* suggests a more collaborative process in which distinct experts bring their specialized skills to a team process in order to address a specific problem of practice comprehensively. It represents more a pooling of unique resources than a merging of perspectives and methodologies. Each method of collaboration, however, represents a formidable challenge in the context of research universities, where specialization rather than collaboration is typically rewarded.

The narrowness of focus within individual professions makes it extremely "difficult to coordinate knowledge and skills for application to multi-dimensional problems that do not fit into a specific category," according to Queeney and Casto (p. 60). However, the increased complexity of technical, economic, and social problems requires more interdisciplinary thinking, as well as increased interprofessional understanding and coordination of skills and services. Thus there is frequently a misfit between workplace needs and professional standards. How to link multiple professional knowledge bases to improve practice may be the central challenge of continuing professional education at the century's end.

A program initiated by the San Diego campus of the University of California in the early 1980s, the Executive Program for Scientists and Engineers, may serve as a useful example. Its development and success may be due in no small part to the fact that it developed in a context where there were no established and competing on-campus professional schools at the time in either engineering or business. The University of California, San Diego, opened in 1964 and is one of the newer campuses of the nine-campus statewide system of research universities, which began with the establishment of the Berkeley campus 125 years ago. The campus is a very successful research university, consistently ranked in the top ten nationally for federal research dollars, with an annual budget exceeding $1 billion, 18 percent of which is state funded. It emphasizes Ph.D. studies at the graduate level and has only two professional schools, each of which was founded with a basic research mission and a highly interdisciplinary vision of professional preparation—the School of Medicine and the Graduate School of

International Relations and Pacific Studies. This context is important to understand because it has resulted thus far in few internal turf wars and an environment that is conducive to allowing innovative and entrepreneurial academic linkages to occur. Such was the case with the establishment of the highly successful Executive Program for Scientists and Engineers.

The idea for an executive program for scientists and engineers grew unexpectedly from informal conversations with industry leaders and was reinforced by survey data in the early 1980s. At that time the San Diego extension service had no provision for engineering and technical education, in spite of the large numbers of defense contractors in fields such as aerospace and the growth of the electronics industry, particularly in telecommunications, in the region. Overtures by the university to the industrial community in the early 1980s were intended to learn more about the professional continuing education needs of the expanding number of engineers and technical personnel working in the area. Conversations made clear, however, that industry professionals and CEOs were concerned not only about the technical competencies of their well-educated workforce but workforce organizational and managerial skills as well.

These CEOs did not see the region's business schools as relevant to their needs. They complained about the youthful inexperience of the students, the nontechnical content of the business curriculum and case studies, and the lack of fit between the needs of technology-based enterprises and the business consulting experience of the faculty at the three other regional universities with advanced management degree programs. Despite protests from UCSD about its having no school of business or management, the message from industry was clear: "That's an advantage because most schools of business and management are not equipped to relate to the challenges facing high-technology enterprises and the needs of technical managers." With such direct encouragement from representatives of enterprises such as Kodak, General Dynamics,

Hewlett-Packard, and Rohr, the decision was made to convene a program development group made up of practitioners and UCSD social science and engineering faculty. The original program was organized and continues to be administered through the Business and Management Department of the university's extension service.

The program development process was genuinely collaborative and was facilitated by a young professional with writing skills and a background in adult learning. The anchor, in terms of academic content issues, was a man who eventually became director of the program but who at the time was a senior professor in a state university business school. His background included engineering and management degrees from Dartmouth and MIT and experience in business as well as many years teaching in an East coast business school and consulting with technical companies. Other members of the planning group included a recent graduate of a short-lived collaborative program at UCLA in engineering management, who was a vice president at a Kodak subsidiary and is now CEO of one of the fastest growing high-tech companies in California; the CEO of an electronics company, who had previously been a professor of engineering at UCSD; senior technical managers from large established companies such as General Dynamics and Hewlett-Packard; the dean of a new engineering division; the dean of the extension service; a professor of economics who had previously taught in a major Midwest business school; and a political science professor with a specialty in government regulatory policy. At first blush, it seems an odd collection of resource people to assume the task of crafting an integrated executive development program, but the program has filled annually for a decade and, in recent years, has been used as a model for degree programs at many institutions including UCSD (in the Graduate School of International Relations and Pacific Studies).

The program takes a full academic year and a commitment of one afternoon and evening a week with an orientation retreat at the beginning. Hundreds of out-of-class hours are spent on reading and special team projects. The program is not based on satisfying a set number of units or courses but is rather an integrated executive development experience with thematic modules organized over the course of the year. There is substantial time given to "nuts and bolts" issues such as budget and finance, marketing, personnel, legal issues, and communications skills. Overall, attention is focused on problem analysis and solutions through team projects dealing with issues mirroring those faced by technical industries functioning in global markets. The group, which is never more than thirty-six people, develops a true sense of esprit de corps and shares dinner each week with a local CEO who talks about his or her enterprise. A cross section of economics, social science, and international relations professors lectures in each of the modules, but the integrative work of the ten-month program is handled by an academic director who has significant technical industry experience. The participants, who must be nominated by their companies to participate in the program, come with a minimum of a master's degree and eight years of work experience. When the program is completed each spring, there is a graduation ceremony at which each participant receives a diploma of completion signed by the chancellor and conferred by the dean of engineering. Family members, employers, and instructors numbering more than 150 usually attend these ceremonies. The cost for this academic-year program is approximately $7,000 and is just sufficient to cover the instruction, coordination, and materials expenses of the program.

The knowledge connections established through a program like this one grow out of a series of encounters, exchanges, and collaborations similar to other forms of professional continuing education. What differs are the actors, the agencies, the resources that must be called upon in order to develop a high-quality curriculum and identify appropriate instructors for these sorts of interdisciplinary programs. At UCSD, the absence of well-established professional schools created an opportunity for an interdisciplinary group to form, develop a common agenda, and achieve consensus as to what the knowledge needs were and how best to serve them. Unless older, more established schools and campuses engage in these sorts of interinstitutional and intrainstitutional efforts, significant learning needs go unmet. Oftentimes when these needs are addressed, it is done through a duplication of scarce resources: an engineering school starts a management program, and a management school starts a technical management program, when what is needed is collaboration between the two schools and appropriate practitioners.

For any of this to happen requires leadership and a willingness to develop or support institutional mechanisms capable of transcending knowledge boundaries on the one hand and facilitating meaningful exchanges in which all parties have a genuine stake on the other. At UCSD, this institutional mechanism proved to be the extension service. At many universities, it could be the colleges and professional schools themselves. In some places, it might be alumni divisions with a strong service orientation that take the lead. What is critical is not so much who does it but how it is done. On different campuses, the personalities, the institutional history and traditions, and the key competencies needed for interdisciplinary work will influence from where interdisciplinary community-oriented academic programs will come.

Another briefer example concerns an area of interdisciplinary knowledge in which many research universities have been exceptionally active and effective. The programs in this area are ones of advanced study for community college and liberal arts college faculty, organized and taught by university scholars, particularly in the humanities and social sciences. As early as 1971, the University of Chicago, for example, instituted the Midwest Faculty Seminar, a faculty exchange and development program, which includes the University of Chicago and approximately sixty liberal arts colleges and small universities from the Midwest. Its objective is to encourage scholarly conversations between the University of Chicago community and faculty members at neighboring institutions. A joint effort by faculty in the humanities and the university extension, the program has supported more than fifty interdisciplinary institutes, typically involving forty to fifty participants each on topics such as "Theories of Literary Criticism" or "What Is a Classic?"

Institutes arise out of consultative conversation among on-campus faculty from a variety of departments. A syllabus is then developed by staff, and programs, typically of two to three days' duration, are scheduled for the visiting faculty. Topics tend to be highly interdisciplinary and of substantial intellectual significance. In the 1980s, the seminars included the program "Interpreting Non-Western History and Culture," which involved twenty-one colleges, thirty-eight participants, and faculty from fields such as history, sociology, South Asian studies, and comparative literature. The following description from an annual report gives a sense of the tone and focus of the seminar.

> Nothing is more characteristically Western than investigating what is distinctive about the "Other," yet nothing is more contemporary than self-consciousness about the extent to which the terms in which we pose the representation run the risk of violating the distinctiveness which we seek to comprehend. This Institute examined three aspects of the interpretation of non-Western history and culture: (1) the invention of the idea of the non-West and the uses of that idea in the formulation of a distinctively Western self-image and world view; (2) the encounters between East and West in terms of some of the characteristic frameworks though which the West has historically structured the encounter; and (3) some of the major interpretative frameworks through which contemporary scholars in a variety of disciplines approach the study of non-Western history and culture.

Another seminar with similar levels of participation was "Critical Issues in the History of the Human Sciences." It drew on University of Chicago faculty from the Divinity School, history, anthropology, psychology, and sociology. The substance of that three-day seminar is described in the annual report as follows:

> The compartmentalization and localization of inquiry into discrete academic disciplines is a distinguishing feature of modern intellectual life. This Institute focused on the problem of discipline formation in the various human sciences: anthropology, psychology, psychiatry, philosophy, sociology, economics, history, religion, and education. In particular, the Institute examined the process by which this "disciplinization" has taken place, and how this reflects epistemological assumptions of the modern academy.
>
> During the course of the Institute, participants examined issues related to the formation and evolution of these disciplines, their boundaries, the nature of their crises and the role myths and values play in their founding and history.

The Midwest Faculty Seminar has in addition sponsored international symposia attracting several hundred scholars over the years. Through an "occasional fellowship" program, it is also possible for faculty from affiliated schools to secure modest grants to conduct original research projects, which include short stays at the University of Chicago campus. A teaching program designed to prepare University of Chicago graduate students for college-level teaching includes short-term teaching positions at the affiliated colleges and represents an important component of the humanities graduate experience for many students. In operation for more than twenty years, the program is administered by a professional who possesses a Ph.D. in a humanities discipline, and its costs are shared by the University of Chicago, the associated colleges, and private foundations. Comparable are the many summer institutes funded by the National Endowment for the Humanities (NEH) for humanities faculty from two- and four-year institutions and offered on campuses around the United States. The main drawback of the NEH Institutes is that they tend to depend upon external funding and are often one-time efforts rather than expressions of an institutionwide commitment to collaboration and conversation with faculty working in primarily teaching institutions. What is impressive about the Chicago program is its long-term institutionwide commitment to interacting with faculty from affiliated institutions on an ongoing basis. It represents a model that could be replicated elsewhere.

Even more complex than the sorts of professional or scholarly interdisciplinary issues just addressed is the problem of appropriately relating to the needs of new and emerging fields of practice. This issue goes beyond just getting people to work together to develop a common agenda. The key challenge is how to identify, access, and engage the proper knowledge resources in the first place. This represents a different type of institutional challenge than the two types of university-based human resources development efforts just described and merits separate discussion.

Knowledge Needed in Emerging Fields of Practice

More and more the academic community is discovering what the business media have been writing about for nearly a decade—the abundance of new careers emerging from a world in a continual state of flux. Whether or not these new careers will be equal in number, satisfaction, and employee compensation to the familiar jobs of the post–World War II economic boom remains to be seen. But clearly the rise and decline of specific occupations and shifts in employment trends within occupations are occurring with such rapidity that it is difficult to know what is really going on. No one adequately anticipated the employment implications of the end of the Cold War, for example. With the dismantling of the Soviet Union and the rapid reordering of national boundaries throughout Eastern Europe, the raison d'être for hundreds of industries employing millions of people has been called into question, particularly for those industries that relate to military preparedness, defense technology, and Cold War notions of national security.

This dismantling also suggests new economic developments which could give rise to new jobs at home and abroad, particularly in the capitalization, manufacture, and distribution of goods and services to which millions of citizens heretofore have had little access. No one as yet has a fix on where this transition or conversion process will lead. While academics and public policy analysts study the process and project the future, the world of work is full of signals about the possibilities. These signals are coming from the new industries forming and the new jobs emerging to respond to the needs triggered by social, technological, and environmental developments.

Ethno-pharmacology has emerged as an area of practice in increasing demand among the world's leading pharmaceutical companies. Realizing perhaps too late that much of the raw material for healing resides in the wisdom of native peoples and the varieties of plant life in endangered regions such as rain forests, companies are investing in ethnological research and field studies as a part of their quest for new and effective drugs for the treatment and prevention of disease. The *Los Angeles Times*, in the fall of 1990, profiled well-educated and well-paid individuals (salaries of $30,000–$50,000) working in the "more high tech, more narrowly defined and more socially conscious" service jobs of the future (New Careers Emerge from a World in a State of Flux, p. 13). One is an information security specialist. As data processing becomes more and more important in organizations as diverse as elementary schools, banking, and aerospace manufacturing, the problem of file damage caused by computer hackers and viruses and by natural disasters has given information security specialists a prominent new role. The profile reported that a company such as Rockwell International with 50,000 computer users employs nearly one hundred people with computer security–related responsibilities.

Research breakthroughs and the move toward a more humanistic response in medicine are giving rise to new areas of responsibility in health care, such as patient advocacy. In the same article, the *Los Angeles Times* profiled a genetic counselor whose job was to fill the gap between doctor and patients by providing counseling on high-risk pregnancy issues, which are increasing. In fact, there is now a licensing program for genetic counselors, which when combined with a nursing or other health degree makes a person highly competitive. There are only about one thousand genetic counselors practicing in the United States today, but with the development of prenatal tests capable of detecting more than four thousand genetic disorders, the need for these professionals is exploding, according to the *Times* (p. 13). A final example from the *Los Angeles Times* profiles is the emerging job of transportation coordinator in response to the stringent air quality guidelines being adopted by metropolitan districts across the United States. Transportation coordinators help their organizations increase ride sharing among employees, through such things as car pools and van pools. They promote commuter alternatives such as mass transit, walking, or cycling, and they develop incentive plans to reduce automobile use. The job includes technical knowledge of transportation, planning skills, marketing know-how, and the ability to work convincingly with people. The *Times* reports that there are between fifteen hundred and two thousand transportation coordinators in the Los Angeles area alone, and the numbers are expected to rise rapidly (p. 13).

These few examples have been selected because they represent not just a new workplace or vocational skill requirement but a set of knowledge-based competencies that are required to perform entirely new functions in the workplace. These functions require critical thinking and the ability to work with a cross section of experts as well as advanced technical knowledge. In this respect, they represent emerging fields of practice with a logical connection to the work of universities from which much of the new knowledge emanates. In fact, the fields of both genetic counseling and transportation demand management represent new programs of continuing education available through University of California campuses throughout the state.

An excellent example of a university that has provided for the knowledge needs of developmental and emerging fields of practice for more than two decades is George Washington University, in Washington, D.C. George Washington University represents one of the leaders in providing postbaccalaureate certificate programs which ensure workplace competencies for persons pursuing new and emerging fields of practice. These programs are often in subjects for which the institution does not typically offer degrees or established curricula, such as paralegal studies. The constituencies for these programs include the highly educated Washington, D.C., population that works for the federal government, national associations, law and accounting firms, and a full range of regional technical- and service-oriented industries. At George Washington University, it is the extension division, originally organized in 1940 to serve the educational need of teachers, which has served as the central linking mechanism over the past fifty years. The focus on new and emerging fields, and in particular the provision of postbaccalaureate certificates in these fields, paralleled the surge in women reentering the university and the workplace throughout the 1960s. This focus was further stimulated by the enormous growth and success of paralegal programs in the early 1970s. In the more than two decades since, George Washington University has greatly expanded its portfolio of programs addressing the knowledge and competency needs of emerging fields of practice. In an article describing the history and character of the programs at George Washington University, Abbie Smith (1991) provides a number of summary descriptions.

She outlines such things as a legal assistant program started in 1972, a publication specialist program begun in 1974, and a landscape design program initiated that same year. Smith describes in addition professional certificate programs in public relations and fundraising as well as a program for child care directors, launched in 1989. Her descriptions of specific programs provide a sense of the focus and appeal of these specific learning experiences. The rationale for the landscape design program, for example, is this:

Washington, D.C., well earns its reputation as the "city in the trees" with its hundreds of tree-lined streets and many formal and informal parks. One of the largest urban parks in the world, Rock Creek Park, runs through the city and into the suburbs. The Washington area as a whole has large numbers of historic homes and gardens, embassy grounds, and suburban and regional parks. With examples of excellent garden design everywhere, Washingtonians tend to focus on their own yards, making gardening a popular pastime.

To serve these interests locally, there are many area landscape architecture firms, landscape contractors, nurseries, and landscape installation and maintenance firms. Until the George Washington University landscape design program was started in spring 1974, the nearest related programs available were a master's degree program in landscape architecture at the University of Virginia [p. 66].

Smith describes the highlights of the public relations program as follows:

Washington, D.C., is the third largest market in the United States for the public relations profession. Promotion of business products, government programs, and association services requires the expertise of public relations professionals. The public relations professional program has two tracks, one for students interested in entering the field and the other for management-level practitioners. Comprehensive training in planning, implementing, and evaluating public relations programs in profit and nonprofit settings prepares George Washington University graduates for the large and diverse community of public relations professionals in the D.C. area. The program has attracted large numbers of students who select individual courses of interest. Approximately ten students complete the full curriculum each year [p. 68].

Each of these programs is highly responsive to workplace skills needed by college graduates in the Washington, D.C., area. Smith's article also includes some guidelines used by the staff at George Washington University, which are useful as an institution considers what fields to work with and how to implement relevant programs.

These brief examples from George Washington University could be expanded to include dozens of similar programs from campuses across the United States. Typically these programs are set up by units not linked to any specific professional school or academic department and carry no campus credit relevant to degree work. Nonetheless, these programs grow out of a circle of experience, expertise, and knowledge that includes the university resource base. Curriculum development is not as directly led by the university as it is in occupations in more advanced stages of professionalization. Programs of this nature represent a valuable service to organizations and individuals, which can enhance appreciation of and support for the university. On some campuses, the fees they generate represent sources of discretionary money, and they are potentially "feeders" into master's degree programs. The imprimatur of the university carries with it a concern for quality and reputation which postbaccalaureate students in particular value. Most importantly, as the need for specific skills and knowledge increases, universities can respond without setting up whole new departments and facilities if they can embrace certificate programs as one of the many ways they organize and disseminate knowledge into society.

The likely expansion in both need for and level of sophistication of academic programs that support the early-stage development of rapidly emerging fields of professional practice is one of the major challenges facing universities in the future. Professions are in large part defined by the standards of performance they set and the competency and knowledge base they require of their incumbents. The process of professionalizing involves participants in the definition of what will ultimately constitute a legitimized new field of professional practice. As advanced knowledge is such a critical component of this defining process, universities could play a critical role by helping identify core competencies and core curricula in these new fields.

In the last few years, an emergent field such as toxic and hazardous waste management is an excellent example of the complexity and advanced knowledge requirements practitioners in professionalizing fields face. Practitioners with degrees in law, chemistry, hospital administration, and general management find themselves linked because of shared needs for knowledge. Their need is to manage toxic and hazardous waste disposal—chemicals, blood, sewage, and garbage—in their organizations and communities. They need technical knowledge, regulatory information, planning and financing skills, all of which emanate from disparate places in the university and in society. Harvesting the knowledge and resources needed to organize a coherent program of study, which equips these diverse practitioners to deal with a complicated workplace problem increasingly common to all organizations in an advanced technological economy, is no easy task. Universities with strong centralized extension or continuing education units and staff who possess content area knowledge, such as those at the University of California and George Washington University, are up to the task. Institutions such as Pennsylvania State University that have colleges designated to take academic leadership for continuing education purposes can be mobilized for collaborative purposes. Many institutions, however, are not capable of responding. Most often this is because they lack people within the institution with sufficient content expertise or access to practitioner networks critical to working with these emerging fields. In the future, as knowledge becomes more and more sophisticated and workplace needs more complex, universities will need academic professionals whose abilities and interests are focused on

- Helping groups articulate their knowledge needs
- Finding the appropriate intellectual and pragmatic resources to address those needs

- Organizing curriculum and programs according to principles appropriate to the experiences and learning styles of advanced practitioners
- Enriching where possible the central research and teaching activities of on-campus academic programs

It is unlikely such professionals can be full-time faculty or generalists out of schools of education. They are much more likely to be academically qualified individuals interested in knowledge applications or practitioners engaged by the world of ideas and reflection.

This brief chapter represents an effort to introduce a more comprehensive way of thinking about how universities might relate to the lifelong human resources development needs of our society, particularly within spheres of professional practice which require advanced skills and continuous learning. Highly effective knowledge linkages have been developed since World War II, primarily through professional schools and associations dedicated to assuring professional updating and the highest levels of professional practice. However, many advanced knowledge needs continue to be unserved or underserved. This is due to the failure of the university as a whole to respond in a timely manner to the radical effects of technical and economic transformations in the workplace as cycles of innovation become shorter and shorter. These changes suggest a possible new role for the university in defining the standards and competencies essential to effective practice in the rapidly increasing range of knowledge intensive practice fields. Oftentimes these transformations involve esoteric knowledge areas and research-related information—genetic counseling, for example—stemming directly from traditional faculty work. Just as often they involve approaches to knowledge and definitions of needs in the world of practice which, once understood by faculty, could result in an enlarged research agenda—both basic and applied—and more flexible approaches to curriculum and instruction, in such areas as toxic waste management, for example.

Enormous gaps in knowledge and experience are developing between the university and the world of practice even in our finest professional schools. These gaps need bridging. As noted at the beginning of this chapter, paradoxically, knowledge within the academy is becoming ever more specialized while knowledge needs in the society are in continuous flux, increasingly interdisciplinary, and related to more and more fields of practice. If we expect to meet the full range of advanced human resource development needs facing us as a nation, universities must develop new institutional mechanisms such as interdisciplinary centers or leverage existing mechanisms such as extension services to play a bridging role both within the university and between the university and society. Experience suggests that institutional efforts to develop advanced professional education opportunities in other than traditional degree programs should possess the following characteristics:

- Leadership by professionals knowledgeable about both intellectual and practice issues
- Assessment of the skills, competencies, and knowledge base essential to effective practice prior to developing curriculum
- Involvement by all relevant stakeholders—faculty, employers, specialists—in the development of curriculum and delivery formats
- Willingness to use skilled practitioners, when appropriate, as instructors in addition to ladder rank faculty
- Support for mature students in the form of targeted communications and marketing, advising and enrollment services, suitable projects and internships, recognition ceremonies and record keeping
- Methods of financing that protect the autonomy of programs rather than structuring them to be cash cows for traditional programs

- A university culture that recognizes and rewards involvement in nondegree programs through reports, publications, institutional reviews, and faculty evaluations

The programs at the University of California, University of Chicago, Pennsylvania State University, and George Washington University described in this chapter all possess these characteristics.

Chapter Seven

Sustaining a Vital Civic Culture

The challenges to civic participation in a postmodern democratic society are formidable. High rates of immigration, geographic mobility, increasing interdependencies in complex urban centers, and the fluidity of the economy give rise to neighborhoods and communities characterized by impermanence rather than stability, fragmentation rather than cohesion, isolation rather than engagement. In their private spheres, most particularly the family, Americans also find themselves meeting demands which detract from time and energy for involvement as informed citizens in civic life. The majority of mothers today are in the paid labor force. More households are run by a single parent. More separated and dissolved families are juggling shared custody of children, stepparent roles, and the management and financial pressures of running separate households. Add to these social trends the extraordinary growth in information relevant to civic discourse and the public policy process in a world dominated by superficial broadcast media, and it is not difficult to see why civic culture as we have known it appears so fragile at century's end.

Simultaneously with these changing social forces and forms, an equally significant shift in the social organization of knowledge and, in particular, the role of intellectuals in public life has occurred. American cultural historian Thomas Bender, in his book *Intellect and Public Life* (1993), provides a series of reflections on the unintended consequences of the "professionalization" and "academicization" of intellectual disciplines such as history, literature, philosophy, economics, and sociology. While these fields have become (1) more intellectually rigorous by developing distinct vocabularies, methodologies, and canons and (2) more prestigious by instituting peer review–based standards of discourse and quality, the progress they have made has been at the "cost of making the parts of American intellectual life more powerful than the whole," according to Bender. He goes on to quote Alfred North Whitehead's pointed remark of the 1920s that "each profession makes progress, but it is progress in its own groove. But there is no groove . . . adequate for the comprehension of human life" (p. 13). Whereas professors and universities participated very actively in civic culture and public life at the turn of the century through institutionally led and rewarded public lectures, forums, and civic action programs, by the 1950s the culture of the academy celebrated and rewarded almost exclusively involvement and achievements inside one's own disciplinary communities. In fact, academic culture often disparages involvement in civil society, in particular the often parochial and putatively intellectually shallow affairs of one's "local" community. Appearing on the "MacNeil/Lehrer News Hour" carries some prestige, but speeches to local community groups rarely do. The consequence, according to Bender, is a much less rich civic culture, particularly at the local level, than is required to sustain a vital democratic society such as ours. Bender states: "The academic disciplines in America have been astonishingly successful in producing new knowledge, but their almost complete hegemony in our intellectual life has left Americans with an impoverished public culture and little means for critical discussion of general ideas, as opposed to scholarly or scientific expertise" (p. 46).

The challenge is how to "reawaken people's sense of caring and commitment at a time when they feel cynical, overworked and extremely isolated," as documented by Bellah and Associates in the widely discussed book *Habits of the Heart* (1985, p. 43). As people are propelled by the growing complexity and impermanence of modern society to focus on their private lives at the expense of community and public concerns, democracy as we know it is seriously threatened. There is a growing consensus that we as a nation are in need of "social renewal" and a "moral revival," which can better equip us to deal with the issues and circumstances of a postmodern society. Sociologists such as Robert Bellah at the University of California, Berkeley; Amitai Etzioni at George Washington University; Benjamin Barber at Rutgers; Alan Wolfe at the City University of New York; and James Q. Wilson of Harvard are raising these important issues, and increasingly, the media and the American public in general are listening as they search for new models of social engagement and community.

The renewal of civic discourse, and with that the increased involvement of citizens in public life, cannot occur without access to and dialogue with the significant ideas and data being developed within the currently self-contained and self-referential academic and intellectual communities. Bender goes so far as to assert that what is required is a renewed commitment to John Dewey's idea of the place of academic expertise in a democratic society, stating that "it must be tested in the public world as well as in disciplinary communities; disciplinary truths must be entered into the conversation of the public" (p. 137). Bender reminds his reader that Immanuel Kant, in "What is Enlightenment?" proposed that human progress could only come from truth telling in public. Only in that way would humans mature (p. 137). Thus the renewal of civic culture requires initiatives that can make critical connections—open up the conversation—between constituencies and community groups seeking perspectives on and solutions to local, regional, and national public issues and the experts and intellectuals who have critical knowledge that can help shed light on fundamental civic issues. Wolfe's work (1989) makes the point that neither markets nor the state can fill the growing moral vacuum underlying the "withering away" of civil society. He argues instead for a reengagement by intellectuals, and especially social scientists, in the moral discourse of the times. This represents a profound challenge for

America's research universities within whose walls the majority of the society's social science research and humanistic scholarship takes place. Finding ways to break down the walls created by the professionalization of academic disciplines is essential.

In addition, as discussed in Part One, there has been a decline in the effectiveness of mediating institutions, through which various private concerns become articulated and addressed as community issues, such as town hall meetings, book groups, and the League of Women Voters. They have been replaced by a proliferation of narrower special interest and lobbying groups. What constitutes the common good is much less clear in a highly diverse and mobile society than in a more homogeneous and stable one. Rutgers political scientist Benjamin Barber stated it this way at a conference entitled "Democracy in Action": "Citizenship is not about simply articulating and aggregating private interests, but about developing public and consensual ways of thinking about problems that, as private persons, we look at from only one point of view. The political question raised by public thinking is not 'what do I want?' but rather 'what is good for us as a community, a community to which I myself belong?'" (Corson, 1988, p. 6).

In a context where "public thinking" is absent, organizations standing between the individual and the state, the family, and society devolve into groups representing subsets of more narrowly defined interests around which it *is* possible to achieve a consensus; battered children, parents without partners, and foster families become the primary focus of subgroups, rather than a shared emphasis on families generally. Issues and interests, which in reality intersect, become polarized, and initiatives pursued on behalf of one set of interests may unduly harm another. Environmental protection and economic development, for example, are issues we as a nation must address simultaneously and with regard for the trade-offs involved in trying to balance desirable outcomes in both arenas. Instead, what we have is a proliferation of pro-environment and pro-business groups and a surfeit of mediating institutions. It is only through such mediating groups that the common good represented by these important issues can be analyzed, discerned, expressed, and ultimately pursued through the public policy process. It is this gap that potentially can be filled by new kinds of knowledge linkages between research universities and the larger society. Such connections must be facilitated by stable institutions that the public perceives as honest brokers. In a society beset by a proliferation of special interests, universities potentially represent such stable institutions. Such a role would also bring professors into conversations with publics in ways that might overcome their isolation and disengaged intellectual pursuits.

In this chapter, three types of knowledge connections will be described, each of which contributes to the ability of individuals to function in a more informed, humanistic, and considered manner. Each also contributes to enhancing the ability of citizens to think more "publicly" in their daily lives as citizens and as members of families and communities. The first represents the creation of opportunities for adult citizens to participate in liberal studies programs, thereby developing lifelong their appreciation of historical, literary, and philosophical issues which can enhance judgment in daily life. The second represents connections built around public affairs and community discourse groups concerned with local, national, and international policy issues. Such efforts can deliver information and perspectives that enable citizens to discern the common good as well as their personal interests and thus empower them to make more informed choices at the ballot box and in other public arenas. The third type represents efforts to connect the unique and undervalued intellectual and moral concerns of retirees, persons living out the final decades of their lives, with the dynamic knowledge resources in their communities so that they can continue to contribute positively to the affairs of their communities as they enjoy the private benefits of retirement.

Liberal Learning Programs

The June 1988 issue of *Johns Hopkins Alumni Magazine* is dedicated to a series of profiles of alumni professionals and the challenges they are facing in a rapidly changing society. One profile is of a prominent Baltimore tax attorney who has enrolled in the School of Continuing Studies master of liberal arts program in order to study ancient Greek history and art. He is studying this topic not because it is required professionally but because, as the attorney comments, "a lawyer's stock in trade is words. It helps sharpen the skills to be exposed to articulate professors." Besides, he points out, reading and studying for him are "fun" ("Café of the 80's," 1988, p. 14). Another student is the president of a major Maryland bank who reentered the classroom at age thirty-nine not because of its practical relevance to his specialty, finance, but because of his belief in the extent to which studying the liberal arts both provides pleasure and helps "develop methods of thinking that are important and useful in a business context" (p. 14).

In their early days, liberal studies programs were primarily havens for returning women students who had not completed college degrees earlier or for mature adults seeking their first college degree. Today's students represent a growing number of highly accomplished adults and well-educated professionals who return in midlife to college campuses to pursue challenging programs of reading and study in liberal arts disciplines, often as ends in themselves. This author has served on visiting committees at two Ivy League universities where there has been a long tradition of liberal studies for adult students. At Harvard, I met a professional woodwind player from the Boston Symphony pursuing a liberal studies degree in Italian history; at the University of Pennsylvania, a "burned-out" psychiatrist exploring possible new directions through studying the classics. As more and more adults achieve more and more advanced levels of education, and as professional life spans grow longer but also less predictable, revisiting the liberal arts becomes a renewing and oftentimes essential midlife step for many people.

According to the *Johns Hopkins Alumni Magazine*, students in these programs are motivated more by the learning experience itself than by earning another college degree. Many liberal studies students have been working in narrowly defined fields and at high levels of responsibility in established careers. For such persons, "skill"-related courses contribute less to career advancement than does intellectual flexibility, the ability to make informed and considered judgments, and a broad frame of reference within which to make decisions. Such students are capable of "seeing the relevance of Plato" and are looking for settings in which reading and conversation about ideas are possible. In fact, the article asserts that "the public places where people once went to talk over ideas have largely vanished. The classrooms of the twenty-five-year-old MLA program fill the void" ("Café of the 80's," 1988, p. 15).

The master of liberal arts program at Johns Hopkins University was begun in 1962 with the help of a three-year Carnegie Foundation grant to establish a nonvocational interdisciplinary liberal arts curriculum. By the early 1970s, many colleges, particularly private ones, were establishing similar programs, lured as often by the income to be gained from adult students as by a central campus commitment to lifelong liberal learning. By the 1990s, the numbers of highly qualified adults interested in this kind of learning and the tightening of academic standards in these interdisciplinary programs has resulted in more than forty such programs at universities around the country and rapid increases in enrollments. Johns Hopkins had over three hundred enrollees in its program in the early 1990s.

The brochure describing the program and academic requirements opens with a statement which captures the important knowledge needs served when mature adults pursue liberal studies.

"Liberal education" wrote John Henry Cardinal Newman in *The Idea of a University* "is simply the cultivation of the intellect and, as

such, its object is nothing more or less than intellectual excellence."
In an age where pursuit of professional excellence can often narrow
one's focus, people yearn for a deeper sense of fulfillment that leads
along the path of intellectual excellence. Adults recognize that specialization in a technological society must be tempered with a
broader vision of knowledge and with an appreciation of the inter-
connectedness of different areas of learning. Johns Hopkins University invites you to explore the ideas—ancient and honored or
radical and new—that provide keen, often provocative insights into
the human condition.

The program is built upon an interdisciplinary history-of-ideas
approach, which has characterized many of the more traditional
degree programs at Hopkins. All students participate in an introductory preseminar, which varies topically from semester to semester but whose intent is to sharpen critical, analytic, and evaluative
skills and to introduce the faculty and intellectual resources of Hopkins. A number of history-of-ideas seminars taught by Hopkins faculty are required. They include titles such as "The Scientific
Tradition" and "The Platonist Tradition." Elective courses can be
taken from the school's general liberal arts offerings, and students
complete the program with an independent project supervised by
a faculty member or with a more conventional master's thesis.

The total program consists of the equivalent of ten three-unit
semester courses. Applicants must have college degrees and a minimum grade point average to qualify, and an interview is required
for admission. The program is directed by a Ph.D. in the humanities, who is responsible for the interface with Hopkins faculty for
purposes of developing seminars and facilitating independent projects. The importance of equivalent academic credentials among
the program's leadership to those of the campus faculty cannot be
overestimated. The director and assistant director at Hopkins are
capable not only of informed discourse with liberal studies faculty
but remain active themselves in teaching, reading, and writing in

their fields. As such, they are superb "intellectual boundary spanners" as well as models for the returning students. The director also administers program budgeting and promotion, and is responsible for such things as coordinating student admissions, advising, and scheduling. Fees in the early 1990s were approximately $700 a course, and students typically pursued one course a semester.

The Johns Hopkins program is reasonably comparable to liberal studies programs at research universities throughout the United States, particularly at many of our more scholarly and research-oriented campuses such as Harvard and Stanford. Programs for the public in disciplines with which the faculty work daily and for which "practitioner" or student input is less essential to the assurance of quality seem to appeal to traditional research university faculty more than the sorts of practice-related interdisciplinary programs described in the preceding chapter. This may in part be due to the faculty's confidence in their ability to judge and control quality in programs whose content mirrors more closely the traditional curriculum. Liberal studies programs can be a very positive way for campuses to introduce faculty to mature learners and off-campus constituencies. On my own university campus, faculty have expressed surprise and, in this increasingly McLuhanesque, visual era, appreciation for the enthusiasm for ideas and the willingness to read and write that mature learners bring to liberal studies. It is one way to begin the very necessary conversation between faculty and the public. It can open faculty eyes and hearts to the concerns of citizens and practitioners. It helps citizens pursue their daily lives with more timely information and broadened perspectives.

The University of Chicago similarly has provisions for mature students to participate in courses in the liberal arts. Of particular interest is their Basic Program of Liberal Education for Adults, which provides off-campus adults the opportunity to participate in seminars and discussions of texts for the sheer reward of studying great books in the company of others who "love ideas." It is a four-year program of reading and conversation with instructors who are discussion guides rather than lecturers and with a focus on texts that are "masterpieces."

The seminars and tutorials meet for ninety minutes each week, and the program also makes available free lectures on important works or ideas throughout the year. It sponsors two weekend retreats a year on works such as Nietzsche's *Thus Spoke Zarathustra* and Mozart's opera *The Marriage of Figaro*. Administered through the Office of Continuing Education at the University of Chicago, the program is an excellent example of an institutionalized commitment to knowledge connections that facilitate liberal learning throughout the community. Programs such as these at Chicago and Hopkins are not passive experiences where educated adults represent an audience for a lecture or a film or a PBS documentary. They represent instead active learning opportunities in which the careful reading of texts, significant discourse, and analysis take place. They are demanding and require a student to be truly engaged. They require significant commitments of time and energy beyond presence in a seminar room once a week.

Many other important but less demanding opportunities for liberal learning exist across the country in addition to the orderly programs of study organized around an association of students or a well-defined curriculum like those just discussed. Institutions such as the New School for Social Research in New York and UCLA offer a rich collection of liberal learning opportunities for the public through courses, lectures, and seminars taught by faculty as well as arts practitioners and leading intellectuals in their communities. These fee-based noncredit programs contribute enormously to the quality of intellectual life in the communities and cities in which they are available and are experiencing significant increases in participation with the increased levels of educational attainment among the general public. But as they do not involve participants as actively in reading, writing, and conversation as coherently planned liberal studies programs do, their effects may be less transformational.

Knowledge linkages of these types can be enormously positive for the quality of life of individuals and communities, as well as relevant to assuring a more generally well-informed and thoughtful citizenry. They represent not merely personal benefits but programs out of which communities of discourse, shared knowledge, and increased tolerance develop. Too often referred to as enrichment or leisure learning by members of the academy, their general social value and specific value to sustaining public understanding and political support for scholarship and the world of ideas should not be underestimated. Additionally, they provide settings within which important ideas emanating from the research and scholarship of highly specialized intellectual disciplines can be discussed from the point of view of citizens and practitioners. In Kant's term they represent a context for "public truth telling."

The benefits of liberal learning opportunities such as those just described are diffuse. Programs designed for the specific purpose of creating settings in which public policy issues and topics of general concern to citizens can be discussed and analyzed tend to be much more focused. They have potential for affecting the direction community planning takes, the rise and fall of policy initiatives, and the behavior of citizens in their community roles and at the ballot box. It is to these we now turn.

Public Affairs and Policy-Focused Programs

MIT policy scientist Dorothy Nelkin (1979) has written convincingly about the extent to which the ability to manipulate complex, esoteric, and scientific knowledge has profound implications for the exercise of political influence in democratic society. In postindustrial societies, there is an increasing need for public awareness and political dialogue in areas formerly seen as "the domain of expertise." This is largely due to the widespread public consequences of many scientific and technical developments in postindustrial societies. However, enlarged participation requires a more informed public. Nelkin points out that "informed dialogue and meaningful negotiation over policy choices require competence to deal with difficult technical information—if only to prevent such choices from being masked as technical imperatives. Scientific knowledge, like land, labor, and capital, is a resource—indeed a commodity— and the ability to manipulate and control this resource has profound implications for the distribution of political power in democratic societies" (p. 118).

In order for public awareness of complex and technical issues to grow and the political dialogue to occur, there must be mechanisms for effectively dispersing information into the larger society as well as into settings in which people can review and evaluate the political and social implications of that information. Whether the issue is widespread in its implications, for example, the risks of casual sex for transmission of a disease such as AIDS; regionalized, such as the economic costs and benefits of immigration along the U.S.–Mexican border; or local, such as the location of a solid-waste management facility in a specific neighborhood, forming an opinion and taking a position on an issue should involve affected publics, not just experts.

How to get information to people who are affected and help them review and use it in socially constructive ways is a significant challenge. As was noted in Part One, the American public probably has more varied, superficial, and contradictory information available than it can handle. There also is less time and fewer neutral mechanisms available to help us make sense of and draw conclusions from information. This is due to the size and complexity but also to the geographic and social mobility of so much of our population. Our commitment to minimal national government and the decentralization of public services, especially education, also makes it very difficult to disperse important knowledge to large groups of people in order to inform and educate. In addition, the forums within which real discussion of issues can take place in order to enhance the development of public thinking are difficult to find.

In contrast, the Swedish government has for decades supported through the Ministry of Education programs to assure an informed citizenry. Through a national system of "study circles" managed by adult education associations, voluntary groups, labor unions, and local folk schools, it is possible to organize public discussions of vital and emerging policy issues. Nelkin cites as an especially significant example the effort of Sweden in 1974 to help citizens acquire more knowledge about nuclear energy. The national government financed a program of public discussion involving approximately eight thousand study groups which met to discuss energy-related issues. Study circles are a regular feature of Swedish democracy. Neutral background materials developed by the Ministry of Education are used in these study circles, and discussion leaders can secure training through government-funded programs. Government funding of study circles allows local groups to hire their own discussion leaders and bring in experts who can address an issue in a way which relates to specific local interests. In this manner, issues of pressing public consequence such as nuclear energy, AIDS, or global warming can be discussed and debated and the ability of even the citizen with modest formal education to have a more informed position on an issue can be enhanced.

I was extremely impressed with the level of interest and information about current affairs that steel workers in Sweden have, for example. While visiting plants there in 1990, I observed worker-led study circles, which clearly make a contribution to the level of civic literacy among Sweden's working people. The voter turnout in Sweden, for example, was 86 percent in 1988 (their lowest in decades), in contrast to barely 50 percent in the United States that same year. Figure 7.1, illustrating voter turnout in industrialized nations, dramatizes the low participation in the United States.

In a report authored by Ross Corson, summarizing the conference "Democracy in Action," held in St. Paul, Minnesota, in 1988, a quotation from Sweden's famed former prime minister (and

Figure 7.1. Voter Turnout Worldwide: Industrial Democracies.

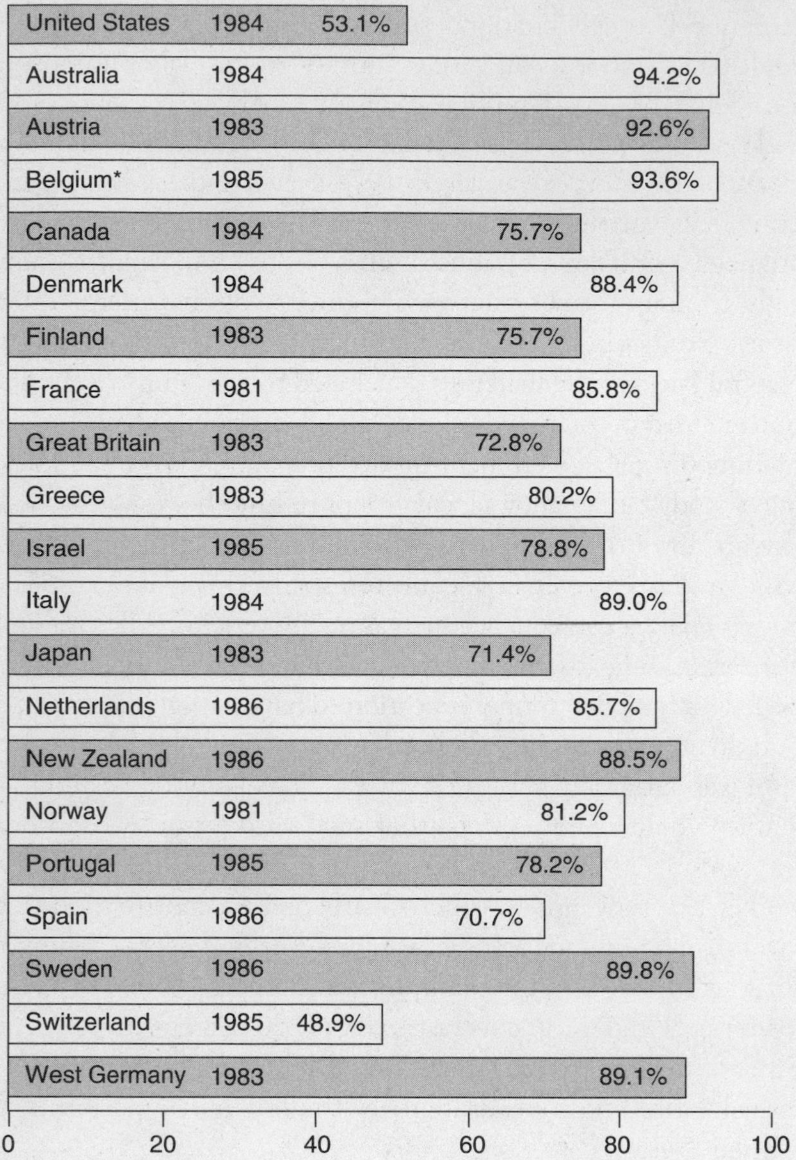

Country	Year	Turnout
United States	1984	53.1%
Australia	1984	94.2%
Austria	1983	92.6%
Belgium*	1985	93.6%
Canada	1984	75.7%
Denmark	1984	88.4%
Finland	1983	75.7%
France	1981	85.8%
Great Britain	1983	72.8%
Greece	1983	80.2%
Israel	1985	78.8%
Italy	1984	89.0%
Japan	1983	71.4%
Netherlands	1986	85.7%
New Zealand	1986	88.5%
Norway	1981	81.2%
Portugal	1985	78.2%
Spain	1986	70.7%
Sweden	1986	89.8%
Switzerland	1985	48.9%
West Germany	1983	89.1%

0   20   40   60   80   100

*Voting is compulsory.

Source: Congressional Research Service, 1986, p. 863.

former minister of education) Olaf Palme appears, which captures the essence of the Swedish way: "Sweden is to a fundamental degree a study circle democracy. It is through study circles that generations have trained themselves in critical analysis so as to be able to reach reasoned decisions in working with one another without abandoning their ideals in the process. It is often in study circles that proposals for changes in society have been first considered" (1988, p. 3).

As a nation, we too have a deep belief in the Jeffersonian ideal that an educated people are the proper repository of decision making. However, assuring that all of the people have access to all of the information they need as well as the skills to arrive at informed decisions is especially daunting in our large heterogeneous society. The closest thing in the United States to the Swedish study circle model is the National Issues Forum (NIF), a national program of civic dialogue initiated by the Ohio-based Kettering Foundation, and the Public Agenda Foundation, whose president is Daniel Yankelovich, the well-known opinion pollster. It is very similar in intent and form to the Swedish model, but it is privately organized and funded rather than federally initiated and funded. It is also administered locally by diverse institutions—libraries, churches, labor unions, and in many instances, universities. The work of the foundation is premised on the assumptions that (1) citizenship skills are greatly enhanced by lifelong learning and (2) a democratic society must have institutionalized mechanisms in place through which issues of civic significance can be discussed and debated by laypeople. The Kettering program in Minnesota and the Institute of World Affairs in Milwaukee, Wisconsin, are excellent examples of institutional initiatives with these characteristics, initiatives that make possible public discourse on significant policy issues. They represent interesting models of how universities might institutionalize policy discourse groups. Each merits some description.

NIF Minnesota is described by Ross Corson as a "loose network linking various groups and individuals throughout Minnesota interested or involved in the National Issues Forum program. NIF is a national nonpartisan program designed to encourage citizen discussion of important public issues—in effect to establish a study circle democracy" (p. 2). At its heart, NIF is an effort to recreate the town meeting idea of public talk and informed public judgment working toward a common ground of public understanding on issues. The goal of this civic education program is to produce better-informed citizens more able to participate in public affairs. Like the Swedish model, it is a highly decentralized program except for the development of study materials and the preparation of local group leaders. Leader preparation emphasizes techniques for guiding discussions that aim to help citizens come to terms with the difficult choices presented by policy issues.

NIF was launched nationally in 1982 with twenty-three local forums. Today more than nine hundred organizations conduct local forums and study circles, and a number of universities have become involved in the development of resource materials, the preparation of study group leaders, and the identification of local experts who can contribute to the policy deliberation process. The Minnesota sites include libraries, adult basic education programs, community colleges, senior citizen centers, churches, and civic groups, all of which rely on a core of materials and issue development strategies provided by NIF. Each year, NIF identifies three important and timely public policy issues for citizen deliberation. For each issue, NIF produces an array of materials to enhance discussion of the trade-offs and implications of alternative policy directions. The key discussion resource is a well-written and well-designed booklet on each issue. Audiocassettes and videocassettes are also available on each issue. The materials are designed to enable participants to move from "private opinions to public judgment." This means a discussion methodology that helps private opinions surface, conflicts to be discussed, relevant information to be introduced, and eventually a process of choosing between alternative courses of action to take place. The result is the ability to make public judgments. Corson describes it this way: "Public judgment represents not the simple sum of views—private opinions—that is measured by public opinion polls. Rather, public judgment depends on integration of diverse points of view" (p. 10).

The NIF model goes beyond the simple amassing of facts and creates a context in which how facts relate to different values is elucidated. Making choices is hard work; it requires "talking through," not just "talking about," according to the NIF methodology. It contrasts dramatically with the "cult of expertise" through which many universities exercise their civic role. By this, I mean university-sponsored public events and lectures at which experts, usually professors, offer information and opinions on policy issues with little opportunity for discussion, much less conflict, involving the laypeople present. In this manner, universities add to the information glut but not to the process of learning to evaluate alternatives and the development of public judgment so necessary to civic life.

Corson's conference summary includes a distinction between schooling and study circles, which though simplistic is very useful in clarifying the sort of knowledge connections that have to be made if the desired outcome is enhancing civic participation rather than just providing more information.

Schooling	Study Circles
Teacher	Study circle leader
Pupil/student	Member/participant
Lesson	Meeting
Classroom	Study room
Teaching	Studies
Textbooks	Study materials
Term	Study season [p. 6]

David Boggs (1988) has studied citizen groups and education over a number of years and has observed that self-learning and community education typically occur without assistance from the formal academic community. In an era of increasingly complex social problems, global interdependencies, and technological change, this gap between citizen groups and knowledge centers needs bridging. Bridging the gap faces two potential barriers, one on the university side, the other on the community side, according to Boggs. Citizen groups are not the typical university constituency and thus require time and negotiation to work with. Faculty in particular need to listen to what citizens' needs are and be able to interact with laypeople in an "egalitarian" as opposed to "superior" manner.

The development of informed public judgment may require settings and formats different from a traditional classroom, and faculty need to be open to new methodologies for sharing knowledge and expertise given the citizenship goals. They also need to understand that because they are experts their knowledge and facts are critical but that political judgments ultimately will come from citizens who incorporate those facts into a larger system of values and community constraints. Finally, the university must avoid the appearance of partisanship or it will lose its credibility as an honest broker.

Boggs points out that a balanced approach to issues will not always be easy to achieve, because citizen groups and special interests will be eager to cite the authority of the university as supportive of their cause. Universities, however, always have had to balance in their research and teaching programs the tendency to perpetuate the status quo with a critical view of things as they are (p. 107). They know how to balance the need to transmit the lessons of the past with the achievements of the present. They are capable of questioning the underlying assumptions framing traditional knowledge, simultaneously pushing the boundaries of knowledge by asking new and challenging questions, according to Boggs. As such they represent excellent conveners of groups facing conflicting alternatives.

On the citizen side, there are also barriers to overcome, which have been documented by researchers such as Boggs. They include a general fear of the higher education establishment and the concern on the part of even very accomplished citizens that they will sound "ignorant" or "uninformed." In addition, there is the perception among many that the university is just another bureaucracy or government agency. There is a concern as well that the university will "take over" and assume control of what is intended to be a collaboration. And there is a persistent concern that what professors like to do is "study problems to death" rather than reach conclusions and take action. Boggs suggests there is much social value to be gained by establishing knowledge linkages between universities and citizen groups. This is particularly the case if the civic group gives priority to "education over agitation," the group leaders are reasonable and credible, and community support in terms of participation and financial backing is likely (pp. 108–112).

The quality of educational programs sponsored by citizen groups is clearly inconsistent, and because of the increasing role of knowledge and expertise in the public judgment-making process, universities could make an important contribution. Campus-based public policy institutes, government study centers, schools of continuing education, and extension services all possess the institutional capabilities required to be effective collaborators. These include the ability to convene planning groups, develop educational formats, and identify and recruit appropriate speakers and experts. They also include the ability to implement programs because of office support and experience in preparing print and audiovisual support materials in education, the ability to summarize complex technical reports, an understanding of the public policy process, and linkages to agencies and key professionals. Many campuses also have well-developed internal marketing systems, mailing lists, and business and foundation contacts who can help with program funding and delivery. For all these reasons, Boggs asserts that an increased role in civic education is currently within the capabilities of universities across the country.

An example of a university-based program that provides, in addition to lectures and seminars conducted primarily by experts, the kind of participation celebrated in the study circle approach is the Institute of World Affairs, administered through the Division of Outreach and Continuing Education at the University of Wisconsin, Milwaukee. Governed by a board of advisers made up of distinguished community leaders and campus faculty, the Institute of World Affairs provides a full schedule annually of programs focused on the most current and important global issues. A small staff at the university works with the board of advisers to identify topics and involve presenters. The institute enjoys broad community support financially from corporations and cosponsorship of many programs with collaborating organizations. Its director, whose position is based in the Division of Outreach, has a Ph.D. in political science and has been active at the local level through service on the board of the Wisconsin World Trade Center and nationally as a board member of the Foreign Policy Association.

What is most interesting about the Institute of World Affairs is that it represents both an ongoing series of lectures, forums, and events, and an "institutional capability"—staff, mailing lists, facilities, and social relationships—on which the university and the city of Milwaukee can draw when (1) an important international event occurs, such as the tearing down of the Berlin wall or the bombing of Iraq; (2) an important international visitor, for example, a Soviet journalist, comes to town on short notice; or (3) state, federal, or foundation resources for special focus international programming become available, for example, for international teleconferencing opportunities on topics such as global warming. For a lively civic culture on international affairs to exist, there needs to be a stable and flexible context in which people can gather, discourse, and learn. The Institute of World Affairs represents such a context in Milwaukee.

The institute's annual report for 1991–92 describes an impressive array of topics and formats over the four quarters of the year. They include lecture series involving faculty from a variety of institutions as well as foreign affairs professionals on topics such as "Nationalism Resurgent: Ethnic Minorities and the Multi-National State." The institute sponsors summer forums and Saturday seminars on geographic areas such as Spain or Germany, at which participants interact informally and in discussion periods with international affairs professionals, country representatives, and faculty area specialists. Special events such as high school international career days, attendance at special cultural functions, diplomatic study tours to Washington, D.C., and dialogues with diplomats over dinner occur with regularity throughout the year. The institute program includes a number of annual programs such as Wisconsin Great Decisions, which recently focused on global issues, such as the refugee crisis and the breakup of the Soviet Union, through a variety of public lectures and parallel newspaper and public radio features. The institute sponsors a number of single-meeting public forums, such as "The Middle East Peace Talks: The Jordanian Perspective," in which differing points of view on policy issues are debated. The institute is the home for the Milwaukee Model United Nations program, as well as the source of local monthly telecasts titled "International Focus," which are interviews with speakers who participate in various institute programs. The conclusion of the institutes' annual report provides impressive numbers on participation and fundraising and sums up institutional activities as follows:

> The programs of the Institute of World Affairs closely paralleled global events. Forums were presented to the public about significant world issues and the evidence of solid community support for the institute was stronger than ever. Established on a foundation of four flagship public programs—the George F. Kennan Forum on International Affairs, Great Decisions, the Milwaukee Global Forum, and the Wisconsin High School Model United Nations—and a successful run of Diplomatic Study Tours to Washington, D.C., the institute is in a strong position to cope with the economic uncertainties of 1992 and the rapidly changing landscape of global politics [Institute of World Affairs, 1992, p. 20].

A program such as this represents a replicable model for

universities and cities across the United States. It is funded largely by individual memberships, corporate sponsorships, and significant business underwriting for specific programs, along with modest fees to participants. It represents the kind of knowledge connection which bridges the worlds of the academic expert, the professional practitioner, and the concerned citizen in a variety of activities encouraging interaction and the development of a more sophisticated appreciation of global issues. Such programs can greatly enhance citizenship skills and a sense of community as they raise the level of discourse in the community at large.

A final very brief example of a program addressing policy issues is one whose focus is regional economic and social development. The program, the San Diego Dialogue, incorporates many of the best elements of programs in Minnesota and Wisconsin. It represents a different model, however, because its focus is linking community leadership and decision makers with the resources they need to envision a new future for a cross-border region, San Diego, California/Tijuana, Mexico.

The establishment of the San Diego Dialogue in 1991 grew out of a series of conversations between leadership at the University of California, editors of the major newspapers, and key members of various local foundations and community leadership groups. The focus of these conversations was a growing despair over the fragmented character and conflictual tone of regional economic development and social planning efforts. What seemed to be lacking was a forum or a body which was capable of transcending parochial special interests in order to deal simultaneously with important long-term regional issues. Of particular concern were the implications of

1. A rapidly increasing and socioeconomically diverse population on the U.S. side

2. Enormous economic expansion and population growth on the Mexican side

3. A transformation of industries and services on both sides of

the border represented by a decline in aerospace, government contracting, military spending, and real-estate development; simultaneously with the rapid expansion of entrepreneurial high tech, especially biotech enterprises, on the U.S. side; paralleled by a tremendous growth in manufacturing, foreign investment, and tourism on the Mexican side

4. The absence of infrastructure—transportation, sewage treatment, education, and health care—capable of dealing with a rapidly expanding border region with a combined population of more than five million people

Previous planning efforts had suffered from a tendency to bite off one issue at a time—the need for more effective and responsive schools, the need for better sewage treatment facilities, the need for an expanded international airport. Special commissions on each topic conducted special hearings and investigations and produced specialized reports with specific recommendations. Little movement occurred, however, because every recommendation could find a detractor and be demonstrated to infringe on another area's needs or concerns. There was no forum for synthesizing or integrating these disparate reports. In addition, none of the special studies and commissions factored in the social or economic implications of the growing and prospering Tijuana region.

What has been happening in San Diego mirrors what is happening in cities across the United States. The complexity of choices and factors influencing choice had become so great that paralysis set in. Cities such as Portland, Phoenix, and Minneapolis have found a way out of this through a process of community dialogue and visioning of alternative regional futures represented by privately initiated and funded civic discourse and planning groups. A small group of San Diegans decided to attempt a similar process in a context as totally free of partisan politics and special interests as it could create.

In San Diego, this meant a critical role for the university because of its access to the diverse knowledge resources—particularly in international affairs and in science and technology—essential to informed dialogue. In addition, the university's reputation for neutrality vis-à-vis regional policy issues is excellent. Perceived in key sectors as an honest broker, the university assumed the role of convener and organizer of the group. To do this meant, in addition to convening a credible organizing committee, identifying a strong professional staff person to guide Dialogue programs and an experienced and respected community leader to chair the group and facilitate developing a clear mission and agenda. The first was accomplished in the person of a sociology Ph.D., whose work and teaching were centrally concerned with civil society and whose experience included a number of years in the newspaper business. The second was achieved by recruiting as chair someone with strong local respect and credibility, a former chancellor of the UCSD campus and for ten years the president of Columbia University.

The idea of San Diego Dialogue was to facilitate the exploration of regional development options through discussion, education, research, and public forums on an agenda defined through a participatory community process. San Diego Dialogue is not a program *of* the University of California, even though the university has been the key linking mechanism. Its appropriateness as a linker is in large part due to its credibility in a variety of disparate communities. Mexico, high-tech interests, the traditional community, business circles, and emerging minority communities perceive the university as fair-minded and relate well to the campus. The university is a guiding force and chief administrator of the San Diego Dialogue on behalf of the community. San Diego Dialogue is governed by a representative executive committee and consists of a community-wide body of approximately one hundred persons who engage in a variety of forums, applied research studies, and policy briefings aimed at arriving at a common vision of regional economic and social development which examines every challenge and opportunity in a binational context.

The goal of San Diego Dialogue has not been to become

another special interest group or advocacy association. It is rather the development of a vision of the "common good" in an international border region undergoing radical social and economic change at century's end. Its mission is to provide community leadership with new and alternative ways of thinking about the future through providing access to ideas, experiences, and models coming from many places in the world. Research and analysis are a part of this process, and the lay leaders participate actively in the definition of research questions and identification of parameters that must be taken into account. Academics then gather, validate, and organize important regional information in reports which receive widespread attention in the media and among political leaders. As important is the ongoing process of community dialogue these reports generate, which is possible because of strong ties with leadership in Mexico and collaborative relationships with community groups throughout San Diego county. The particular institutional capabilities of the university—its credibility, its faculty in relevant areas, and the outreach and program administration capabilities of its extension service—make all this possible.

Programs Serving Retirees

Before concluding our discussion on knowledge connections that help sustain a vital civic culture, a brief acknowledgment of the significance to civic culture of college- and university-based programs for retirees is relevant. The demographics of the American population are changing, with the most dramatic fact being the increasing size and significance of the cohort of citizens aged sixty and older. As discussed in Chapter Three, well-educated, affluent retirees, with as many as thirty years of active life in retirement, represent a significant new knowledge constituency. If this cohort continues to remain up to date on important economic, social, and technological issues and trends, they can continue to live intellectually active lives *and* make informed decisions as citizens and voters. If, however, their primary interests in retirement become the promotion of their self-interests they can potentially become a retrogressive influence in society, given their increasing numbers. Connections to sources of new knowledge are as significant for the retiree as the midcareer professional, both because of the life-enhancing benefits of an active mind to the individual and because of their potential to keep retirees active and informed participants in civic culture.

One of the earliest knowledge linkages established to relate to the intellectual needs of retirees was the Institute for Retired Professionals (IRP), founded in the 1960s by Hyman Hirsch at the New School for Social Research. That such a program would be founded at the New School is not surprising, given its unique beginnings and its significant role through most of the twentieth century in the intellectual life of New York City and the nation. The New School began as a result of the firings and resignations of key professors at Columbia University in 1917 due to their opposition to President Wilson's decision to enter into World War I. The school was founded to be the complete antithesis of Columbia at that time. As such, it committed itself to fostering among American social scientists a desire to participate in the "democratic social reconstruction" of western society (Rutkoff and Scott, 1986, p. 3). The ideological foundations of the New School were a commitment to freeing people from outdated habits of mind so that they could act intellectually and consistently with present needs and purposes (p. 7).

This tradition of social criticism, progressivism, and concern with education as a means to informed action has always characterized the culture at the New School. Fifteen years after its founding, the New School created an affiliate "University in Exile" that provided a haven for a generation of scholars fleeing Hitler and Mussolini's domination of Europe. Becoming the home for many of the most original and cosmopolitan thinkers of the twentieth century further established the New School as an intellectual center of criticism, controversy, and "liberalism." The curriculum and research programs of the New School always have been highly interdisciplinary and experimental. Over the years, some of this century's greatest intellectuals and artists have been faculty there— Thorstein Veblen, Claude Lévi-Strauss, Hannah Arendt, Leon Festinger, John Cage, Robert Heilbroner.

Since the early days of the New School, its primary focus has not been college degrees but creating a more open academic context in which the population of New York City could engage the "challenging and innovative" through a highly sophisticated program of classes, lectures, seminars, and special events. While other colleges and universities have built disciplinary boundaries and implemented complex academic degree requirements, as well as narrowed their lifelong learning focus to the continuing education needs of professionals, the New School has managed to sustain a lively program of creative, oftentimes esoteric, and intellectually challenging knowledge connections throughout New York. Its innovative program of learning in retirement was a natural extension of this view of knowledge and learning as essential tools for a rewarding life and responsible citizenship.

At the heart of the IRP is an array of self-taught courses and self-directed discussion groups. Based on the assumption that retirees have a richness of experience and intellectual resources to call upon, the program's central focus is to create study groups within which this wisdom and experience can be shared. The program is based on annual memberships and is guided by its own board of directors and a curriculum committee who plan and schedule the programs for each quarter. The IRP model has spawned hundreds of similar university-based programs of cooperative education across the United States. Not all are as participatory as the New School model, and many have elaborated programs and activities to include intellectual linkages with faculty, undergraduate and foreign students, and community leaders.

The Evergreen Society at Johns Hopkins University, for example, includes in addition to study/discussion groups social activities, lunchtime lectures, and access to the library and computer center, as well as the opportunity to enroll on a complimentary basis in two continuing studies courses a year. The Institute for Continued Learning, established twenty years ago at the University of California, San Diego, includes weekly lectures by prominent citizens and professionals on current affairs, four ten-week lecture programs by UCSD faculty, and a variety of regional, national, and international study tour opportunities for members. Many programs provide opportunities for retirees to provide service to their campus or surrounding community. The University of North Carolina, Asheville, involves retirees in undergraduate tutoring and as research assistants in faculty research. Program members also provide retirement preparation programs in the community as well as reading and tutorial assistance to regional public schools. The program at the University of Delaware has more than seven hundred members and a beautiful dedicated facility in Wilmington housing its offices and programs. Retired executives provide pro bono assistance to not-for-profits and small businesses as a part of Delaware's program.

Common Characteristics of Programs That Enhance Civic Culture

What these three brief examples of programs focused on civic issues have in common is (1) a commitment to community participation in the setting of agendas and formats; and (2) a methodology which assures active participation, lively discussion, and debate between faculty, experts, and citizens. Without these two critical components, civic culture and the development of a communitywide consensus as to the common good cannot be significantly enhanced. It is bringing the knowledge resources of the university into "conversation" with the larger society that promises the greatest gains in the development of public judgment. The liberal studies programs and civic education initiatives described in this chapter portend well for the future of civic culture. However, if they remain idiosyncratic examples rather than models for many institutions in many of our cities and communities, little can happen.

In all these cases, the university is the "home" for the programs because of the significant role of knowledge, of teaching and learning, in all of them. It provides a knowledge connection that is clearly enriching for the individual participants but that also represents something more. And that something more is the tremendous social benefit that comes from having an informed and active citizenry or retiree community: a community capable of contributing to the development of public judgment and vital community needs, as well as one which receives benefits from the university and the community. Research universities are appropriate settings for these programs because of the central role of knowledge in the life of these programs, not just because of the new knowledge they develop but because of their libraries, media resources, campus facilities, and most importantly, their tradition of fair-mindedness and open debate.

There is a dominant theme echoed in the brief descriptions of all these programs: the theme of participation and interaction in what are truly "learning communities." These communities may be a cohort in a liberal studies program, members of a liberal learning society, associates of an Institute of World Affairs, or participants in an ongoing community dialogue group. In each case, information is not just transmitted but shared and engaged as part of a social experience. Out of the sociability and "talk," come new perspectives and shared understandings based as much on a "feeling" of shared concerns as an intellectual grasp of significant issues. Universities can help create these communities, because of their depth and maturity as centers of knowledge and because they are comfortable settings for well-educated adults. The examples provided also underscore that such programs can be essentially self-funding and self-managing. As the key knowledge centers of their communities, universities are properly one of the conveners, one of the important links in sustaining a vital civic culture in a democratic society.

Without a nationwide commitment to the renewal of civic discourse at the local level on critical regional, national, and international issues, there is likely to be further erosion of participation at all levels of society. Richard Lyman, who spent a decade as president of Stanford University and eight years as president of the Rockefeller Foundation, in a speech on the profession of continuing education and the public, exhorted those responsible for the outreach and lifelong learning programs of universities to take a more active role on behalf of their campuses in civic education.

> For the continuing education profession to fulfill its mission to serve the public will require your enlistment in the struggle to restore a sense of public responsibility across America that has sadly eroded in our time. And this must inevitably be grounded in knowledge of and respect for human potential as it has been demonstrated by the greatest thinkers and doers of many ages and many cultures. A rejection of the world's complexity won't do it. Pursuit of the higher selfishness through such euphemisms as "personhood" won't do it. Focusing entirely on one's professional backyard won't do it. Only by raising our sights and taking command of our destiny midst a puzzling, complicated and fast-changing world can we hope to survive, let alone prosper [1988, p. 10].

John Maguire, the innovative president of Claremont Graduate School in California, has argued throughout his career that the university has a "debt to society" and that "a great university brings its resources to bear on the problems of the community" (Hendrix, 1985, p. 1). In addition to teaching values and citizenship to undergraduates, in addition to conducting research that can benefit social and economic development, in addition to designing professional school programs that are socially responsive, universities have an ongoing role to play in community discourse about matters of civic importance. Such matters require a supportive and neutral context in which to be discussed. They benefit as well from the information and insights the work of scholars and researchers can contribute to the discourse (Maguire, 1982, p. 281). Maguire offers his own alternative to the traditional conceptualization of the mission of the university as teaching, research, and public service. He emphasizes the importance of *invention*, *recovery*, and *reform* as the central impulses of a responsible academic institution. A commitment to invention involves "pressing towards the future"; recovering, reclaiming, and honoring the past; reforming; and "seeking to address social needs with powerful understanding" (Hendrix, 1985, p. 1). The institutions and programs just described are attempting to do the latter through ongoing interactions with citizens throughout their communities.

Chapter Eight

Building Effective Linkages Between Universities and the Public

The data and ideas presented in Part One and the program examples in Part Two suggest that there are expanding knowledge needs that are intellectually compelling and socially significant *and* that there are ways for universities to address them which enhance rather than detract from traditional programs of research and teaching. The data, ideas, and examples also underscore that, in order to achieve the proper fit between traditional functions and new needs, there must be an organizing framework which relates to mission and values, not just "markets" and political expediency. What is needed are new institutional initiatives capable of providing the sorts of linking functions not now in place, which will allow universities to increase interaction with off-campus publics simultaneously with sustaining traditional commitments to basic research and traditional degree programs.

A compelling case for extending learning opportunities and reconceptualizing the knowledge work of the modern university can be made purely on the basis of the social implications of the transformations and reconfigurations of knowledge coming out of the ongoing research and teaching programs of these institutions. The need to better integrate nonuniversity-based knowledge resources, such as research results from industry and expertise from practitioners, and the ever-changing global political and economic pressures facing this nation make an even stronger case for an expanded commitment to knowledge extension, exchange, and collaboration between the university and its publics. However, this expanded mission should in no way encumber the autonomy and integrity of the research and scholarship that has fueled our social and economic development to date. As Bartlett Giamatti, for many years president of Yale University, so convincingly argued, universities for most of their history have resisted "giving in" to outside political pressures, because the university traditionally has been the one place in society "where the most free swinging and intense intellectual exchange takes place without any intent to damage or coerce other human beings and as a place where the larger goal of intellectual training is a civic one" (1988, p. 12).

Thus it behooves those of us concerned about society's knowledge needs to develop models that enrich the central work of research universities and that enhance the production and preservation of knowledge as well as its dissemination and application. However, these four traditional functions can no longer proceed effectively without better connections to the larger society, because advanced postindustrial societies produce and use knowledge in many more places and in many more interrelated ways than agricultural and industrial societies do. If universities wish to continue their central knowledge role in American society in the rapidly changing future, they must find ways to engage these knowledge resources more effectively, simultaneously with preserving their traditional neutrality and autonomy.

The various programs described in Part Two prosper within the context of some of this country's finest research universities as much because they reinforce the traditional knowledge activities of their universities as because they serve society. They tend to be idiosyncratic for the most part. They deserve to be a more integral part of their university's mission and identity. Because they represent examples of knowledge linkages that benefit their campuses as well as the publics they serve, they merit replication on campuses in communities throughout the nation. How to replicate them elsewhere can be addressed by drawing out their common themes and organizational characteristics. Together they represent a set of principles and recommendations that may be relevant to communities and institutions interested in expanding the institutional mechanisms through which universities and colleges relate to expanding publics.

It is important to reiterate the intellectual rationale for this expanded mission. Part One provided a lengthy description of the types of knowledge transformations and the changes in society and the economy that argue for expanded interactions of this type. The half-life of the technical and scientific knowledge and skills transmitted in the course of undergraduate and graduate education is shrinking. Dealing with global problems and change—including economic trends, immigration and migration patterns, environmental and natural resource contingencies, ethnic and religious conflicts—requires access to new forms of knowledge at more accelerated rates and in more interactive forms than we currently provide citizens. Emerging fields of specialization spring up faster than traditional college curriculum committees and faculty recruitment and reward mechanisms can respond. For these reasons, colleges and universities need to find ways of connecting to the society which are complementary to their established programs. Many in the academy resist relating to these expanded needs, as much because they cannot imagine how to relate to them, given current structures and traditional commitments, as because of indifference toward the everyday concerns of the sponsoring society. The examples in Part Two of university-based programs that *are* providing successful links between the academy and society in a variety of contexts for a variety of social and economic benefits represent promising avenues for institutions still struggling with how to serve their publics most effectively.

Common Intellectual and Organizational Themes

Ten critical characteristics, which unite the diverse programs described in Chapters Five, Six, and Seven, need to be present in institutional initiatives linking research universities with their publics:

1. There are persons and/or academic departments within the university that have a flexible view of knowledge and acknowledge the variable sources of relevant expertise inside and outside the academy.

2. There is a desire to learn *from* these nonuniversity sources as well as teach *to* them.

3. There is a genuine commitment to collaboration expressed through broadly representative founding boards and governing committees who set program priorities and formats, and identify appropriate sources of expertise.

4. There is a commitment to a social dynamic characterized by exchanges, interaction, and networking, and thus an acknowledgment that programs must support informal as well as formal activities, and a belief that a "community" needs to be developed.

5. There is a commitment to flexible and varied formats for information dissemination and knowledge exchange.

6. There is an ongoing process of self-evaluation and tracking of program effects, which often means research and evaluation functions.

7. There are multiple sources of funding—private, university, corporate, membership, fees for services—in all the programs.

8. There are components in all of the programs that directly or indirectly enhance the central intellectual preoccupations and resource needs of the university.

9. Programs are staffed and facilitated by highly educated full-time professionals, who are as at home with academic as with off-campus constituencies and who possess credibility among all the partners in the knowledge exchange.

10. There is a significant component of campus leadership support, typically in the person of the provost or the president, associated with every program.

Fuller discussion can help elucidate the dimensions of each of these essential characteristics.

Knowledge Comes from Many Places

A flexible view of knowledge and the recognition of multiple sources of expertise as needing to be factored into any institutional initiative is the central issue in every example given. With regard to supporting postindustrial economic development initiatives, case studies of successful regional development cite again and again the importance of mutual understanding, cooperation, and collaboration among a variety of experts. This is especially true in high-tech economic development. The significance of knowledge exchanges to the development of mutual understanding and the evolution of techniques for enhancing regional growth cannot be overestimated. Scientists and engineers often lack the financing and management information needed to grow businesses, just as accountants, attorneys, and marketing professionals may lack the knowledge of scientific and technical facts needed to provide appropriate guidance and business services. Equally significant is the need for civic leaders and government officials who understand both the unique scientific and the special business formation problems facing new industries. Thus, before collaborations can occur and joint strategies develop, a powerful amount of learning and knowledge exchange needs to take place. This is where universities can play a unique convening, brokering, and synergizing role, which can add real value to regional economic development efforts. Ongoing knowledge linkages such as those described in Chapter Five can greatly enhance a community's readiness to respond to new economic opportunities.

Similarly, the discussion of how to better serve human capacity development needs lifelong emphasized the important interactions between academics and practitioners in the development of programs that assure professionals have up-to-date skills and competencies. Equally important, however, is the problem of setting up programs capable of crossing disciplinary lines so that practitioners can have access to the knowledge, skills, and interpretative frameworks they need in the largely interdisciplinary world of professional practice, of which engineering management is such an excellent example. Finally, as we vision the future, there is a growing phenomenon of new and emerging fields of practice, which are arising with increased rapidity, in response to real world economic and social trends in environmental fields, for example. For these sorts of emerging advanced practice knowledge needs, existing faculty and curricula are not yet in place. These needs require extraordinary reliance on approaches that draw from the best resources from a variety of places within the academy and from the world of practice in order to help define the standards and competencies appropriate to areas certain to become major professional areas of practice. Examples such as toxic and hazardous waste management and transportation demand management were cited earlier.

Sustaining a vital civic culture through university initiatives that foster liberal learning opportunities and programs of civic education and discourse also must possess this consultative/collaborative quality, because of the importance of participation on the part of laypeople in the analysis of ideas, the study of texts, and in debate and conversation on critical intellectual and civic issues. Linkages must be forged to accommodate this kind of give-and-take, and experts must be prepared to draw on the experiences, values, and political realities which laypeople often bring to the conversation. The program in liberal studies at Johns Hopkins University, the Institute of World Affairs at the University of Wisconsin, and the Institute for Retired Professionals (IRP) at the New School for Social Research are superb examples.

Points 2 and 3 in the list of essentials flow quite naturally from this first point. University activities seeking to draw on diverse and multiple sources of information and experience must of necessity be guided and governed by a cross section of representatives from various resource bases. All the programs described in Part Two are characterized by collaborative governance, agenda setting, and support in securing resources—financial and expert—on behalf of the effort. Knowledge linkages supporting economic efforts involve academics, business leaders, and government. Those supporting human resources development involve academics, professional associations, and hands-on practitioners, especially in the development of initiatives addressing the knowledge needs of interdisciplinary and emerging practice needs. The National Issues Forum (NIF), Institute of World Affairs, and the liberal arts learning programs at places such as University of Chicago and Johns Hopkins University all draw on diverse expertise and knowledge sources as they develop priorities, agendas, and curriculums, not just for the delivery of programs and services.

Importance of Learning Communities

A commitment to developing a community (point 4), is a more difficult case to make, and yet it may be what is most critical to any institution effort that works. Decades of social science research suggests that, as people begin to develop relationships and "feelings" for one another, they are more likely to develop empathy, a sense of common destiny, and a commitment to building a shared future (Homans, 1950). The argument of this book has been that such feelings of mutual interest and a shared future flow from the opportunity to examine facts, information, and ideas in a shared context that leaves room for not just information and data transmission but talk, debate, and socializing. Out of the talk and socializing comes the potential for the development of mutual respect and empathy and ultimately a shared agenda. These are the ideas upon which our own democracy was built. There is no reason why the fragmentation of contemporary urban life and the information explosion of our technological age should signal the end of relevance for these founding principles.

What has been argued and demonstrated through program examples is that effective inistitutional programs create communities of overlapping expertise and interests. They can be structured in such a way that participants discover their common interests, develop respect for different forms of expertise, and begin to work toward a common good. The CONNECT program at UCSD, the fine professional certificate offerings at George Washington University, the Midwest Faculty Seminar at the University of Chicago, the liberal studies program at Johns Hopkins, the Institute of World Affairs at Wisconsin, the IRP at the New School for Social Research, all represent much more than conventional "classroom" experiences or briefing sessions in which ideas and technology get "transferred" in a one-way relationship between academic experts and lifelong learners. They represent rather a community of learning in which ideas, experiences, and expertise are shared and out of which new perspectives on major questions on "What is to be done?" evolve. People develop respect and affection for the limits as well as the potential of one another's spheres. They develop a "feeling for" as well as an "idea of" one another's worlds. It is this combination of feelings and ideas that allows for the kind of compromise and collaboration so essential to building a sense of the common good, whether it is in the service of economic growth, human capacity development, or sustaining a vital civic culture.

Importance of Organizational Supports and Funding

The four points just discussed are perhaps the most critical in the list of ten because they represent the underlying assumptions that need to govern university initiatives capable of addressing the needs we face at century's end. The remaining six points relate primarily to organizational and staffing issues and flow quite naturally from the assumptions just laid out. Clearly, if information transmission and exchange, opportunities for informal exchange and socializing, and a commitment to developing a sense of community are among the desired outcomes, they need to occur in a variety of settings, in a variety of formats, and through a variety of media. The examples given in Part Two all have this variety in common. The CON-NECT program offers courses and seminars, but it also sponsors breakfast research briefings, late afternoon lectures, international symposia, quarterly reports, the publication of occasional papers, the dissemination of audiotapes, a monthly television show, and a newsletter on the Internet. The interdisciplinary programs at the University of Chicago include—in addition to classes and seminars—weekend retreats, lecture programs, independent study opportunities, and tutorials with distinguished faculty. The Institute of World Affairs at the University of Wisconsin has a similarly varied format and also incorporates programs for high school students and an international affairs television series. Civic education programs such as the National Issues Forum and learning in retirement programs such as the Institute for Retired Professionals provide leaderless discussion formats and volunteer teaching opportunities. The point is that the purposes of the knowledge exchange give rise to the formats and ways of communicating; it is not some fixed notion of teaching and learning or principles of adult education that governs the process.

Each of the programs described in Part Two has also built in ways of measuring program success and progress. This is in large part because they all have multiple stakeholders and financial backers who require feedback. Programs that depend on state allocations or exclusively on student fees often rely primarily on conventional measures such as student evaluations of classroom experiences. However, in the sorts of institutionalized efforts described in this book, different kinds of indicators appear to be needed. All track enrollment and participation figures, and all seek evaluative input from participants. However, a program such as CONNECT, for example, collects and reports data on a regular basis on regional business developments, particularly with regard to new businesses in developing fields such as biotechnology and multimedia. They regularly issue reports on number of companies, level of capitalization, number of employees, and future prospects. They also report on financing outcomes for companies participating in their two annual financing forums as well as on issues such as acquisitions, mergers, patents, and licenses among the companies in the CONNECT network.

Programs such as NIF and the Institute of World Affairs report participation data but also prepare annual reports in which underwriters and members are acknowledged for their contributions and a full description of previous years' programs and participants is given. San Diego Dialogue conducts applied research on regional issues, which is regularly reported in the regional press and broadcast media and provides a basis for the briefing books utilized in community forums. Johns Hopkins supports an active alumni program for its liberal studies graduates, as does UCSD for the graduates of the Executive Program for Scientists and Engineers. These programs allow the institutions to keep track of the progress of their former participants and also to provide additional learning opportunities for them and use them as resources in future program planning. These sorts of formal and informal mechanisms all contribute to assuring continual feedback to the staff managing the programs and also to sustaining a sense of ongoing commitment among key stakeholders and participants.

Having multiple sources of funding is another characteristic of all of these programs. It may be a significant reason for their longevity and stability. Just as a local community that is dependent on a single industry—agriculture, or tourism, for example—can be economically derailed by a natural disaster like a drought or by declines in consumer spending due to a recession, boundary-spanning initiatives that rely on only one sector for resources are overly dependent on the uncontrollable forces affecting that sector. State budgetary crises can force profound cutbacks in state-funded programs; the withdrawal or decline of key industries such as aerospace can have profound implications for fee-based programs.

Plummeting interest rates can affect the level of foundation giving and private philanthropy. Corporate restructuring and downsizing can affect willingness to underwrite programs. Unemployment and the absence of salary and wage increases can lead individuals to be reluctant to pay fees or membership dues. Thus programs that have a mix of funding seem to have a better chance of survival. All the programs described in Part Two either deliberately or out of necessity have variable sources of funding.

Benefits for Traditional Campus Programs

The programs also share the characteristic of generating returns to their campuses in intellectually and oftentimes financially significant ways. The CONNECT program works intimately with the UCSD office of technology transfer, organizes faculty research briefings for industry on a regular basis, employs campus graduate assistants, and includes faculty as guests at all functions. Staff review upon request campus research initiatives that have potential industrial implications and facilitate industrial partnerships where appropriate. They also schedule as many events and briefings on the campus as possible to increase the business and government communities' identification with the campus.

The University of Chicago Midwest Faculty Seminar provides an invaluable service to graduate programs by facilitating paid teaching assignments for Chicago graduate students at the campuses of many of the participating small colleges and state universities. In addition to identification of opportunities and placement, the seminar provides orientations which prepare graduate students for future college teaching. The wide array of continuing professional-education programs such as those at Pennsylvania State University and George Washington University also represent additional sources of income for faculty. Faculty who participate in providing this advanced education as often use the income to offset the costs of their labs, research programs, and graduate students as to enhance personal earnings. When semester-long courses in liberal studies are offered, the additional income to faculty often represents travel funds or book funds not always available to faculty in the arts, humanities, and social sciences. Program participants or graduates also become campus advocates and donors to more traditional research and teaching programs.

All these programs also represent access to practice settings and communities of interest not always available to campus faculty through regular programs of undergraduate and graduate teaching and research. Even very established universities and professional schools benefit from access to new practitioner settings and new industries, which represent the employers, applied research settings, and corporate contributors of the future. Finally, the programs all create access to settings in which student interns can have meaningful experiences and graduates can potentially find employment. Campuses are uneven in the extent to which their research faculty, placement offices, alumni affairs, and development functions leverage these community-focused programs for institutional purposes; but over time, campuses are discovering what an invaluable resource the programs represent.

Professional Staffing

Of special significance in all of the programs described in Part Two is point 9 on the list of essentials: the existence of highly competent professional staff with credibility in a variety of communities to lead programmatic efforts. These staff members are rarely conventional faculty but rather persons who possess advanced academic credentials and whom faculty respect but for whom the bridging and interpreting role is the primary vocation rather than teaching and research. Such persons are absolutely essential for the kinds of knowledge-focused initiatives we as a nation need as we face our uncertain future. They are persons who possess the requisite expertise in the areas for which they are responsible, but whose values and professional commitments are to facilitate the application and use of knowledge in society rather than to expand knowledge through basic research or diffuse it through teaching in conventional degree programs. There is no set job description or professional association for persons such as these, but they are to be found on college and university campuses across this nation. They are also often found on the staffs of magazines and newspapers that deal with sophisticated advanced knowledge issues. They can also be found as producers in the documentary television and film world and as staff to highly specialized congressional committees. They work as librarians and research aides at our most research-oriented institutions and as program directors in the extension services of our great research universities. The things they must know how to do include identifying appropriate sources of expertise and information on a given topic; conversing with experts; convening and organizing knowledge-based agendas; summarizing and synthesizing information and knowledge in actionable forms such as curricula, lecture series, research reports, or events; and securing the political, financial, and managerial support essential to initiating a new program. Thus a combination of intellectual, communication, and organizational skills are essential.

Persons who help formulate and lead these sorts of efforts are typically animated less by the impulse to expand the knowledge base or relate to the particular needs of students—traditional or nontraditional—than they are animated by a commitment to serve as interpreters, brokers, and linkages in the important process of putting knowledge to work in a democratic society. In fact, University of California management professor Judith Rosener describes a new style of leadership, "linking leadership," which she expects to be common to all types of advanced organizations. This style recognizes that leaders have to manage nontraditional linkages and must think horizontally and diagonally as well as vertically, according to a 1994 *Los Angeles Times* feature.

Looking at the staffs of the various programs profiled in Part

Two, a number of common characteristics emerge. The directors of the CONNECT program, the Midwest Faculty Seminar, the programs in advanced professional education at Pennsylvania State University, the Executive Program for Scientists and Engineers, the Institute of World Affairs in Wisconsin, San Diego Dialogue, and the liberal studies programs at Johns Hopkins University and the University of Chicago all come from previous roles and experiences in the academy or society which uniquely qualify them for the linking roles they play. They bring academic or professional school credentials equivalent to those possessed by key players in the communities they will be serving and bring as well a component of relevant practice experience. Their significant knowledge of content issues and familiarity with the practices, ideas, and data characterizing the fields for which they are responsible give them intellectual credibility. In addition, as my personal interviews revealed and their reputations indicate, they are professionals who know how to speak the language of whatever community they are dealing with, and as such, are excellent interpreters and synthesizers of different types of knowledge.

They are also learners themselves, more inclined to be well read and informed about developments in the fields for which they are responsible than in organizational and interpersonal issues such as management, organizational development, or principles of adult learning. This observation is in no way meant to diminish the importance of management, organization, and learning issues so much as it is to emphasize the overriding importance of content issues when the objective is the development of the kinds of diverse and innovative knowledge-rich activities described in Part Two. In fact, the staffs of these programs also possess superb communication, interpretation, and facilitation skills which they are able to use in the service of building collaborative programs once they have established their credibility based on content knowledge among all the partners in the knowledge exchange. All also operate within the context of a larger outreach function—a professional school, academic institute, school of continuing studies, or extension service—which provides the financial, managerial, marketing, and program implementation resources needed to deliver academic support services to the community in an ongoing and cost-effective manner.

Campus Leadership Support

Finally, campus-based leadership is a significant element in all of the programs described in Part Two. That leadership is not necessarily in the actual initiation of boundary-spanning programs so much as in the provision of intellectual and political support for such initiatives, whether they come from the faculty, the community, or the university's outreach functions. The deep and significant support of the provosts at the University of Chicago and Johns Hopkins University, of the chancellors at UCSD and the University of Wisconsin, and of the vice president at Pennsylvania State University were identified in interviews as critical to the early-stage development of innovative institutional initiatives. Opening doors to foundation contacts, convening community groups, signing letters soliciting community financial backing, hosting receptions, and keynoting important events are all ways in which campus leadership contributes. Sometimes that leadership includes commitment of institutional discretionary funds and internal advocacy with department chairs and faculty members. More often it is a diffuse but clearly articulated commitment to the value of knowledge linkages for the campus as well as for the larger society.

In brief, these points represent some of the key characteristics that emerge from a close examination of campus programs that appear to be having a positive effect in their communities, whether for the purpose of supporting economic development, enhancing human resource development across the life span, or sustaining a vital civic culture. What do the characteristics all mean in terms of concrete recommendations to communities and universities

committed to building similar linkages capable of serving important knowledge needs?

Recommendations for Action

Drawing upon my own decade-long experiences as a professional
committed to increasing the social benefits of the research university, my intellectual preoccupations as a reflective social scientist,
and the research and campus visits that provided the raw material
for this book, the summative recommendations I would offer relate
to three issues: planning, philosophy, and structure.

Planning

It is the rare research university that includes the provision of institutionalized knowledge connections to off-campus publics as an
important component of its central academic conversations or long-
range institutional planning efforts. Recently, campuses such as the
University of Minnesota and Michigan State University have
released campuswide plans defining what they mean by "service"
and "outreach" and how they plan to implement and measure it.
Universities such as the Universities of Georgia and Wisconsin
have long traditions of having very senior administrators charged
with public service and extension responsibilities. However, these
examples, while encouraging, are exceptions among research universities. On most campuses, the outreach, service, and linking
issues only arise episodically and usually when faculty and administrators perceive a need for political support for a new research
agenda or financial support for a new program initiative. Even in
those cases where it does become a priority, nonfaculty expertise
and support is usually sought only after faculty have determined
what it is they want and need. Such an approach curtails the opportunity for any real collaboration of the type being advocated in this

book. If this situation is going to change, colleges and universities, starting at the most senior levels of academic administration, will have to begin to see their intellectual interests, not just their political and financial interests, as served by these new kinds of relationships. Once that cultural change takes place, as it is increasingly in fields such as biology and in professional schools and extension programs, a wider circle of experts from industry, government, and knowledge-based organizations, as well as traditional academics, can be invited to the head table, as it were. What is absolutely critical is that a wider circle of perspectives and intellectual competencies needs to be included when discussing important academic priorities related to developing an institutionwide commitment to initiatives whose intent is to better serve the sponsoring society.

Books like this are an effort to help change that culture. Exhortations by business leaders and funding priority shifts in state legislatures and within federal agencies are other ways the culture is being forced to change. As a member of the academy, I would prefer to see institutions of higher education take the leadership role in defining and organizing institutional initiatives that will allow us to meet the social and economic challenges of the century ahead of us. However, this will not be possible without a deep and wide commitment to factoring in the concerns of expanding publics for knowledge in our conversations about the future of the university. There need to be serious internal conversations about (1) the value of institutionalized knowledge linkages; (2) which types represent the highest priorities for a given campus, division, or department in a particular community; and (3) how a given campus can leverage existing campus and community resources to build these linkages. These internal conversations need to include the voices of academic professionals who often have been marginalized because of the peripheral importance given to outreach functions. They also need to include appropriate expertise and input from significant resources outside the academy.

Philosophy

The second recommendation relates to philosophy and flows from the observation of successful programs at major universities across the United States. This is simply a reiteration of points 1 to 4 on the list of essential characteristics spelled out in the previous section. A recognition of diverse sources of expertise and the inclusion of that expertise in the planning, implementation, and ongoing evaluation of knowledge-linking initiatives is absolutely critical. This is a major challenge because of the extreme specialization and self-referential character of so much of the work inside academic disciplines today. However, face-to-face encounters between faculty and parallel experts—government economists, museum curators, documentary film producers, high-tech industry researchers—often begin the intellectual boundary spanning that is required. I am not advocating that practitioners and community leadership play a decisive role in establishing research priorities. In fact, this book argues just the opposite: that experts from outside the academy must not unduly influence the content of the liberal arts and graduate education curricula. However, once an institution makes a major commitment to expanding knowledge connections with the larger society, it must do so in a manner that includes the kind of heterogeneous inputs represented in the program examples provided. The purpose of these knowledge linkages is not one-way transfer but rather the fostering of interactive and exchange relationships involving both the users and producers of different kinds of knowledge, in ways that are productive of improved social action. Thus, as deans of schools and outreach functions such as extension services increase their work in this area, they need to constitute planning and governance groups that are broadly representative of the various participants in these knowledge transactions, rather than develop concepts internally, which they then try to "sell" to a hurriedly constituted group of outside advisers. Real time and professional competency needs to be invested, and most universities already have within their staff and faculty people with the skills and sensitivities necessary to play these bridging roles.

Structure

Finally, the recommendations for organization and structure refer back to the discussion of points 5 to 10. Clearly, the expanded provision of collaborative and multidimensional programs such as these described in Part Two, requires new kinds of institutional mechanisms and new kinds of knowledge workers. The mechanisms can be built upon programs and divisions many campuses already have in place. They may simply need a more collaborative approach, a better connection to central campus priorities, and more imaginative approaches to financing and program evaluation. Identifying a cadre of professionals capable of guiding these initiatives is also within our current capabilities if we can begin to spell out more effectively the competencies required in an effective leader in a given knowledge area and to spell out more clearly the desired outcomes. Such professionals need the managerial and program implementation support of ongoing academic divisions with outreach capability, but in addition to that, they need to be extremely competent in content areas and effective interpreters across a variety of sectors. As the program examples confirm, a solid institutional home and effective professional leadership result in activities that can be relatively self-managed and self-funded.

Whether or not these sorts of expanded academic functions should be centralized or decentralized depends largely on the history, the culture, and the resources of the campus. Harvard University, one of the most effective universities in the world when it comes to reaching off-campus constituencies is highly decentralized. Through each of its schools, including the Faculty of Arts and Sciences, it provides deep and varied connections to the larger society through a wide array of programs involving practitioners and citizens. The Business School, the Kennedy School of Government, the School of Education, and the Faculty of Arts and Sciences Extension School all serve dozens of publics in programs that complement on-campus research and teaching. These programs represent millions of dollars to Harvard annually, superb opportunities for faculty to interact with significant practitioners on a regular basis, and enormous goodwill toward Harvard from a variety of sectors. The programs are designed and administered by well-educated professionals responsible for outreach in each of Harvard's schools. These linking professionals are included as well in the central academic conversations about issues affecting their particular schools and in long-range planning efforts. They also meet periodically as a group to assure campuswide communication about service and outreach. In contrast, the University of Wisconsin has a long history of a highly centralized extension service, which provides extremely effective knowledge services across a variety of disciplines and sociotechnical problem areas statewide. However, it too is characterized by a highly professionalized staff of academics who guide the programming efforts, by a highly consultative planning culture, and by participation of extension leadership in the highest levels of planning at the university. It is for these reasons that the issue of how a campus ultimately organizes all of these bridging activities seems less critical than the issues of professionalism, collaboration, and participation in long-range academic planning.

The case studies provided in this book, and the hundreds of similarly effective programs not included in this book, speak to the incredible flexibility and capacity for interacting with diverse publics which exists within American research universities. Over recent decades a number of disconnections and knowledge gaps have developed as a result of the fragmentation of the knowledge work universities do and the legacy of concern from the fifties and sixties about the potential negative effects of the intrusion of political and special interests on the work of the university. As we approach century's end and enter a world entirely different from that characterizing the decades immediately following World War

II—the heyday for higher education generally and the research university in particular—we need to revisit our assumptions and our strategies for connecting the university in meaningful ways to society, while continuing to preserve its essential neutrality and autonomy. Institutional initiatives are needed that can serve knowledge needs in new and different ways. Such efforts, properly developed and managed, can contribute to the continued significance and prosperity of the university as well as the enhancement of economic and social life in postindustrial America.

In the university of the twenty-first century, it is likely that the functions connected with serving the economic, workplace, and civic knowledge needs of the public will be as central as those connected with research, undergraduate, graduate, and professional education today. The increased importance of the needs of the public to the central preoccupations of the research university will be an inevitable outcome of the forces of change at work in society today. Universities have been the breeding grounds for some of the most exciting radical and innovative ideas of this century. They have also organizationally been one of the more conservative institutions of this century. They must and can change. That change means embracing new functions, not abandoning old ones. For it is only in broadening its vision of its role that the university can effectively serve its many publics.

References

Aaron, H. J., and Schultze, C. L. (eds.). *Setting Domestic Priorities: What Can Government Do?* Washington, D.C.: The Brookings Institution, 1992.

Abetti, P. A., LeMaistre, C. W., and Smilor, R. W. (eds.). *Industrial Innovation, Productivity, and Employment.* Austin: IC2 Institute, The University of Texas, 1987.

Barber, B. R. *An Aristocracy of Everyone: The Politics of Education and the Future of America.* New York: Ballantine Books, 1992.

Barnard, C. *The Function of the Executive.* Cambridge, Mass.: Harvard University Press, 1938.

Bell, D. *The End of Ideology: On the Exhaustion of Political Ideas in the Fifties.* New York: Free Press, 1961.

Bell, D. *The Coming of Post-industrial Society: A Venture in Social Forecasting.* New York: Basic Books, 1976.

Bellah, R., and Associates. *Habits of the Heart.* New York: HarperCollins, 1985.

Bender, T. *Intellect and Public Life: Essays on the Social History of Academic Intellectuals in the United States.* Baltimore, Md.: Johns Hopkins University Press, 1993.

Bennett, W. J. *The Devaluing of America: The Fight for Our Culture and Our Children.* New York: Summit Books, 1992.

Bennett, W. J. *The Book of Virtues.* New York: Simon & Schuster, 1993.

Bergquist, W. H. *The Four Cultures of the Academy: Insights and Strategies for Improving Leadership in Collegiate Organizations.* San Francisco: Jossey-Bass, 1992.

Bingham, R. D., and Mier, R. (eds.). *Theories of Local Economic Development: Perspectives from Across the Disciplines.* Newbury Park, Calif.: Sage, 1993.

Blakely, E. J. *Planning Local Economic Development: Theory and Practice.* Newbury Park, Calif.: Sage, 1989.

Blauner, R. *Alienation and Freedom.* Chicago: University of Chicago Press, 1964.

Bluestone, B., and Harrison, B. *The Deindustrialization of America.* New York: Basic Books, 1982.

Boggs, D. L. "Citizen Groups: A Challenge to Public Service." *Continuing Higher Education Review,* Spring 1988, pp. 105–113.

Bok, D. C. *Higher Learning*. Cambridge, Mass.: Harvard University Press, 1986.

Bok, D. C. *Universities and the Future of America*. Durham. N.C.: Duke University Press, 1990.

Bok, D. C. *The Cost of Talent: How Executives and Professionals Are Paid and How It Affects America*. New York: Free Press, 1993.

Botkin, J. W., Dimancescu, D., Stata, R., and McClellan, J. *Global Stakes: The Future of High Technology in America*. New York: HarperBusiness, 1982.

Boyett, J. H., and Conn, H. P. *Workplace 2000: The Revolution Reshaping American Business*. New York: Plume, 1991.

Braverman, H. *Labor and Monopoly Capital: The Degradation of Work in the Twentieth Century*. New York: Monthly Review Press, 1974.

Bush, V. *Science, the Endless Frontier*. A Report to the President on a Program for Postwar Scientific Research. Washington, D.C.: National Science Foundation, 1980. (Originally published 1945).

"Café of the 80's." *Johns Hopkins Alumni Magazine*, June 1988, pp. 14–16.

"Can America Compete?" *Business Week*, Aug. 10, 1987, pp. 45–69.

Carnevale, A. P., Gainer, L. J., and Meltzer, A. A. *Workplace Basics: The Essential Skills Employers Want*. San Francisco: Jossey-Bass, 1990.

Chapman, J. W. (ed.). *The Western University on Trial*. Berkeley: University of California Press, 1983.

Charner, I., and Rolzinski, C. A. (eds.). *Responding to the Educational Needs of Today's Workplace*. San Francisco: Jossey-Bass, 1987.

Christensen, C. R., Garvin, D. A., and Sweet, A. (eds.). *Education for Judgment*. Boston: Harvard Business School Press, 1991.

Cohen, S. S., and Zysman, J. *Manufacturing Matters: The Myth of the Post-industrial Economy*. New York: Basic Books, 1987.

Cole, R. *Work, Mobility, and Participation—A Comparative Study of American and Japanese Industry*. Berkeley: University of California Press, 1979.

Cole, R. *Strategies for Learning: Small-Group Activities in American, Japanese, and Swedish Industry*. Berkeley: University of California Press, 1989.

Congressional Research Service. "Voter Turnout Worldwide: Industrial Democracies," *Congressional Quarterly*, Apr. 2, 1986, p. 863.

Corson, R. "Democracy in Action." Conference report on lifelong learning and citizenship in Sweden and the United States, National Issues Forum, St. Paul, Minn., October 1988.

Democratic Staff of the Joint Economic Committee of the U.S. Congress, Report on the U.S. Economy. Washington, D.C.: Government Printing Office, July 1986.

Dertouzos, M. L., Lester, R. K., Solow, R. M., and the MIT Commission on Industrial Productivity. *Made in America: Regaining the Productive Edge*. Cambridge, Mass.: MIT Press, 1989.

Dorf, R. C. "Models for Technology Transfer from Universities and Research Laboratories." Unpublished paper presented at the Annual Conference of the American Society of Engineering Management, University of California, Davis, 1987.

Dornbush, R., Paterba, J., and Summers, L. *The Case for Manufacturing in America's Future*. Rochester, N.Y.: Eastman Kodak, 1987.

Drucker, P. F. *Managing in Turbulent Times*. New York: HarperCollins, 1980.

Drucker, P. F. *The Changing World of the Executive*. New York: Times Books, 1982.

Drucker, P. F. *Post-Capitalist Society*. New York: HarperCollins, 1993.

Etzioni, A. *The Active Society: A Theory of Societal and Political Processes*. New York: Free Press, 1968.

Etzioni, A. *The Semi-Professions and Their Organization; Teachers, Nurses, Social Workers*. New York: Free Press, 1969.

Etzioni, A. *Social Profile: USA Today*. From *The New York Times*. New York: Van Nostrand Reinhold, 1969, 1970.

Etzioni, A. *An Immodest Agenda: Rebuilding America Before the Twenty-First Century*. New York: McGraw-Hill, 1983.

Eurich, N. P. *Corporate Classrooms: The Learning Business*. Carnegie Foundation Special Report. Princeton, N.J.: Carnegie Foundation for the Advancement of Teaching, 1985.

Fairweather, J. S. *Entrepreneurship and Higher Education: Lessons for Colleges, Universities, and Industry*. ASHE-ERIC Higher Education Report No. 6. Washington, D.C.: Association for the Study of Higher Education, 1988.

Fallows, J. "America's Changing Economic Landscape." *Atlantic Monthly*, 1985, 255(3), 47–70.

Fallows, J. *More Like Us: Making America Great Again*. Boston: Houghton Mifflin, 1989.

"Fastest Growing Jobs." *American Demographics*, Apr. 1986.

Galbraith, J. K. *The Culture of Contentment*. Boston: Houghton Mifflin, 1992.

Giamatti, A. B. *A Free and Ordered Space: The Real World of the University*. New York: Norton, 1988.

Gibson, D. V., and Kozmetsky, G. "Networking the Technopolis: Cross-Institutional Alliances to Facilitate Regionally-Based Economic Development." *The Journal of Urban Technology*, Spring 1993, 1(2), pp. 21–39.

Glaser, E. M., Abelson, H. H., and Garrison, K. N. *Putting Knowledge to Use: Facilitating the Diffusion of Knowledge and the Implementation of Planned Change*. San Francisco: Jossey-Bass, 1983.

Gold, G. G. *Business and Higher Education: Toward New Alliances*. San Francisco: Jossey-Bass, 1981.

Halberstam, D. *The Next Century*. New York: Morrow, 1991.

Hendrix, K. "Profile of College President John Maguire." *Los Angeles Times*, June 20, 1985, p. 1.

Hodgkinson, H. L. "Reform? Higher Education? Don't be Absurd!" *Phi Delta Kappan*, Dec. 1986, pp. 271–274.

Holt, M. E., and Lopos, G. J. (eds.). *Perspectives on Educational Certificate Programs*. New Directions for Adult and Continuing Education, no. 52 (entire issue). San Francisco: Jossey-Bass, 1991.

Holzner, B., and Marx, J. H. *Knowledge Application: The Knowledge System in Society*. Needham Heights, Mass.: Allyn & Bacon, 1979.

Homans, G. *The Human Group*. Cambridge, Mass.: Harvard University Press, 1950.

Houle, C. O. *The Design of Education*. San Francisco: Jossey-Bass, 1972.

Houle, C. O. *Continuing Learning in the Professions*. San Francisco: Jossey-Bass, 1980.

Houle, C. O. *Patterns of Learning: New Perspectives on Life-Span Education*. San Francisco: Jossey-Bass, 1984.

Institute of World Affairs. *Annual Report 1991–92*. Milwaukee: The University of Wisconsin, Division of Outreach and Continuing Education, 1992.

Jacoby, R. *The Last Intellectuals: American Culture in the Age of Academe*. New York: Basic Books, 1987.

Johnson, L. G. *The High-Technology Connection: Academic/Industrial Cooperation for Economic Growth*. ASHE-ERIC Higher Education Report No. 6. Washington, D.C.: Association for the Study of Higher Education, 1984.

Johnston, W. B., and Packer, A. H. *Workforce 2000: Work and Workers for the 21st Century*. Indianapolis, Ind.: Hudson Institute, 1987.

Kanter, R. M. *The Change Masters: Innovations for Productivity in the American Corporation*. New York: Simon & Schuster, 1983.

Kates, R. W. "The Great Questions of Science and Society Do Not Fit Neatly into Single Disciplines." *Chronicle of Higher Education*, May 17, 1989, p. B2.

Kenney, M. *Biotechnology: The University-Industrial Complex*. New Haven, Conn.: Yale University Press, 1988a.

Kenney, M. *Los Angeles Times*, Mar. 24, 1988b, editorial page.

Kennedy, P. M. *The Rise and Fall of the Great Powers: Economic Change and Military Conflict from 1500 to 2000*. New York: Random House, 1987.

Kennedy, P. M. *Preparing for the Twenty-first Century*. New York: Random House, 1993.

Kerr, C. *The Uses of the University*. Cambridge, Mass.: Harvard University Press, 1964.

Kotler, P. *Marketing for Nonprofit Organizations*. Englewood Cliffs, N.J.: Prentice Hall, 1982.

Kutscher, R. *Monthly Labor Review*, 1993, *16*(11), 3–10.

Lawrence, R. Z. *Can America Compete?* Washington, D.C.: The Brookings Institution, 1984.

Lederberg, J. "Does Scientific Progress Come for Projects or People." Address at the 100th anniversary meeting of the National Association of State Universities and Land Grant Colleges, Nov. 7, 1987.

Leontief, W. W., and Duchin, F. *The Future Impact of Automation on Workers*. New York: Oxford University Press, 1986.

Levine, A. (ed.). *Higher Education in America 1980–2000*. Baltimore, Md.: Johns Hopkins University Press, 1993.

Levinson, M. "America's Edge." *Newsweek*, June 8, 1992, pp. 40–43.

Louis Phillips and Associates. "1993 Mandatory Continuing Education Update." Summer 1993 Newsletter, p. 4.

Lyman, R. W. "The Profession of Continuing Education and the Public." Occasional Paper 6. National University Continuing Education Association, Washington, D.C., 1988.

Lynton, E. A. *The Missing Connection Between Business and the Universities*. New York: American Council on Education/Macmillan, 1984.

Lynton, E. A., and Elman, S. *New Priorities for the University: Meeting Society's Needs for Applied Knowledge and Competent Individuals*. San Francisco: Jossey-Bass, 1987.

Machlup, F., 1962. *The Production of Knowledge in the United States*. Princeton, N. J.: Princeton University Press, 1962.

Magaziner, I. C., and Patinkin, M. *The Silent War: Inside the Global Business Battles Shaping America's Future*. New York: Random House, 1989.

Maguire, J. "Toward a Definition of the Civic." *Liberal Education*, 1982, 68(4), 281–283.

Markusen, A., Hall, P., and Glasmeier, A. *High Tech American: The What, How, Where, and Why of the Sunrise Industries*. London: Allen & Unwin, 1986.

Marshall, F. R. *Unheard Voices: Labor and Economic Policy in a Competitive World*. New York: Basic Books, 1987.

Marshall, F. R., and Tucker, M. *Thinking for a Living: Education and the Wealth of Nations*. New York: Basic Books, 1992.

Matkin, G. W. *Technology Transfer and the University*. New York: Macmillan, 1990.

Matthews, D. *Politics for People: Finding a Responsible Public Voice*. Urbana: University of Illinois Press, 1994.

Matthews, J. B., and Norgaard, R. *Managing the Partnership Between Higher Education and Industry*. Boulder, Colo.: National Center for Higher Education Management Systems, 1984.

Melkers, J., Bugler, D., and Bozeman, B. "Technology Transfer and Economic Development." In R. D. Bingham and R. Mier (eds.), *Theories of Local Economic Development: Perspectives from Across the Disciplines*. Newbury Park, Calif.: Sage, 1993.

Mintzberg, H. *The Nature of Managerial Work*. New York: HarperCollins, 1973.

Mitroff, I. I. *Stakeholders of the Organizational Mind: Toward a New View of Organizational Policy Making*. (1st ed.). San Francisco: Jossey-Bass, 1983.

Morse, S. W. *Employee Education Programs: Implication for Industry and Higher*

284 References

Education. ASHE-ERIC Higher Education Report No. 7, Washington, D.C.: Association for the Study of Higher Education, 1984.

Naisbitt, J. *Megatrends: Ten New Directions Transforming Our Lives*. New York: Warner Books, 1982.

National Alliance for Business. Advertising supplement to the *New York Times*, Sept. 10, 1987.

National Center for Education Statistics. "The Condition of Education." U.S. Department of Education, 1993.

National Commission on Excellence in Education. *A Nation at Risk: The Imperative for Educational Reform: A Report to the Nation and the Secretary of Education*. Washington, D.C.: Government Printing Office, 1983.

National Governors Association. *Making America Work*. Washington, D.C., Center for Policy Research, 1987.

National Governors Association. *The Role of Science and Technology in Economic Competitiveness*. Washington, D.C.: National Science Foundation, 1989.

Nelkin, D. "Scientific Knowledge, Public Policy, and Democracy." *Knowledge Creation, Diffusion, Utilization*, Sept. 1979, *1*(1), 106–122.

"New Careers Emerge from a World in a State of Flux." *Los Angeles Times* special supplement, Sept. 25, 1990, pp. 1–25.

Newman, F. *Higher Education and the American Resurgence*. Carnegie Foundation Special Report. Princeton, N.J.: Carnegie Foundation for the Advancement of Teaching, 1985.

Nowlen, P. M., and Queeney, D. S. "The Role of Colleges and Universities in Continuing Education." Washington, D.C.: National University Continuing Education Association, 1988.

Nowlen, P. *A New Approach to Continuing Education for Business and the Professions*. New York: Macmillan, 1988.

Ohmae, K. *The Borderless World: Power and Strategy in the Interlinked Economy*. New York: HarperCollins, 1990.

Oliver, L. P. *Study Circles: Coming Together for Personal Growth and Social Change*. Washington, D.C.: Seven Locks Press, 1987.

Osborne, D. *Economic Competitiveness: The States Take the Lead*. Washington, D.C.: Economic Policy Institute, 1987.

Oxford Analytica. *America in Perspective: Major Trends in the United States Through the 1990s*. Boston: Houghton Mifflin, 1986.

Parnell, D. *Dateline 2000: The New Higher Education Agenda*. Washington, D.C.: Community College Press, 1990.

Pavalko, R. M. *Sociology of Occupations and Professions*. (2nd ed.) Itasca, Ill.: Peacock, 1988.

Peterson, P. G. "The Morning After." *Atlantic Monthly*, Oct. 1987, pp. 43–69.

Peterson, P. G. *Facing Up: How to Rescue the Economy from Crushing Debt and Restore the American Dream*. New York: Simon & Schuster, 1993.

Price, D. K. *The Scientific Estate*. Cambridge, Mass.: Belknap Press, 1965.

Public Policy Center, SRI International. *The Higher Education-Economic Development Connection: Emerging Roles for Public Colleges and Universities in a Changing Economy*. Washington, D.C.: American Association of State Colleges and Universities, 1986.

Queeney, D. S., with Casto, R. M. "Interprofessional Collaboration Among Professionals of Different Disciplines." In *An Agenda for Action: Continuing Professional Education Focus Group Reports*. University Park: Office of Continuing Professional Education, Division of Planning Studies, The Pennsylvania State University, 1990.

Queeney, D. S. "Professional and Occupational Practice Requirements." (4th ed.) Pennsylvania State University Office of Continuing Professional Education, Planning Studies, Dec. 1987.

Reich, R. B. *Minding America's Business: The Decline and Rise of the American Economy*. New York: Vintage Books, 1982.

Reich, R. B. *The Next American Frontier*. New York: Times Books, 1983.

Reich, R. B. "The Real Economy." *Atlantic Monthly*, Feb. 1991a, pp. 35–52.

Reich, R. B. "Secession of the Successful." *New York Times Magazine*, Jan. 20, 1991b, pp. 16–45.

Reich, R. B. *The Work of Nations: Preparing Ourselves for the 21st Century Capitalism*. New York: Vintage Books, 1992.

Roberts, E. B. *Entrepreneurs in High Technology: Lessons from MIT and Beyond*. New York: Oxford University Press, 1991.

Rogers, E. M., and Larsen, J. K. *Silicon Valley Fever: Growth of High Technology Culture*. New York: Basic Books, 1984.

Rorty, R. "Intellectuals in Politics." *Dissent*, 1991(Fall), pp. 483–490.

Rosener, J. "Watch for a New Style in the Workplace—'Linking Leadership.'" *Los Angeles Times*, Sept. 11, 1994, business section, p. D2.

Rosenzweig, R. M., and Turlington, B. *The Research Universities and Their Patrons*. Berkeley: University of California Press, 1982.

Rostow, W. W. *Rich Countries and Poor Countries: Reflections on the Past, Lessons for the Future*. Boulder, CO: Westview Press, 1987.

Rutkoff, P. M., and Scott, W. B. *New School: A History of the New School for Social Research*. New York: Free Press, 1986.

Schor, J. B. *The Overworked American: The Unexpected Decline of Leisure*. New York: Basic Books, 1991.

Schwartz, G. G., and Neikirk, W. *The Work Revolution*. New York: Rawson Associates, 1983.

Scott, A. J. *Technopolis: High-Technology Industry and Regional Development in Southern California*. Berkeley: University of California Press, 1993.

Segal, N. S. "The Cambridge Phenomenon: Universities, Research and Local Economic Development in Great Britain." In R. W. Smilor, G. Kozmetsky, and D. V. Gibson (eds.), *Creating the Technopolis: Linking Technology Commercialization and Economic Development*. New York: Harper-Collins, 1988.

Simerly, R. G., and others. *Strategic Planning and Leadership in Continuing Education*. San Francisco: Jossey-Bass, 1987.

Sivasy, A., and Hymowitz, C. "Education Mismatch: The Workforce Revolution." *Wall Street Journal* special supplement, Feb. 9, 1990, pp. R5–R12.

Skyes, C. J. *Profscam: Professors and the Demise of Higher Education*. New York: St. Martin's Press, 1988.

Smilor, R. W., Kozmetsky, G., and Gibson, D. V. (eds.). *Creating the Technopolis: Linking Technology Commercialization and Economic Development*. New York: HarperCollins, 1988.

Smith, A. O. "An Institutional History of Certificate Programs at George Washington University." In M. E. Holt and G. J. Lopos (eds.), *Perspectives on Educational Certificate Programs*. New Directions for Adult and Continuing Education, no. 52. San Francisco: Jossey-Bass, 1991.

Smith, P. *Killing the Spirit: Higher Education in America*. New York: Viking/Penguin, 1990.

"Southern California Job Market." *Los Angeles Times* special supplement, Sept. 25, 1990.

State of California Economic Development Corporation. *California's Higher Education System: Adding Economic Competitiveness to the Higher Education Agenda*. Background paper prepared for California Economic Development Corporation by SRI International, Meno Park, Calif., March 1988.

State of California Economic Development Corporation. *Vision: California 2010: A Special Report to the Governor*. Sacramento: State of California Economic Development Corporation, 1988b.

Stern, M. R. (ed.). *Power and Conflict in Continuing Professional Education*. Belmont, Calif.: Wadsworth, 1983.

Sykes, C. J. *The Hollow Men: Politics and Corruption in Higher Education*. Washington, D.C.: Regnery Gateway, 1990.

Toffler, A. *Future Shock*. New York: Random House, 1970.

Touraine, A. *The Post-industrial Society: Tomorrow's Social History: Classes, Conflicts and Culture in the Programmed Society*. (L.F.X. Mayhew, trans.). New York: Random House, 1971.

"The 21st Century Executive." *U.S. News and World Report*, 1988, *104*(9), 48–51.

U.S. Bureau of the Census. *Current Population Reports*. Series P-20, No. 432. Washington, D.C.: U.S. Bureau of the Census, Sept. 1988.

U.S. Bureau of the Census. *1980 Census of the Population, Handbook of Labor Statistics*. Washington, D.C.: U.S. Bureau of the Census, 1985.

U.S. Department of Commerce. *Population Profile of the United States*. Washington, D.C.: U.S. Department of Commerce, Bureau of the Census, 1993.

U.S. Department of Labor, Bureau of Labor Statistics. *Handbook of Labor Statistics, 1985*. Washington, D.C.: U.S. Department of Labor, 1985.

U.S. Department of Labor, Bureau of Labor Statistics. *Monthly Labor Review*. Washington, D.C.: U.S. Department of Labor, Sept. 1987.

U.S. Senate Committee on Aging. *Aging in America: Trends and Projections*. Washington, D.C.: U.S. Department of Health and Human Services, 1988.

United Way of America. *What Lies Ahead: Looking Toward the '90s*. Alexandria, Va.: United Way of America, Strategic Planning and Marketing Division, 1987.

University of Chicago, Internal Report Division of Continuing Education. "Summaries of Topics and Activities of Midwest Faculty Seminar Institutes 1982–1987." Chicago: University of Chicago, Internal Report Division of Continuing Education.

Wall Street Journal, July 25, 1986.

Walshok, M. L. "Evaluation and Quality Control in Certificate Programs." In M. E. Holt and G. J. Lopos (eds.), *Perspectives on Educational Certificate Programs*. New Directions for Adult and Continuing Education, no. 52. San Francisco: Jossey-Bass, 1991.

Wenk, E., Jr., *Tradeoffs: Imperatives of Choice in a High-Tech World*. Baltimore, Md.: Johns Hopkins University Press, 1989.

Wilson, J. Q. *The Moral Sense*. New York: Free Press, 1993.

Wolfe, A. *Whose Keeper? Social Science and Moral Obligation*. Berkeley: University of California Press, 1989.

Wolfe, A. (ed.). *America at Century's End*. Berkeley: University of California Press, 1991.

Zuboff, S. *In the Age of the Smart Machine: The Future of Work and Power*. New York: Basic Books, 1988.

Index

294   Index

54–77, 165, 193–224; for established fields of practice, 202–207; in general education, 141; and global economy, 92–97; for interdisciplinary knowledge brokering, 145–146; for interdisciplinary practice needs, 207–215; and key outcomes, 138–139; leveraging existing resources to serve, 154–155; and sociological trends, 91–136; summative matrix of, 137–143; for supporting economic development, 40–54, 164–191; for sustaining a vital civic culture, 77–85, 225–255; and technological innovations, 97–100; for technological updates, 146–147; underserved, 143–154

Knowledge networks, 28–33

Knowledge organization, 19–24; barriers to new forms of, 25–28

Knowledge resources: for basic education, 141; for certification/credentialing, 142; for civic culture needs, 150–152; for continuing education, 144–145; for general education, 141; for interdisciplinary knowledge exchange, 145–146; for professionals, 198, 200–202; for quality-of-life education, 151, 152–153; summative matrix of, 137–143; for technology updates, 146–147; universities as, 86–87. *See also* Educational institutions; Programs for linking universities with publics; Research universities

Knowledge society, 6–7; implications of, for research universities, 8–12, 25–33; and industries, 15; versus information and learning society, 26; and occupations, 15; types of knowledge needed in, 22–23

Kozmetsky, G., 54, 170, 172–173

Kranzler, B., 180

Kutscher, R., 113–114

L

Labor and Monopoly Capital (Braverman), 56

Labor market, 55–57. *See also* Workforce

Landscape design certificate program, 218–219

Larsen, J. K., 54, 179

Latin American literature, 79–80

Lawrence, R. Z., 56

Leadership, campus-based, 271

Learning communities, 253–254, 263–264

Learning society, 26

Lederberg, J., 43, 44–45

Leontief, W. W., 56

Lester, R. K., 30, 39

Lévi-Strauss, C., 251

Levinson, M., 41

Liberal learning: knowledge needs related to, 79–81; postgraduate, 78, 230–235; programs for, 230–235, 252–253; for quality-of-life enhancement, 152–153

Licensing/patenting, 49, 52

Lifelong learning: for professionals, 61–63; in the workplace, 59–60. *See also* Adult education; Continuing professional education

Los Angeles Times, 216–217, 269

Lyman, R. W., 254

Lynton, E. A., 27, 39

M

McClellan, J., 39, 97

Machlup, F., 15

Made in America: Regaining the Productive Edge (MIT Commission on Industrial Productivity), 30, 43

Magaziner, I. C., 55, 97

Maguire, J., 254–255

Management systems, and global competitiveness, 52, 93

Managing in Turbulent Times (Drucker), 97

Manufacturing sector, 103, 104–105: decline in U.S., 42–43, 67–68; strengthening, 165

Manufacturing modernization, 26

Markusen, A., 54

Márquez, G. G., 80

Marriage patterns, 121–124, 125

Marshall, F. R., 7, 9–10, 52, 55, 56, 59, 60, 92–93, 95

Marx, J. H., 17–19

Math education, 68–69, 74–75

Matkin, G. W., 39, 54

Mediating institutions: for connecting research to society, 19–20, 28–33; decline in, 228; for linking individuals